"From battle, murder and sudden death; Good Lord, deliver us."

Allied Military Chaplains Killed in WW2

By

The Rev Dr Thomas D Wilson

Anglican Chaplain of Saint-Raphaël & the Var, France

Copyright © 2023
All Rights Reserved.

Dedication

To my loving wife, Dawn Cornelio, who brought me to France in 2006 on my first visit and has since then accompanied me on many visits to France, to battlefields, and to war grave cemeteries in both Northern and Southern France. She has endured listening to untold military conversations with good grace and humour! She also is a fantastic translation professional, as well as a wonderful proofreader, and I thank her for her great assistance in my literary works!

Acknowledgements

Paul Rowcliffe
Owen Sound Ontario
Canada
for his almost 50 years of friendship
and his financial support that has helped
make this book possible

All those who backed the
publication of this book
through supporting the
Kickstarter Campaign that
made it possible.

Gregory Pique
OREP Editions, Bayeux
for permitting the inclusion of the information from my
first book
No Guns, Just God's Glory

This book would not have been possible without the
influence, encouragement and expertise of the best tour
guides in Normandy:

Paul Woodadge—www.ddayhistorian.com

Sean Claxton—www.normandyinsight.com

Nigel Stewart—www.Nigel-Stewart.com

Geert Van den Bogaert—www.normandyheroes.com

Magali Desquesne—www.dday4you.com

Special thanks to:

David Blake—Curator of the Museum of Army Chaplaincy
Amport, Hampshire
https://www.chaplains-museum.co.uk

Pierre Lagace
Trois-Rivieres, Quebec Canada
for providing detailed information on a Chaplain

David Pearson and Frank Vanpaemel
from Findagrave.com
for providing pictures of grave stones that I needed

Ian MacAulay
Ottawa, Canada
for providing information on the Macaulay Family

Albert Trostorf
Langerwehe, Germany
&
Heidi Reiss Smith, Zelienople, PA, USA
for providing information on Pastor Clarence G Stump

Robert and Susan Tribit
Glen Mills, PA, USA
for providing information on Pastor John R Kilbert

Patrick J. Hayes, PhD.
Redemptorist Archives
Philadelphia, PA, USA
for providing information on Father Clarence Vincent

Emilie Wyel, Berchtesgaden Germany
for her hospitality and interest in World War Two Chaplains

Paul and Eliane Metz
Frejus, France
for proof reading the French manuscript

National Library and Archives,
Government of Canada, Ottawa, Canada

The Ministry of Defence Army Personnel Centre
MS Support Unit,
P & D Branch Historical Disclosures,
Glasgow, United Kingdom

Nathalie Worthington
Directrice – Centre Juno Beach
Normandy France
for her, and her staff's hospitality and encouragement

Mark Worthington
Curator – Pegasus Memorial
Normandy France
for his and his staff's hospitality and encouragement

Monsieur et Madame P Metz
pour leur aide avec la correction de la traduction en français

"From battle, murder and sudden death; Good Lord, deliver us."

- Anglican Book of Common Prayer

Introduction

In World War Two, a war that truly did span the globe and had many millions of soldiers involved, there have been many books written about the generals who planned and ordered their various armies, corps and divisions into battle. Then there are the more personal stories that have been written about individual regiments and battalions and their actions in the war, and finally, there have been thousands of books written since the end of the war detailing the stories of individual soldiers of all the nations involved.

A war is not just won by the soldiers on the frontlines. For the Allies, for every frontline soldier, there were up to 10 individuals behind the lines unloading ships, bringing supplies of food, ammunition and all the little items that are needed by an army at war to the front. Additionally, there are the soldiers on the home front, providing the training for the combat soldiers, running the administration of the war, and so many other things as well.

In all of these situations, from the combat soldier on the frontlines to the new recruit being turned from a civilian into a fighting soldier on the home front, there was also a unique class of soldier, the Chaplain: an ordained minister, pastor, priest, or rabbi who was there to provide spiritual care and moral guidance to the men of the unit they were assigned to.

In this work, I am concentrating on the British chaplains who were killed in Northwest Europe in the British and French retreat to Dunkirk in 1940, American and British chaplains who were killed at sea in the Atlantic Ocean, two chaplains who died in England but are counted as battle casualties, and those chaplains killed between 6 June 1944 (D-Day) and VE (Victory in Europe) Day on 8 May 1945.

These men of God in uniform are the focus of this work. There are some who might be surprised to know that clergy, including Roman Catholic, Anglican/Episcopalian, Baptist, Church of Scotland, Methodist, Free Presbyterian, and other denominations, as well as other faiths – notably Jewish – served in all the western Allied armies in World War Two. What is unique about their service is that the chaplains in the Allied armies did not carry any weapons.

Both the Hague Convention of 1907 and the Geneva Convention of 1929 on the rules of war do not actually state that chaplains cannot carry weapons. However, clergy in military service are specifically noted as non-combatants and, therefore, must, if captured, be returned to their respective countries unless retained by the capturing country to minister to prisoners of war. This non-combatant status has been interpreted by the Allies in both the First and Second World Wars to mean that military chaplains are not permitted to carry any form of weapon, including a pistol or revolver, to protect themselves. While the Hague and Geneva Conventions on the rules of war do not permit military medical staff to carry any weapons while wearing the red cross symbol anywhere on their bodies, chaplains were forbidden from carrying any sort of firearm, whether they were wearing a red cross symbol or not.

Spiritual care of soldiers was also an important part of maintaining morale. Each Commonwealth infantry division was authorized fifteen chaplains: on average, two-thirds were Protestant and one-third Catholic; Jewish chaplains comprised less than 3% of the chaplain corps and generally ministered on the divisional (10,000 – 15,000 soldiers) or even corps (2 or more divisions) level. In the American army, the authorized strength (although never achieved in World War Two) for the American Army was set at 1 Chaplain for every 1,000 personnel.

Chaplains performed a range of pastoral services, ministering to the wounded and conducting services. Behind the lines, in addition to access to religious services, as many as 25% of the soldiers received personal counselling from a chaplain. Occasionally Chaplains were able to make use of churches and chapels near the front lines, but as church steeples made excellent observation posts and places for snipers to shoot from, many churches were damaged by Allied tank or artillery fire striving to destroy these vantage points. More often, a stack of empty ammunition boxes, the hood of the chaplain's jeep, or the tailgate of a truck would become an altar. Helmets, ammunition cases, logs or rocks served as pews. Beyond holding services, chaplains also wrote letters to relatives, fiancées, and friends of soldiers and helped with inquiries through the Red Cross to notify a soldier of the birth of a child or the death of a parent in their home country. Chaplains also assisted or often were responsible for, organizing sporting events, amateur stage and musical shows, unit libraries, reading rooms (rooms where soldiers could sit quietly and write letters and relax, etc.) Sometimes the chaplain was also the designated sports or special service officer whose role was to keep the soldiers busy while they waited to be sent overseas, or were preparing for embarkation onto a landing craft, or waiting for ships to transport them home from the war and back to civilian life.

In battle, stretcher-bearers or, more often, ordinary soldiers carried the casualties to the battalion aid station, where the battalion surgeon, or regimental medical officer, attended them. The chaplain was usually also stationed at the aid station to provide spiritual support, although more often, he could be found assisting the doctor and the medics. In these aid stations, the lightly injured soldiers were quickly patched up and returned to the frontlines while the seriously wounded were stabilized and evacuated to the rear areas to larger field hospitals or evacuation to the United Kingdom and even the United States for further care.

While clergy serving alongside soldiers have a long history, going as far back as the Roman Empire, it is only in the 20th century that they became an official part of the table of organization of military forces. Prior to this, clergy members were unofficially attached to military units. During the First World War, Commonwealth chaplains, who were not even initially considered to be sent to the front, turned out to be some of the bravest men on the front lines, and many were awarded with the Military Cross. This is the third-highest award for bravery in action in the British Commonwealth. It was awarded to chaplains, often for their actions in rescuing wounded men and the retrieval of dead bodies in no-man's land. However, when World War One ended, the Commonwealth military chaplaincy was effectively terminated as a department of the British and Commonwealth armed forces, and the clergy that survived returned to civilian life and generally took up congregational appointments in the churches of their various denominations. During the interwar period, a few of those chaplains who had served in World War One retained a connection by serving as honorary chaplains to battalions, especially those of the reserve, territorial or militia (depending upon which Allied country they lived in), but these were few and far between.

In the American armed forces, the Chaplain Corps continued, but at a very much reduced form, with the few chaplains who continued in military service assigned not to battalion-level units but more often to permanent military bases in the continental United States and the few overseas dependences, such as Hawaii, the Philippines or Alaska.

Within a generation, the winds of war again began to sweep across Europe and by early 1939, military chaplaincies became a part of the military establishment in the Commonwealth armed forces once more. As the Allied forces began to mobilize and young men answered the call of their countries to their armed forces, clergy serving in congregations were not immune to this call. These men of God knew that the young men enlisting would need spiritual and moral support and guidance, as well as the understanding that if they were killed in battle, they would receive a proper burial and at least a quick funeral service as well during which their sacrifice and life would be commended to their God. Unlike the beginning of World War 1, at the beginning of WW 2 military authorities were blessed in that they had the experience of clergy who had served in WW 1 on the frontlines and were still young enough to provide leadership and support to the younger clergy that would be recruited to minister to the troops on the front lines.

In the British Army in World War Two, 3,314 men served as chaplains on all fronts. Of those that served, 102 died, 144 were wounded, and 142 were held as prisoners of war. This is a loss rate of almost 12%, which is one of the highest by branch of service in the whole war. The high rate of injury or death was especially critical because there were limited numbers of clergy available for replacements. In the Canadian Army in World War Two, 1,253 men served as chaplains, 9 died, and an unknown number were wounded in action or taken prisoner. It is worth noting that in World War Two, the Canadian armed forces had over 1 million people in uniform from a nation of only 11 million people. So chaplains were few and far between in the American Army. In World War Two, there were 8,896 men who served as chaplains, and 100 died. An unknown number were wounded or taken prisoner.

In the early days of World War Two, the British and Canadian armies had to establish a system of leadership for chaplains, so a reporting hierarchy was established. These were equivalent ranks to those of the military, as chaplains did not actually hold a rank in Commonwealth Forces, but were given a class from 4th class, the equivalent of a captain, to 1st class, the equivalent of a Colonel.

However, in the American Armed Forces, chaplains were a specific part of the Table of Organization of Divisions and were given actual ranks beginning as First Lieutenants on up to the rank of Colonel for field formations such as Divisions or Armies. Chaplains were paid at the same rate of pay for the rank as their equivalent in armed service and in the American Army, the same as other officers of the same rank.

As the war began in 1939 for the British and Canadians, and after the Americans entered it in December 1941, there was much involved in rebuilding Army chaplaincies by all

Western powers, including determining what group within a denomination could recommend a minister, priest or pastor for service as a chaplain; finding space on rapidly expanding military bases for locations to hold worship services, and training these new military chaplains in the ins and outs of military life, including official military church parades and other services.

In the rush to re-arm and send troops to the front lines, chaplains went overseas with their battalions and regiments. Some of these clergy were not necessarily suited to military life, no matter how keen they might have been to serve. However, in Europe, after the invasion of Poland at the beginning of September 1939, the war settled into an uncomfortable but stable frontline and chaplains not suited to frontline service were able to be transferred to base areas, and younger, more suitable clergy were able to take their place at the front. The chaplains at the front were able to tend to the moral and spiritual needs of the troops under their care while in static positions.

When the blitzkrieg of the German forces overran the Low Countries and France in the spring of 1940, chaplains accompanied the men of their units during the retreat to Dunkirk and most of the chaplains were evacuated to England. A significant number, however, did end up in German captivity, where they spent the next five years ministering to all the British troops taken prisoner in that uncertain time, even though they could have sought reparation from the United Kingdom. In fact, some even volunteered to remain behind with the wounded soldiers so as to let more much-needed British medical personnel escape to the United Kingdom. It should be noted that as chaplains were non-combatant personnel, they were not actually prisoners of war. They were on "parole", giving their word to the German authorities that they would not try and escape to neutral countries. In return, they were permitted to travel to the various prisoner-of-war camps, often by German railways or military vehicles. In fact, there are accounts of British chaplains being assigned two German soldiers to travel with them to the various camps. These soldiers were not guards for the chaplains but rather were there to protect the chaplains from harassment or assault by German civilians or soldiers, as the chaplains were travelling in British army uniform.

As the British and Commonwealth Armies began to rebuild themselves, the chaplains of the forces also began to learn their ministry as military chaplains more thoroughly. As in civilian life, chaplains were still responsible for religious services and specifically for what was called "divine worship", a service that offered prayers and hymns and was acceptable to all Christian denominations. They were also responsible for ensuring denominationally specific worship was available, as often as possible, for the soldiers in their units. This may have included arranging Roman Catholics in their units to attend Confession and Mass at a local Catholic church or for Church of England (Anglican/Episcopal) troops to receive Communion from a local civilian minister. They also arranged for troops of other denominations to have time, as military needs dictated, to visit places of worship of their own denomination or faith as well.

While in camp, the chaplains, or as they are more commonly known in Commonwealth armies, Padres, also often performed what today are called social work functions. They, along with the medical officers, did not have to go through the chain of command but had direct access to unit commanding officers, and this meant they could act as intermediaries between the ordinary soldier and the military bureaucracy. This included supporting requests for compassionate leave due to the serious illness or death of a loved one, or emergency leave so a soldier could be with his wife if a baby was being born, etc. The padre sometimes even provided a payday loan service to the troops of his unit, especially when they might have lost all their pay in the inevitable games of chance soldiers play to while away the waiting times in their lives. Although the padres did not charge any interest on these loans, there were few who defaulted on them because of how well respected the padres were.

Another role of a padre was to help the moral welfare of their men. This included the development of what was called the "Padre's or Chaplain's Hour", which was time allocated in the training regime for, ideally, each platoon to meet informally with the padre on a weekly basis, who would prepare a brief address on a current affair topic, which was sometimes very controversial, such as premarital sex, and sometimes more specifically religious, such as the existence of heaven and hell. Then the padre would take questions from the troops and answer as honestly as possible, or, if he could not provide an answer, he would seek one out and get back to the questioner later in the week.

Of course, most of the padres would accompany their units on training exercises and learn all the fieldcraft techniques that the troops were learning as well. Most chaplains attached to combat units also were trained to high standards of first aid (generally to the level of what was called a stretcher bearer in Commonwealth armies or a corpsman in the American army.) This training enabled them to act as extra medics for their unit in combat.

After training, as units were dispatched from the United Kingdom to the various battle fronts, the chaplains accompanied their men on the often long and often hazardous sea journeys across the globe. As the Americans began their build-up of army and airforces in Britain beginning in 1942, chaplains crossed the ocean with the men of their Divisions as well.

After the battles in Normandy, where 33 Allied chaplains lost their lives, there were certain battles that took more chaplains' lives than others. One of these was Operation Market Garden, the Allied plan to seize three bridges over the northern Rhine River in mid-September 1944. There were substantial numbers of chaplains killed and wounded, both as parachute and glider regimental chaplains, as well as those accompanying the British XXX corps as it fought its way north to relieve the beleaguered 82nd and 101st American parachute divisions and the doomed 6th British Airborne Division at Arnhem.

The next major battle that involved substantial losses of Allied chaplains, all American, was the Ardennes Offensive, as it was called by the Germans, or the Battle of the Bulge by the Allies. This sudden attack in the Ardennes Forest of Luxemburg and Belgium in mid-December 1944 led to many losses of wounded, captured and killed chaplains. Furthermore, the battles in the dense forests of Western Germany, described as the Reichswald and Hochwald battles, as well as those in the Ruhr pocket, also led to the wounding and death of Allied chaplains.

In late March 1945, when the Allies stormed across the Rhine, Operation Varsity, which included mass parachute drops by the Americans and British (including the 1st Canadian Parachute Battalion), led to many chaplains being wounded and killed in action, especially within the parachute units. During April of 1945, the Allies began to sweep eastward into the heart of Germany, and by the beginning of May, much of the fighting was over. However, even in the last few days of the war, some chaplains were killed. There is, in fact, a very distinct possibility that the last Canadian killed before VE-Day was a chaplain in

Holland on May 4, 1945. Also, possibly the last American soldier to die before VE-Day was declared was a chaplain.

The chaplains accompanied their troops right to the frontlines as often as possible. In fact, many chaplains had to be ordered by the unit commanding officer to remain behind the lines at regimental aid posts and first aid stations where the wounded soldiers would be brought. The loss of a chaplain tended to have a serious effect on the morale of Allied units, and being aware of this, commanding officers did all they could to try and keep their chaplains from being wounded or killed. They also knew that as each battalion or regiment only had one chaplain, obtaining a replacement might be difficult, especially as the war ground on and there were fewer and fewer qualified clergy to take the place of those captured, wounded or killed.

In the following work, I have arranged the information on the Commonwealth, American and Polish chaplains who died during the periods mentioned above in chronological order of their dates of death. If more than one died on the same day, I have endeavoured to record it by what time of day they died.

For some of these brave men, there is quite a bit of information available about their lives before entering military chaplaincy and during the war, but for others, there is very little. I obtained some service records from the United Kingdom Ministry of Defence Personnel Records Centre in Glasgow, but, unfortunately, there was not much more detail about the lives of some chaplains before they volunteered for service with the army in WW 2. I also obtained the records of some of the Canadian chaplains who died from the records held by the National Library and Public Archives of Canada in Ottawa, which were exhaustingly complete – some even including the chaplains' dental and medical records!

The reader may note that in some of the pictures of the chaplains' headstones, there is quite a bit of weathering and pitting. For American chaplains laid to rest in military cemeteries, their graves are tended in perpetuity, and any weathering of the information inscribed into the headstone is repaired as needed. American chaplains lying in private cemeteries do not have this care, and their headstones have begun to suffer from the effects of weather over the past 70-80 years, especially as immediate family members have passed on. In the Commonwealth War Graves Commission (CWGC) cemeteries, the headstones have also suffered from the effects of weather and been damaged by acid rain, eating away at the Portland limestone that was originally used in the 1950s for the headstones. The CWGC has a program of replacing these worn headstones. This has included both World War One and World War Two cemeteries. In the 1990's they began using Botticino stone, which often resembles a high-end kitchen countertop and has a marbled effect. However, recently the CWGC has been using Bulgarian Vratsa limestone. According to the director of the CWGC, when showing the Canadian minister of Veterans Affairs the CWGC headquarters in the summer of 2016, they use almost all the Vratsa limestone quarried in the world! This Vratsa stone is more resistant to acid rain and pollution than the original Portland limestone, yet retaining the more original light tan appearance of the original headstones than the Botticino did.[1]

Notes Concerning Chaplains

The Service Number, or Serial Number in the American Army, is a unique identifying number issued to all ranks in the Armies. The numbers were only used to refer to enlisted soldiers or non-commissioned officers, as officers were never identified by their Service Numbers or Serial Numbers; they were always identified by their rank and name.

Officers in the Canadian Army, including honorary ranks, such as chaplains, had a Service Number, but it was never used in identifying them, even on the Identity Discs that were issued to the officers and chaplains. This is why Canadian officers do not have their service number listed on the Commonwealth War Graves Commission Website.

Chaplain Rank Comparison

British and Canadian		American
		2nd Lieutenant
		1st Lieutenant
Chaplain 4th Class	Honorary Captain	Captain
Chaplain 3rd Class	Honorary Major	Major
Chaplain 2nd Class	Honorary Lieutenant Colonel	Lieutenant Colonel
Chaplain 1st Class	Honorary Colonel	Colonel

Sometimes, in British and Canadian usage, a chaplain would be identified as follows: H/Captain Rev John Smith. However, on Commonwealth War Graves Commission headstones, British and Canadian Chaplains are identified as *The Rev John Smith, CF* (Chaplain to the Forces), indicating they were different from a standard army officer, and held only an honorary rank. On headstones in the American Battlefield Monuments Commission cemeteries, a chaplain is identified as *Capt. (Rev) Joe Smith*, indicating they were commissioned officers.

Within his unit, in the British and Canadian armies, a chaplain would be addressed as Padre. In the American Army, as Chaplain or Chappie. In the Polish Army, they were addressed as Father since there were no Protestant Polish chaplains due to the fact that 90% of Poland's population identified as Roman Catholic.

Chaplains in all three armies wore the rank that was the equivalent of the corresponding officer in the table above and were to be treated as officers, but especially in the Commonwealth armies, they were granted special dispensations, as the rank was purely honorary and gave no command rights or privileges. For example, in the British and Canadian Armies, one dispensation was that a chaplain could enter the Non-Commissioned Officers and the Other Ranks messes (dining halls) without an invitation. Other officers, including the Commanding Officer, had to be invited unless they were fulfilling a specific task related to their duty (such as Officer of the Day).

Commonwealth and American governments handled the disposition of the remains of soldiers who had died in different manners. Commonwealth troops have traditionally been buried in cemeteries close to where they died. The Commonwealth War Graves Commission was established to maintain these graves in perpetuity, with annual funding supplied by the various Commonwealth nations. American service personnel who died overseas until the end of the Korean War were initially interred in the country where they died. A few years after the end of hostilities, United States Military Cemeteries were established, generally where large numbers of American soldiers' remains had been interred. However, American servicemen and women's families had the right to request the government return the remains of their loved one to the United States for burial either in a military cemetery or in a community cemetery, and approximately 60% of the remains of American WW 2 casualties in Europe were repatriated to the United States for burial. From early 1947 until 1950, there was a steady stream of American transport ships with their holds full of caskets, repatriating the remains of Americans killed overseas.

For the almost 3,500 mostly land forces of the Commonwealth, both men and women, who have no known grave, including a number of chaplains, they are commemorated on the Brookwood 1939-45 Memorial, located 30 miles from London and located in the Brookwood Military Cemetery near the village of Pirbright. Those memorialised on the Brookwood Memorial died in the campaign in Norway in 1940 or in the various raids on enemy-occupied territory in Europe, such as Dieppe and St Nazaire. Others were special agents who died as prisoners or while working with Allied underground movements. Some died at sea, on hospital ships and troop transports, in waters not associated with the major campaigns, and a few were killed in flying accidents or in aerial combat.

It is worth noting that beginning with the Vietnam War for Americans and the wars in Iraq and Afghanistan for the Commonwealth soldiers, all remains of soldiers killed in action are returned to their home country, and there are now no new burials of soldiers overseas.

Academic Abbreviations

BA Bachelor of Arts Degree
BD Bachelor of Divinity Degree
BTH Bachelor of Theology Degree
MA Master of Arts Degree

PhD/DPhil Doctor of Philosophy Degree
LTH Licentiate of Theology (especially from Canadian Theological Colleges; presented to candidates for ordination when the Seminary was not a degree-granting institution)
AKC Associate of King's College, London (equivalent to a BA)

Religious Terminology

Father The term of address for a Roman Catholic priest and for some Anglo-Catholic clergy of the Church of England and the World-wide Anglican Communion.

Priest In episcopal (Bishop-led) denominations (Anglican and Roman Catholic especially), the second level of ordination after being ordained a deacon. A priest can officiate at a Communion Service, pronounce Blessings in the name of God, hear Confessions and provide Absolution of Sins.

Minister A clergy person. However, the term is generally used for the ordained leader of a congregational church congregation (as opposed to an episcopally-led denomination). However, it can and is used interchangeably with priests in Anglican/Episcopal Churches. It may also be used interchangeably with "pastor".

Pastor A clergy person, most often the ordained leader of an evangelical congregation in Baptist and Pentecostal traditions. It may also be used interchangeably with "minister".

Curate A priest in an Anglican congregation or parish who normally has a few years of ordained experience.

Assistant Curate A newly ordained priest acting as an assistant priest in a congregation or a parish in the Anglican Communion.

Vicar/Rector The Anglican or Roman Catholic priest in charge of leading a congregation on behalf of a bishop. During World War 2, many Vicars and Rectors in Britain and Canada were men beyond the age for military service, although not exclusively. Clergy were exempt from being conscripted in the British, Canadian and American armed forces.

CssR, The Congregation of the Sons of Most Holy Redeemer (Filii Sanctissimi Redemptoris), is a Roman Catholic Order of priests and lay monks.

FFC The Franciscan Friars Covenantal is a Roman Catholic order of priests and monks who follow the Order of St Francis of Assisi.

OFM The Order of Friars Minor is a branch of the Order of St Francis of Assisi and consists of priests and lay monks.

SSE The Society of Saint Edmund is a small Roman Catholic order located in the state of Vermont.

SJ The Society of Jesus (Jesuits) is a Roman Catholic order of Priests.

SSJE The Society of Saint John the Evangelist was a Church of England order of priests.

SSH The Servants of the Sacred Heart is a Roman Catholic Franciscan religious community of priests.

OMI The Missionary Oblates of Mary Immaculate is a Polish Roman Catholic order of priests.

Military Terminology

Medals Awarded to Chaplains in WW 1 And WW 2

AMERICAN

Purple Heart The Purple Heart Medal is the oldest medal awarded to American troops. All branches of the American military forces are eligible to receive it. It is awarded for wounds incurred by enemy action. Each of the American Chaplains in this book was automatically awarded the Purple Heart Medal due to them being wounded or killed by enemy action.

Bronze Star The Bronze Star Medal is a United States decoration awarded to members of the United States Armed Forces for either valour or exceptional service in a combat zone. When awarded for valour in a combat zone, a "V" emblem is attached to the medal ribbon. It can also be awarded to foreign nationals (in this case, Commonwealth chaplains) if they performed a heroic act on behalf of the American Armed Forces.

Silver Star The Silver Star Medal is the United States Armed Forces' third highest decoration awarded for exceptional heroism in action against an enemy of the United States.

Distinguished Service Cross The Distinguished Service Cross is the second-highest military award of the United States Army for extreme gallantry and risk of life in actual combat with an armed enemy force.

Four Chaplains Medal This medal was specifically authorized for the award (in 1960, by the Congress of the United States) to the 4 American Army Chaplains who demonstrated extraordinary heroism in the sinking of the

SS Dorchester in February 1943. They had been nominated for the Medal of Honor, the highest American award for valour but were deemed ineligible, as they did not risk their lives in direct combat with enemy armed forces.

BRITISH AND COMMONWEALTH

Mentioned in Dispatches (MiD) This is the lowest-ranking award for either heroism or notable service for members of the British Commonwealth armies in World War Two. The Dispatches are the daily reports sent by the military commanders to the reigning monarch of the United Kingdom and the Commonwealth. It was one of only 2 awards for heroism in the Commonwealth that could be awarded after death in WW 2. The other is the highest award for exceptional, life-risking heroism in the face of the enemy, the Victoria Cross.

Military Medal (MM) The Military Medal was a military decoration in WW 2 awarded to personnel of the British and Commonwealth Army Non-commissioned officers and below for valour on the battlefield. The equivalent medal for officers was the Military Cross.

Military Cross (MC) The Military Cross is the third highest military decoration for gallantry awarded to officers of the British Commonwealth forces for an act of exemplary gallantry during active operations against the enemy on land.

FRENCH

Croix de Guerre (CdG) The Croix de Guerre is a medal created by the French Government in 1939 to honour people who fought against the Axis forces in World War Two. It was awarded also to Commonwealth and American forces for services rendered to French military units or citizens of France. It appears to have been awarded to Allied Roman Catholic chaplains, who officiated at Masses (Communion Services) that French citizens attended or aided French civilians in the areas where they were stationed with their units in France.

Casualty Treatment Units and Unit Size Designations

RAP A British Regimental Aid Post is an immediate treatment station, normally located within a kilometre or two of the front lines, with the medical officer (doctor) of a regiment and first aid assistants. It is where wounded soldiers were stabilized, had their wounds assessed and pain medication administered, and before they were transported further back to a Casualty Clearing Station. Those with minor wounds were transferred to a Field Dressing Station.

FDS A Field Dressing Station is slightly further back from the front lines. The RAP evacuated wounded troops here for assessment and further treatment of what were deemed minor injuries by the RAP staff.

BAS An American Battalion Aid Station is equivalent to a RAP; its wounded were evacuated to a Divisional Casualty Clearing Station.

CCS An American Casualty Clearing Station is a small hospital unit normally located a few miles behind the frontline and normally beyond the range of enemy artillery fire. It is similar to a Field Dressing Station in the Commonwealth armies. Lightly wounded soldiers would be treated here until they had recovered to return to the front lines, or, if their wounds were too severe, they were stabilized before being transferred further back to Field Hospitals where they would be treated and recover (from a wound such as a broken arm or leg). Severely wounded soldiers were evacuated from the Field Hospitals to the General Hospitals. General Hospitals were located in the United Kingdom or in the United States. Only the most serious were evacuated to the UK or the US, and normally were so badly injured that they would not return to the battlefield, and often, after recovery, they would be discharged from the armed forces.

Platoon A platoon is a small military unit of approximately 25-40 soldiers in infantry units. It is generally the smallest unit in the army, led by an officer (a 2nd or 1st Lieutenant).

Troop A troop is a small armoured military unit of approximately 25-40 soldiers in units of the British Commonwealth (and American Cavalry units), similar to an infantry Platoon and led by an officer.

Company A company is a military unit of 3 or more platoons and is generally commanded by a Captain.

Squadron A squadron is an armoured military unit comprising 3 or more Troops, generally commanded by a Major, due to the unit having numerous attached supporting soldiers, such as mechanics, radio technicians, etc., who help maintain the armoured vehicles.

Brigade A brigade is a combined unit of a number of Infantry Battalions along with attached units from other branches such as Armour, Artillery, or other specialized units in the Commonwealth Armies.

Due to the confusion of war in times of retreat, or heavy, sustained battle, such as after a parachute landing, sometimes the exact date of death of a chaplain is not known, and a range will be given. Some sources will give an exact date, but this is often just a best guess by the authorities long after the war ended.

Any errors in the information provided are mine, and I accept responsibility for them. If you have information that you would be willing to share about the chaplains I have written about, please feel free to contact me at <u>tomdwilson@gmail.com</u>.

I would as soon think of going into battle without my artillery as without my chaplains.

> \- Field Marshal Bernard Montgomery
> *(at the dedication of Chaplains War Memorial, Bagshot Park, 19 July, 1951)*

The Battle for France and the Dunkirk Evacuation

23 May 1940

Reginald Thompson Podmore, BA, BTh, SSJE. Service number 111748. Age 38. Chaplain 4th Class, Royal Army Chaplains' Department. Attached to 3rd Corps Ammunition Park. Buried in the Divion Cemetery, grave 8, Divion, France.

Reginald Podmore was born in Broughton, Kettering, Northamptonshire, in 1902 to Rev Claude Podmore and his wife Ella V. Podmore (nee Wainwright). His father was the Rector of the Broughton Parish, located a few miles south of Leicester. Reginald had a younger brother, John, and three younger sisters, Violet, Elfrida and Muriel. As a boy, Reginald attended Haileybury Boarding School in

Hertfordshire. He originally studied engineering at the University of Leeds but then felt called to the priesthood and transferred to Keble College of the University of Oxford for his Bachelor of Arts degree, which he earned in 1923. He then entered Ely Theological College, from where he graduated in 1926. Rev Podmore was ordained a deacon in Ripon Diocese in 1927 and made a priest in 1928. His first posting was as curate of All Saints Anglican Church in Leeds from 1927 to 1931.

Upon finishing his curacy, Father Podmore decided to join the Anglican Society of Saint John the Evangelist. In 1866, the Anglican SSJE was the first monastic religious order to be established in the Anglican Church after the 16th century Reformation of the Church of England. Due to the location of its mother house in Cowley, the members of the Society of Saint John the Evangelist are often referred to as "the Cowley Fathers". Rev Podmore spent 6 years with the City of Oxford branch of the Cowley Fathers at their Mission House on Marston Street in Oxford. While there, Father Podmore was in charge of youth work, which included being the Scoutmaster of the 26th Oxford Scouts sponsored by the Mission House. He also instituted the St. John's Club at the Oxford Mission and organised an annual camp for the boys. He then moved to London to live and minister at the London headquarters of the Society of Saint John the Evangelist, St Edward's House, on Great College Street.

Chaplain Podmore joined the Royal Army Chaplains' Department on 8 January 1940. It is interesting to note that there is no mention of Chaplain Podmore undergoing any specific chaplain or military training, although this may have occurred between his joining the Chaplains Department and being assigned to Southern Command in England on 30 January 1940 and attached to the 3rd Army Corps rear area at Aldershot. It was noted by a colleague that Padre Podmore had his hair go prematurely grey by the time he joined the Army. By April 1940, Chaplain Podmore was with the British Expeditionary Force in France and attached to 3rd Army Corps Ammunition Park in and around the Artois village of Divion, on the edge of the Bethune coalfield complex in northern France. Chaplain Podmore established a small chapel in one of the rooms off the main hall in the village *salle de fetes* (Function Hall), opened a canteen for many of his 'parishioners' and also organized occasional boxing matches. The Ammunition Park that Padre Podmore was assigned to was responsible for issuing all ammunition to the various units that comprised the British 3rd Army Corps.

Chaplain Podmore based himself with the medical staff attached to the 3rd Ammunition Park and, while in Divion, acquired the necessary material to construct a portable altar that would fit in the back of his assigned car. He commissioned the lady of the house with whom he was billeted to make a beautiful cover for the altar. He also persuaded a local café owner to let him hold services in her establishment, having overcome her qualms about his not being a Roman Catholic. As Chaplain Podmore was of the Anglo-Catholic persuasion, while the café owner would not have spoken much English, the pattern of Anglo-Catholic worship is very similar to that of Roman Catholicism.

Chaplain Podmore's unit advanced into Belgium on 17 May 1940 to help counter the German attack that began on 10 May 1940. On May 21, Chaplain Podmore was given permission to travel back to Divion, France, where the 3rd Ammunition Dump was still in use by the British Army, to pick up some items left there, so he could distribute them to the men of his unit. Chaplain Podmore and his driver/assistant George Randell had travelled 30 miles south and reached the edge of Divion when they were ambushed by members of the 3rd Infantry Regiment of the 3rd SS (Totenkopf Division) Panzer Division. That the SS troops had arrived in Divion would have been a shock to Padre Podmore and Private Randell, as the Germans had advanced much more quickly and further than had been reported to Chaplain Podmore. The Totenkopf Division was one of the most notorious of the SS Divisions. In 1940, the majority of its members had formerly been guards at the early concentration camps. In fact, the Totenkopf Division commander, Theodor Eicke, was acknowledged as the creator of the brutality used in the running of the concentration camps to keep the prisoners subservient. The SS Totenkopf Division was also eager to prove itself as a front-line unit alongside the Wehrmacht (German Army) and even to prove they were superior to the Wehrmacht.

One account of Chaplain Podmore's death states that he and his batman (personal assistant), Private Randell, had been able to jump from their car and take cover in a ditch. However, the SS Troops threw a grenade at the ditch, which exploded near Padre Podmore's legs, severely wounding him. However, the more accurate account was told in a letter by Private Randall to the Society of St John the Evangelist in February 1941 from the prisoner-of-war camp where he was being held captive. Private Randall wrote that Padre Podmore was severely injured by 4 bullet wounds in each leg during the ambush. The German stretcher-bearers immediately sent for an ambulance, but it was held up by heavy German traffic moving forward toward the front on the roads. Within 4 hours, Padre Podmore died due to loss of blood and shock. Private Randall, with the aid of two French civilians, buried Padre Podmore. The German SS Officer had told Private Randall that his unit thought Padre Podmore's car was the beginning of an English attack, and if they had known it was a chaplain, they would not have opened fire.

With so many accounts regarding chaplains' deaths being second-hand, there can be inconsistencies. One account provided by the Society of St John the Evangelist's archives says that the family of Edouard Mathon, the Chief Engineer of the coal mine in Divion, insisted upon taking the wounded padre into his house. With the help of Private Randall, they carried Chaplain Podmore into their living room and made him as comfortable as possible on their sofa, and he died at about 5 pm on May 23.

However, as Private Randall noted previously, his account has Padre Podmore dying when he was wounded and only was buried in the garden of M. Mathon. As both Private Randall and Edouard Mathon give this account, it is probably the more accurate account of his death and burial. The one provided by the Crowley Brothers perhaps gives Chaplain Podmore a more heroic and sacrificial death, as often happened when stories of soldiers' deaths were recounted 2nd or 3rd hand.

After having Chaplain Podmore buried, the SS troops seized the car that he and Private Randall had been in and discovered that it still was in running condition. They threw all Padre Podmore's vestments, religious items and personal items out of the car and drove off. Chaplain Podmore was listed as missing in action until September 1940. M Mathon and his family gathered up Chaplain Podmore's vestments which were used in celebrating Communion Services, and his personal items, including his uniform hat and hid them in their home.

In 1942 the German occupation authorities learned through an informer that M Mathon and his family had hidden in their house some of Padre Podmore's and Private Randall's military equipment, which had been discarded by the SS Troops in the street after they seized the padre's car. German occupying troops returned to Divion and arrested M Mathon and his family, intending to send them to a concentration camp. While searching the Mathon home, the German troops overlooked Padre Podmore's vestments (being more colourful and religious in nature, and which had been hidden separately from his military equipment) probably because they did not realize what they were. However, M Mathon was well-liked and respected by the workers at the coal mine where he was the chief engineer, so the workers went on strike, refusing to work unless M Mathon, and his family, were released. As the Germans needed the output of the mine for war production, they reluctantly released Mr Mathon and his family and let them return home.

After being liberated in the fall of 1944, M Mathon notified the British authorities that Chaplain Podmore was buried in the garden of his family home. Eventually, Chaplain Podmore's remains were removed and re-interred in a proper Commonwealth War Grave in the Divion Communal War Cemetery. M Mathon

also searched for an address for Chaplain Podmore's religious order, as he had found a reference to the SSJE on the front page of a bible of Chaplain Podmore's that he had hidden. In 1946 M Mathon was able to contact the Mother House of the Cowley Fathers and arrange to return Chaplain Podmore's vestments and bible to them.

Padre Podmore is the only British person buried in the Divion Communal War Cemetery, although there are 6 graves from the battle of Loos in 1915 during World War One.

31 May 1940

Geoffrey Gervase Hobson-Matthews, Mentioned in Dispatches, Service number 96035. Age 36. Chaplain 4th Class, Royal Army Chaplains' Department. Attached to the 1st Battalion, The King's Shropshire Light Infantry. Buried in the Town Cemetery, plot 2, row 19, grave 2, Dunkirk, France.

Geoffrey Hobson-Matthews was the son of John and Alice Hobson-Matthews (née Gwyn-Hughes) and born in Monmouth, Wales, in 1903. Geoffrey's father had converted to Roman Catholicism as a young man and, after studying at Cambridge, had become a lawyer in Cardiff, Wales. Geoffrey's father died when he was 11 years old. Geoffrey also had 3 brothers and two sisters.

Rev Hobson-Matthews was an ordained monk of the Roman Catholic Order of St Benedict at Downside Abbey in Somerset. While living at Downside Abbey, he was a teacher at the school his order ran there, along with also teaching at their second school at Ealing. He had volunteered to serve as a chaplain in September 1939, shortly after World War Two began. After his initial training, he was sent to France in October 1939 with the British Expeditionary Force (BEF). He reasoned upon joining the Royal Army Chaplains' Department that he needed to be with those boys he had taught at school, as they would be fighting for their lives.

Chaplain Hobson-Matthews was initially attached to the British 1st Infantry Division Headquarters and its attached Royal Artillery Units. However, on 5 April 1940, Chaplain Hobson-Matthews was transferred to the 1st Battalion of the King's Shropshire Light Infantry. He was on leave in Britain when the blitzkrieg attack by Germany began on 10 May 1940. He was told he did not have to return to France to be with his unit, but he managed to find a way across the channel in mid-May and rejoined the King's Shropshire Light Infantry as they began to retreat towards Dunkirk. In late May 1940, the BEF had been forced to retreat from Belgium to Dunkirk on the coast of France with its back against the English channel, and a total of 300,000 British, French and Belgian troops were trapped there awaiting evacuation.

Padre Hobson-Matthews kept a diary while serving in France. Here are a few of his entries:

"May 29 Wednesday. Abandoned belongings and, with skeleton kit, led marching column to the sand dunes; thence in convoy to the coast (Coxyde) and to La Panne, where destroyers and other boats are beginning to take troops to England. Opened up the Casualty Clearing Station (CCS) in a large air-raid shelter on (or rather under) the sea front. Billeted in a house overlooking the sea and the evacuation— men wading waist-deep to boats to take them to the destroyers and troop ships. British ships bombarded the German lines towards Ostend. Intense anti-aircraft fire from innumerable guns on the shore, as German planes flew overhead. Incredible noise. Shells and bullets whizzing in all directions! Tracer bullets at night.

May 30 Thursday. I was able to say Mass for the first time since the church at Steenvoorde was destroyed on Sunday. Lord Gort (the commander of the BEF) visited the Casualty Clearing Station.

May 31 Friday. (I) was with the wounded from 3 am till 6.30 am. Peter Hardy, 150th Field Ambulance Royal Army Medical Corps (RAMC) died and I buried him later in the improvised military cemetery. We had to throw ourselves to the ground during the burial to avoid fire from enemy planes and our own shrapnel from the Anti-aircraft guns. The Boches began to shell the evacuation. A bomb fell very close after lunch and our windows were smashed. Saw a German plane dive into the sea during a colossal air battle. Fathers (RC Chaplains) Ford, Gigan, Callaghan, and I with some non-Catholic chaplains, drew lots for who should remain in the town—all troops are being otherwise, if possible, evacuated. Callaghan was selected to remain. Two non-Catholic chaplains declined to take part in the draw. If one of us had not drawn the 'cross' to remain, we were going to draw among ourselves, as a priest has certainly to stay.

Padre Hobson-Matthews did not escape with the rest of the British Expeditionary Force and part of the French Army did at Dunkirk though he had "won" the draw to remain with the wounded at the CCS. Hours after agreeing to remain behind, he was killed by a random German shell that hit the CCS where he was ministering to the wounded.

1 June 1940

Jonathan Maynard Knowles, BA, MA, Mentioned in Dispatches, Service number 95803. Age 26. Chaplain 4th Class, Royal Army Chaplains' Department. Buried in the New Oostende Cemetery, plot 9, row 4, grave 2 Oostende, Belgium.

Jonathan Knowles was the son of Captain Jonathan and Viva B. Knowles (nee Bagot) of Bordon, Hampshire and was born in Billericay, Essex, in October 1913. He had two older sisters, Nina and Viva.

His father, Captain Jonathan Edward Knowles, had an illustrious career with the British army, serving with distinction during the Boer War in South Africa. Johnathan's father was serving with the 4th Battalion Duke Of Cambridge's Own (Middlesex Regiment) at the beginning of the First World War during the defence of Mons, Belgium and on 23 August 1914, just after the war began, he was killed in action. This means that Jonathan never knew his father, as he was just ten months old when his father was killed.

Jonathan attended Radley College in Oxfordshire as a boy. Upon graduation, he then attended Corpus Christi College at the University of Cambridge, where he was a member of the 1st eight of the rowing team. After earning his Bachelor of Arts Degree, he went on to take a Masters Degree in Theology. After finishing university Rev Knowles was ordained in 1936 in the Priory Church of St Mary, Church of Wales in Usk, Monmouthshire, where he was the curate until he joined the Royal Army Chaplains' Department on May 19, 1939.

Padre Knowles was caught up in the retreat to the coast of France centred on Dunkirk. He ended up with the British troops in the Belgian port of Ostend, which was also under heavy attack by the German air and ground forces. While the author has found no indication of how Padre Knowles was killed, it is safe to presume that he was killed in the heavy German bombing and shelling of the Allied positions in Ostend as the armies were forced into an ever-shrinking perimeter and could not retreat towards Dunkirk.

Leslie Philip Riches, BA. Service number 101549. Age 30. Chaplain 4th Class Royal Army Chaplains' Department. No known grave. He is remembered in column 131 of the Dunkirk Memorial.

Leslie Riches was the son of Philip T. and Rosetta J. Riches (nee Sturgess) and was born on the 27 June 1909 at Northumberland Heath, Erith. He was the eldest of the three children, and they suffered the tragedy of their mother dying in November 1918 when Leslie was just nine years old. As his father could not cope with raising 3 children while also working full-time, the children were raised by their mother's parents, James and Sarah Sturgess.

Rev Riches was ordained in the Church of England in 1932. Rev Riches married Dorothy Evelyn Frances Brown, on 7 August 1937, in Christ Church, Erith, located in south-east London, the church that Leslie had attended as a boy. At the time of his marriage, Leslie was living in Highfield Road, Luton, and was curate at St Mary's Anglican Church, Luton. At the completion of

Rev Riches' curacy in Luton, the newly married couple moved to Banstead, Surrey, where Leslie became curate at the larger All Saints Church. He soon became an active member of the Church Institute Committee, which ran a large hall and meeting room facility on the High Street in Banstead.

Rev Riches joined the Royal Army Chaplains' Department on the 24 October 1939. It is not known how Chaplain Riches died, although there are suggestions that he was killed either by a German bomb or by machine gun fire as a German plane strafed the soldiers waiting on the beaches at Dunkirk for evacuation.

6, 7 or 8 June 1940

Arthur Currie Gordon, MA, BD. Service number 91866. Age 36. Chaplain 4th Class, Royal Army Chaplains' Department. Attached to 1st Battalion, The Black Watch (Royal Highlanders), 51st Highland Division. Buried in the Blangy-sur-Bresle Town Cemetery, in grave 3, Blangy-sur-Bresle, France.

Arthur Gordon was born in 1904 to Rev William Gordon and Alison Gordon (nee Jollie) of Barhill, Ayrshire, Scotland. Chaplain Gordon attended George Watson's College, Edinburgh, from 1915 to 1920 and then went on to Edinburgh University and graduated with a Bachelor of Divinity in 1924 and a Master of Arts in 1926.

Rev Gordon was ordained in the Church of Scotland shortly after his graduation from Edinburgh University in 1926 and was appointed the assistant minister to Rev Albert A. Diak at Saint Bernard's Church in Edinburgh for two years. In 1928 he was then called to become the minister at Kells Parish Church, Kirkcudbrightshire. While there, he married Agnes Doreen Gordon (nee Mathers) on 20 April 1929. In 1932 he was called to Foveran Parish Council Church at Newburgh, Aberdeenshire.

Rev Gordon joined the Royal Army Chaplains' Department on 8 February 1939 (before the war was declared). After training, he was assigned to the 1st Battalion of the Black Watch (Royal Highlanders). His unit was part of the defensive perimeter by the 51st Highland Division around the English Channel port of Le Havre, and his unit was doomed to either death or imprisonment, as they formed the rear guard of the British Army in France and their sacrifice prevented the German army from overrunning the Dunkirk and Le Havre ports. Their holding the Germans back permitted the maximum number of men to be evacuated from the Dunkirk beaches further along the Channel coast.

It was a chaotic time in Le Havre as the Highland Division was under constant shell fire and aerial bombardment. It is not clear if Chaplain Gordon was actually killed on 6 or 7 June. The probate of his will records his death as either date, but the United Kingdom Army Roll of Honour lists him as dying on 6 June. One account notes that Chaplain Gordon was ministering to a wounded soldier when an artillery shell landed near them and killed both men.

After World War Two ended, a bronze mural tablet was erected in memory of Padre Gordon in the Foveran Parish Council Church at Newburgh by his widow Agnes, accompanied by her two children. Mrs Gordon also presented the congregation with two brass vases in memory of her husband.

12 June 1940

Theodore Douglas Emslie, BA, BTh, Military Medal (WW1), Mentioned in Dispatches, Service number 111056. Age 41. Chaplain 4th class, Royal Army Chaplains' Department. Attached to the 51st Highland Division. Buried in the St. Valery-en-Caux Franco-British Cemetery, grave 33, St Valery-en-Caux, France.

Theodore Douglas Emslie, called Douglas by his family, was the son of the Rev William and Jessie Douglas Emslie. Douglas Emslie was born on 15 March 1899 in Nweichow, China, where his parents were Church of Scotland (Presbyterian) missionaries.

During the First World War, Douglas travelled from China to join the British Army as a Highland soldier, enlisting as soon as he was old enough on 16 April 1917. He served with the Cameron Highlanders, the Gordon Highlanders and the Argyll and Sutherland Highlanders. In a particularly hazardous operation, he was severely wounded in the chest and was hospitalised for six months. He was awarded the Military Medal for valour in the field of action.

After World War One, Douglas married his wife, Anna Emslie (née Nikolina) of Crieff, Perthshire and returned with his bride to China to pursue a business career. However, in the 1930's, he had a brief stint in British politics. Douglas Emslie has a unique claim to fame in Scottish history: he was the first person to stand in any Scottish election as a member of the Scottish Nationalist Party. The election took place for the Montrose Burghs seat, and Douglas made his Campaign Headquarters at Arbroath Railway Station since the station master there was the first person he met as he got off the train from Aberdeen. The station master was also a Scottish Nationalist and offered the use of the British Rail waiting room to Douglas for his Campaign Headquarters.

After Douglas' failure to be elected to the Westminster parliament, he felt the call to ordained ministry and took up studies at the University of Aberdeen for his Bachelor's Degree and then at the university's Christ's College for his theological studies. In 1937 Douglas was called as the minister for West Church in Crieff, where he remained until the outbreak of World War Two. On 2 January 1940, Rev Emslie volunteered for the Royal Army Chaplains' Department, and, after training, he was attached to his former World War One unit, the Gordon Highlanders, then serving in France with the 51st Highland Division.

On 11 June 1940, Padre Emslie was shot in the chest (as he had been in World War One) and severely wounded. He had been assisting with the wounded and helping to rally the troops on the beaches at Saint-Valery in the hope that they would be evacuated as the troops further up the coast at Dunkirk had been. Padre Emslie died of his wounds the next day, shortly before the surrender of the 51st Highland Division at Saint-Valery, as they had been the rear guard and were not able to be evacuated from the beaches as they had hoped. As it was a chaotic time in France, news of Chaplain Emslie's death did not reach his wife until September 1940 when a letter was received from one of the doctors who had been in the advanced dressing station with Chaplain Emslie and was now a prisoner of war in Germany. He wrote, "Tell Mrs Emslie, West Manse, Crieff, that her husband died as nobly as he had lived, on 12 June in our Advanced Dressing Station. He was a fine chap."

There is a memorial plaque to Chaplain Emslie in the Crieff Parish Church, but it was originally inside The West Church, Crieff, where he had been the minister before entering the army.

The Cold, Cruel Waters of the Atlantic

16 September 1942

William Robert Copland, MA, Service number 94093. Age 31. Chaplain 4th Class Royal Army Chaplains' Department. Died at sea. Remembered on panel 15, column 2 of the Brookwood Memorial.

William Copland was the son of John and Mary Copland (nee McKay) of Greenock, Scotland, where he was born on 7 March 1911. He grew up and attended Greenock High School. His father was a civil engineer in the town. After high school, William attended the University of Glasgow and was ordained in the Church of Scotland following his graduation. He was married to Agnes (known as Nancy) Copland (née Mitchell) of Gourock, Scotland. Prior to his enlistment in the British Army, Rev Copland was the minister in Logie Pert, near the town of Brechin, in eastern Scotland. After her husband's death, Agnes Copland decided to dedicate her life to the Church of Scotland and went on to graduate from St Colm's College, Edinburgh, as a deaconess and became the first female Elder in the Church of Scotland. She served for many years as an assistant chaplain at Gateside Prison. She was awarded a Member of the British Empire medal in 1974 for her services to church and state.

Rev Copland joined the Royal Army Chaplains' Department on 10 August 1939. He died in the sinking of the Royal Mail Ship (RMS) Laconia, formerly of the Cunard Steamship Line, when it was torpedoed by the German Submarine U-156 northeast of Ascension Island in the south Atlantic Ocean as it was returning from the Middle East via the Suez Canal to Mombasa, Durban, Cape Town, Sierra Leone and finally to Canada. The RMS Laconia was travelling without escort as it was felt to be fast enough in speed to avoid German submarines, and there had not been any reports of U-boats near Ascension Island. The RMS Laconia was carrying 1,809 Italian prisoners of war (from the campaign in North Africa), as well as 268 British soldiers and 160 Polish soldiers (who were guarding the prisoners of war) who, along with the crew of the Laconia totalled almost 2,500 people.

After torpedoing the RMS Laconia, the commander of U-156, Kapitänleutnant Werner Hartenstein, staged a dramatic effort to rescue the passengers and the crew of Laconia. This involved an additional German U-boat (U-506) and an Italian submarine (Regio Sottomarino Cappellini) and became known as the "Laconia Incident". Before the RMS Laconia sank, U-156 surfaced. When Kapitänleutnant Hartenstein realized civilians and prisoners of war were on board the sinking ship, he radioed the U-Boat Headquarters in France and asked for help. Both U-boats and the Italian submarine were flying Red Cross flags, and Captain Hartenstein radioed in plain English to the Allies on the central African Coast. that a rescue operation was underway. The three surfaced submarines, with RMS Laconia survivors on their decks and being towed in lifeboats behind, slowly headed for the Vichy French ports in Cameroon to debark those they had rescued.

The next morning, 17 September, a U.S. B-24 Liberator plane sighted the rescue efforts. Captain Hartenstein signalled the pilot for assistance, who then notified his superiors at the American base on Ascension Island of the situation. The senior officer on duty there, who was unaware of the German radio message indicating they were on a mission of mercy, ordered that the U-boats be attacked. Despite the Red Cross flags, the survivors crowded on the surfaced submarines decks and the towed lifeboats; the B-24 started attacking U-156.

The Captains of the three submarines ordered the tow ropes attached to the lifeboats cut and their vessels to dive, abandoning the survivors they had rescued back to their fate in the sea.

It is not clear, from the few records of this incident, if Padre Copland was killed in the initial attack on the RMS Laconia or was rescued by the submarines and then subsequently died after being returned to the water when they dove to avoid the air attack.

After this incident, the German submarine force commander, Grand-Admiral Karl Dönitz, issued what is regarded as an infamous order, known in English as the "Lanconia Order". It stated that henceforth, German submarines were not to attempt to assist or rescue the survivors of the ships they sank, as some U-boat captains had been doing until September 1942.

Between the 17 and 20 of September 1942, the French cruiser Gloire, the minesweeper Annamite, and the sloop Dumont d'Urville, all stationed in the Vichy port of Douala, Cameroon, rescued 837 persons from the lifeboats and floating in the ocean out of the 2,500 on board the RMS Laconia, and took them to Dakar. However, approximately 1,658 people died in either the initial torpedo attack, in the

American air attack on the U-boats, or they were killed by sharks, attracted by the blood of the wounded who were floating in the water.

14 October 1942

EDWARD FRANCIS HAND, Purple Heart. Service no. O-385280. Age 39. Captain, United States Army Chaplain Corps. Lost at sea. Commemorated on the Tablet of the Missing, Cambridge American Cemetery, UK and the East Coast Memorial in Battery Park, Manhattan, New York, USA.

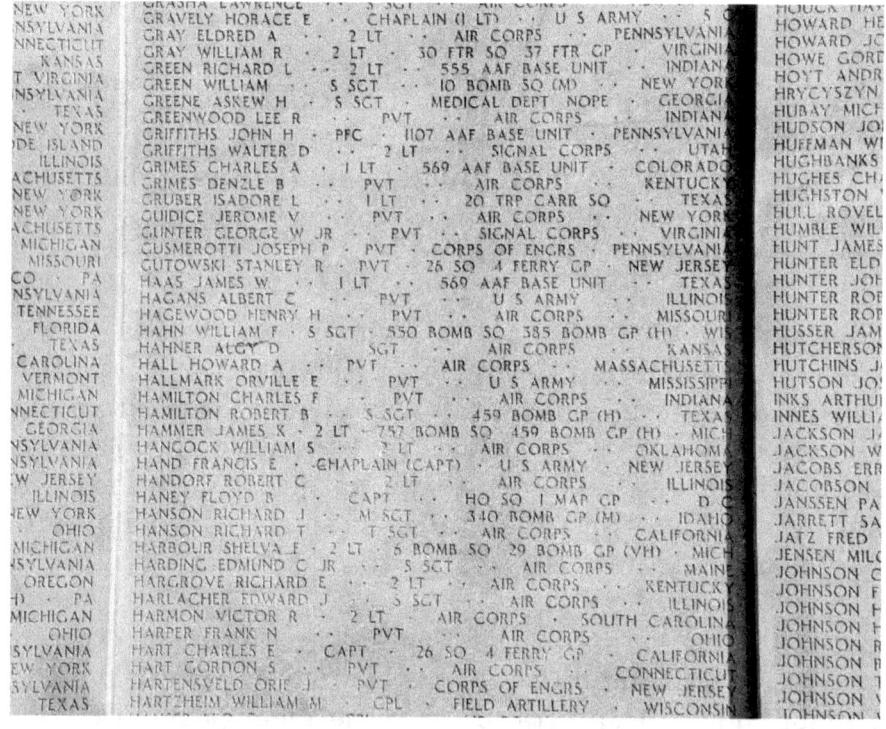

Edward Francis Hand was born in 1905 in Atlantic City, New Jersey, to John and Annie Hand (nee Schneider). At some time in his early adult life, Francis, whose first name at birth was Edward, reversed his name and used Francis as his first name from that point on until his death. This reversal of names is not reflected in his military records but does appear in genealogical reports. In 1920 the Hand family was living in Massachusetts, where Francis' father was a lawyer.

Francis married Idella Hand (nee Cramer) in 1923 in Atlantic City, New Jersey. Francis and Idella had a daughter born in 1930. When his daughter was born, Francis was attending Wheaton College in Chicago and working as an elevator operator to support his family. Francis graduated in 1935 and was ordained in the Methodist Church that same year. In the year before his ordination, he served as student pastor at Central Methodist Church, Point Pleasant Beach, New Jersey. Later, Pastor Hand took up ministry at Neptune City Memorial Methodist Church in Neptune City, New Jersey, in 1935-36. Francis and his family then moved to the joint congregations of Clarksboro Methodist Church and Milton Methodist Church, in Jefferson, New Jersey, in 1938. However, the Hand family did not remain there for long and in 1939, they moved to the Bayville-Ocean Gate Methodist Church in Ocean County, New Jersey. Francis was then commissioned in the United States Army as a reserve chaplain in late 1938. In 1940, Chaplain Hand had been called to duty and was serving with the 3rd Infantry Regiment at Fort Snelling, Minnesota.

In September 1940, the United Kingdom and the United States entered an agreement to transfer 50 American destroyers to the British Navy in exchange for 99-year leases on British bases along the western Atlantic coast and in the Caribbean, including Bermuda, the British West

Indies, the Bahamas, Jamaica, Saint Lucia, British Guiana, Trinidad and most importantly for Chaplain Hand, Newfoundland, off the Canadian east coast.

In January 1941, Chaplain Hand was reported to be temporarily posted to New York City in preparation for a move with his family to the American army and navy bases in Newfoundland, at that time a separate dominion from Canada in the British Commonwealth. Chaplain Hand was assigned to the Army Air Force bases that had been leased to the American government in the September 1940 agreement with Britain mentioned above. However, in the fall of 1941, Chaplain Hand and the 3rd Infantry Division were moved into the newly constructed Fort Pepperrell near Saint John's while his wife and daughter returned to the United States, as the North Atlantic campaign and the danger of U-boat torpedo attacks on the ferries from Newfoundland became more likely. This possibility of attacks on the ostensibly neutral American naval forces was that they were taking an active role in convoy escort to the mid-Atlantic and attacking U-boats that attacked the convoys they were guarding. Mrs. Hand and her daughter returned to Ocean City, New Jersey, where Rev Hand had his last civilian pastorate.

When The United States officially joined the war on 7 December, 1941, Newfoundland became a very active place, as convoys often formed up in St John's Harbour before setting off across the North Atlantic under the cover of American aircraft flying from Newfoundland bases. These convoys were also guarded by American Navy ships.

As Newfoundland is an island, there were ferry services that ran between both Quebec and Nova Scotia from the island. One of the most popular ferry routes was from Port aux Basques, Newfoundland, to Sydney, on the northern tip of Nova Scotia, which then permitted travellers to access the railway network across North America, both in Canada and the United States.

The ferry service between Port aux Basques and Sydney continued during World War Two, but it became a convoy route known as the Sydney Port aux Basque (SPAB) route. Generally, this meant that the ferry SS Caribou was escorted by Royal Canadian Navy ships three times per week, always sailing in darkness for more safety from attack by German U-boats. The Caribou was a fairly large ship, as it was able to carry railway cars and livestock and other cargo, as well as passengers. On the night of 13 October 1942, Chaplain Hand was on returning from leave with his family in New Jersey and was onboard the SS Caribou which had sailed from Sydney and was nearing its destination at Port aux Basques, under escort only by the HMCS Grandmère, a Bangor-class minesweeper, which is a very small naval ship. The Caribou was less than 20 nautical miles (37 kilometres) from its destination in Newfoundland. U-69 was on the surface in the Gulf of Saint Laurence, looking for shipping to attack. Against the lightening early morning sky, U-69 saw the telltale sign of the smoke from the SS Caribou's smokestack and began to plot a torpedo attack on the vessel at 3:51 a.m. Newfoundland Summer Time, U-69 fired one torpedo at the SS Caribou, hitting it squarely in the middle of the ship. The devastation caused by the torpedo hit was so severe that the SS Caribou, with Chaplain Hand and 190 other civilian and military passengers, including women and children, as well as a crew of 46, sank in less than 5 minutes. Of the 237 people on board the Caribou, 137 were killed in the sinking, but 100 others were rescued by the HMCS Grandmère. Chaplain Hand was one of those killed, and his body was not recovered.

In December 1944, Chaplain Hand's wife married Harvey Ford, a businessman in Ocean City, New Jersey.

1 or 2 December 1942

REV. ROLLIN GOODFELLOW

ROLLIN GOODFELLOW, Purple Heart. Service no. O-411496. Age 43. Captain, United States Army Chaplain Corps. Attached to the US Army Transportation Corps. Commemorated on the Tablet of the Missing, Cambridge American Cemetery, UK.

Rollin Goodfellow, and his twin brother Simeon, were born on 12 November 1899, in McConnellstown, Pennsylvania, to Addison and Letitia "Lettie" Goodfellow (née Stouffer). Rollin had an older sister, Anna, and a younger sister, Irene.

In July of 1918, Rollin, 17 years old, applied for a passport to permit him to travel to Cuba to be the private tutor for the children of a wealthy family there. However, he never made it to Cuba but rather enlisted in the US Army in October 1918 in the Students' Army Training Corps. World War One ended a month later, and Rollin was discharged in mid-December 1918.

Rollin married Esther Goodfellow (nee Engelmann) in 1925. They had two daughters, Eunice, who was born in 1927 and Maria, who was born in 1932.

Pastor Goodfellow's ministry was one of helping churches in their growing and changing. His first ministry as pastor was at Goss Memorial Reformed Church (now Evangelical and Reformed) in Akron, Ohio, where he was the pastor between 1927 to 1929, at a time when Goss Memorial was building a new church after outgrowing its previous location. In 1929, from Akron, Pastor Goodfellow and his family moved to Bedford, Ohio, where he became the pastor of the Reformed Church there. In November 1935, Pastor Goodfellow again moved, this time to Pine St Congregational Church in Lewiston, Maine, where he was instrumental in the merger of the Pine Street Church and the First Universalist Church. After shepherding the successful merger of the two congregations, Pastor Goodfellow, in 1936, moved on to the Second Congregational Church in Biddeford, Maine, where he served until volunteering for the Chaplain Corps in 1941.

Sources indicate that Chaplain Goodfellow died at sea when the ship he was a passenger on was sunk. The author believes that Chaplain Goodfellow was on the passenger ship SS Coamo, which had been chartered by the US Navy as a troopship and was torpedoed on Dec 2, about 150 miles west of Ireland. The SS Coamo had been sailing with a convoy between Gibraltar and the United Kingdom but was ordered to leave the convoy in the mid-Atlantic and proceed independently to New York. It was felt that its speed as a passenger ship would help protect it from a U-boat attack. It was carrying supplies and a small number of US troops from North Africa back to the United States. Chaplain Goodfellow must have been serving in the American invasion of North Africa but was recalled to the United States for some reason.

On the evening of 2 December 1942, German U-boat U-604 fired one torpedo at the SS Coamo. The torpedo struck below the water line under the bridge of the ship and, according to the report on the sinking by the U-boat captain, caused the SS Coamo to sink in about five minutes. The ship had eleven officers, 122 crewmen, as well as 37 men to man the defensive guns mounted on the ship, and 16 US Army passengers (of which, the author believes one was Chaplain Goodfellow). The U-boat captain reported seeing a few men leaving the ship on life rafts, but there were no survivors ever found, as a very strong storm swept the area of the SS Coamo, sinking for three days beginning early late in the evening of 2 December.

Besides being remembered on the Cambridge (UK) Memorial to the Missing, Chaplain Goodfellow is remembered in a stained glass window at Fort Eustis, Virginia's chapel. Fort Eustis is the home of the US Army Transportation Corps, which Chaplain Goodfellow was serving with when he died.

As the following entries show, the first week of February 1943 was a disastrous one for the United States Army Chaplain Corps. In two separate ship sinkings in the North Atlantic, they lost 9 highly trained chaplains to the icy waters of the North Atlantic.

4 February 1943

Captain **GEORGE LANSING FOX, BTh, Four Chaplains Medal, Distinguished Service Cross, Silver Star, Purple Heart (with Oak Leaf Cluster), Croix de Guerre,** Service no. O-485690. Age 42. United States Army Chaplain Corps. Commemorated on the Tablets of the Missing, Cambridge American Cemetery, Cambridge, UK and commemorated in the Chapel of the Four Chaplains, Philadelphia, PA.

George Lansing Fox (Cassatta) was born on 15 March 1900 to Charles J Cassatta and his wife, Mary C Cassatta (nee Reichert), in Lewistown, Pennsylvania. George had a sister, Gertrude, and 3 brothers, Bert, Leo and John. Sometime in his early adulthood, George changed his last name from Cassatta to Fox, but there is no reason recorded for this change. The rest of George's siblings retained the last name of Cassatta. One can imagine that he may have changed his name to a more English-sounding one due to his becoming a Methodist minister.

When the United States entered World War One, George was only 17, but he felt he needed to support his country in the war, so he lied about his age, saying he was 18, and joined the US Army Medical Corps, where he served as a medical orderly. On 3 December 1917, George embarked from Camp Merritt, New Jersey, and boarded the troopship, the USS Huron, en route to France. George served as a frontline medic and was awarded the Silver Star for rescuing a wounded soldier on the battlefield where a gas attack was taking place. He was wounded in World War One and awarded the Purple Heart. He also received the Croix de Guerre from the French Government for his heroism on the French battlefields.

After the end of World War One, George returned to America and his parents' home in Altoona and completed his high school education and went to work for the Guarantee Trust Company. However, In 1923 he answered the call to ordained ministry and enrolled in the Moody Bible Institute in Chicago, Illinois. In that same year, he married Isadore Gertrude Fox (Hurlbutt) in Winona Lake, Indiana. Isadore Fox was originally from Hyde Park, Vermont and had been married before to Charles J Breer when she was 18; the couple had a daughter who died less than a year after she was born in 1916. It appears that Isadore had then divorced Charles Breer and moved to Chicago.

Having a family led to George withdrawing from his studies at the Moody Bible Institute and becoming an itinerant preacher in the Methodist Church. George and Isadore had a son, Wyatt, who was born in November 1924. However, George had not given up his determination to finish his studies, and he took on a student pastorate at the Methodist Church in Downs, Illinois. George then entered Illinois Wesleyan University in Bloomington in 1929 and graduated with a Bachelor of Arts degree in 1931. George and his family then moved to another student pastorate, this time in Rye, New Hampshire, and George enrolled in the Boston University School of Theology. George graduated with a Bachelor of Sacred Theology degree and was ordained a Methodist minister on 10 June 1934. While at seminary, George, who was only 5' 7" (173cm), earned the nickname "The Little Minister". Following his graduation and ordination, George was appointed the pastor of the Methodist Church in Waits River, Vermont. While there, George and Isadore had their second child, Mary. In 1936, George and his family moved to Union Village, Vermont. His next pastorate was in Gilman (part of the town of Lunenburg), also in Vermont, in 1939. While there, Rev Fox joined the American Legion and was appointed chaplain for the whole of the Vermont Legion.

On 7 December 1941, upon hearing of the Japanese attack on Pearl Harbour, George commented to his wife, "I've got to go. I know from experience what those boys are about to face. They need me." He volunteered for the Chaplain Corps and was commissioned as a chaplain on 24 July 1942 (the same date as his son joined the United States Marine Corps). Chaplain Fox was sent to the Harvard Chaplains School and, upon graduation, was assigned to the 411th Coast Artillery Battalion at Camp Davis, where soldiers were trained in the use of anti-aircraft artillery. However, as the American Army began to move overseas to North Africa and Europe, there was a need to have chaplains go with the troops, and Chaplain Fox was assigned to go and replace more experienced American chaplains who had been stationed in Iceland and were to accompany their units to Great Britain. The Americans had taken over the occupation of Iceland in June 1941 from the British to prevent the Germans from occupying this strategically important island. Chaplain Fox was assigned to Camp Myles Standish in Taunton, Massachusetts, where troops were gathered before being assigned to transport ships and sent overseas. From there, Chaplain Fox was assigned to the SS Dorchester, along with 3 other chaplains and 901 sailors and soldiers.

 **ALEXANDER DAVID GOODE, BA, BH, Four Chaplains Medal, Distinguished Service Cross, Purple Heart.** Service no. O-485093. Age 31. Captain, United States Army Chaplain Corps. Commemorated on the Tablets of the Missing, Cambridge American Cemetery, Cambridge, UK and commemorated in the Chapel of the Four Chaplains, Philadelphia, PA.

Alexander Goode was born in Columbus Ohio on 10 May, 1911 to Rabbi Hyman Sulman Goodkowitz and his wife Fannie "Fay" Goodkowitz (née Aronin). Alexander had two brothers, Joseph and Moses, and a sister, Agatha.

As a rabbi, Alexander's father moved, as many clergy do, to a variety of synagogues in the eastern United States, including Rocky Mount, North Carolina, and then New York City. As a teenager, Alexander's family moved to Washington DC, where he attended Eastern High School and was a star athlete winning medals for tennis, swimming and track. Besides being a good athlete, Alexander was an excellent scholar, as he planned to become a rabbi, following in his father's footsteps. The neighbourhood where Alexander spent his teenage years was quite diverse, and he had friends who were Jewish, Protestant and Catholic. Alexander shortened his name from Goodkowitz to the more generic-sounding Goode sometime in his early adulthood.

In 1929, Alexander entered the University of Cincinnati and graduated in 1934 with a Bachelor of Arts degree. On 7 October 1935, he married his teenage sweetheart from Eastern High School, Theresa Goode (nee Flax), in Washington, DC. That same year, Alexander entered the Hebrew Union College (HUC) of the University of Cincinnati and earned a Bachelor of Hebrew degree in 1937. While at Hebrew Union College, in his last year of study, Alexander was appointed as the student rabbi of the synagogue in Marion, Indiana. After his graduation from HUC, he was ordained a rabbi and assigned to the Beth Israel synagogue in York, Pennsylvania, where, besides being the Rabbi, he was also a PhD candidate at Johns Hopkins University in Baltimore. Rabbi Goode was awarded his doctorate in 1940. It was in York that Alexander and Theresa's only child, their daughter Rosalie, was born. While in York, Rabbi Goode established a multicultural Boy Scout troop, which was the first troop in America to have boys earn religious awards in Catholicism, Judaism, and Protestantism.

In January 1941, after reading of the plight of Jewish people in occupied Europe, Rabbi Goode applied to the US Navy as a chaplain but was not accepted. In December 1941, after the attack on Pearl Harbour, Rabbi Goode applied to the US Army as a chaplain and was accepted. He was commissioned on 21 July 1942 and was sent to the Harvard Chaplain School in August 1942. After his graduation from the school, Chaplain Goode was assigned to the 333rd Airbase Squadron in Goldsboro, North Carolina. As the American buildup of troops in Europe and North Africa began, Rabbi Goode was assigned to Camp Myles Standish in Taunton, Massachusetts, where troops were gathered before being assigned to transport ships to be sent overseas. From there, Chaplain Goode was assigned to the SS Dorchester, along with 3 other chaplains and 901 sailors and soldiers.

CLARK VANDERSALL POLING, BA, BD, Four Chaplains Medal, Distinguished Service Cross, Purple Heart. Service no. O-477425. Age 42. 1st Lieutenant, United States Army Chaplain Corps. Commemorated on the Tablets of the Missing, Cambridge American Cemetery, Cambridge, UK and commemorated in the Chapel of the Four Chaplains, Philadelphia, PA.

Clark Poling was born 7 August, 1910, in Columbus, Ohio. He was the son of Daniel A. Poling and Susie Jane Poling (nee Vandersall). Clark had a brother, Daniel, and sisters, Mary and Elizabeth. As a young boy, Clark's family moved to Auburndale, Massachusetts, where he was noted for both his maturity and his caring for others. Unfortunately, in 1918 Clark's mother died, and in 1919 Clark's father, an Evangelical (Pentecostal) Minister, remarried Lillian Diebold Poling (nee Heingartner), who became stepmother to Clark, his brother, and his sisters. In 1936, Clark's father left the Pentecostal Church and joined the Northern Baptist denomination and became a Baptist minister.

As a teenager, Clark and his family lived in Poughkeepsie, New York, where he attended Oakwood Friends School, a private preparatory Quaker high school in Poughkeepsie. Clark was noted to be a good student and an excellent football halfback. While at Oakwood, he also became president of the Student Council.

In 1929 Clark graduated from Oakwood, and he enrolled at Hope College in Holland, Michigan. Hope College is a private college affiliated with the Reformed Church in America. However, in 1931, he transferred to Rutgers University in New Brunswick, New Jersey, graduating in 1933 with a Bachelor of Arts degree. Clark entered Yale University Divinity School in New Haven, Connecticut and graduated with his Bachelor of Divinity degree in 1936. Obviously, Clark was greatly influenced as a young man by his time at Hope College, for he did not follow his father into ministry in the Baptist Church or even the Pentecostal Church but chose instead to seek ordination in the Reformed Church in America. Clark was ordained a minister in 1936, and his first congregation was the First Church of Christ, New London, Connecticut. Shortly thereafter, he accepted the assignment of Pastor of the First Reformed Church in Schenectady, New York. Clark was married to Elizabeth "Betty" Poling (nee Jung) of Philadelphia, Pennsylvania, in 1936, and the next year, Clark, Jr. (Corky) was born.

In December 1941, with America now at war, Pastor Polling talked with his father, who had served as a chaplain in World War I, and who warned Clark that chaplains in that war had sustained very high casualty rates. However, Pastor Polling still felt the call to serve in the US Army and was commissioned on 10 June 1942 as a chaplain with the 131st Quartermaster Truck Regiment and reported to Camp Shelby, Hattiesburg, Mississippi. However, within two months, Chaplain Poling was reassigned to the Chaplains School at Harvard University for training as a chaplain. It is not clear why Chaplain Polling did not immediately attend the Chaplains School after his commissioning. It is possible that Chaplain Polling's attendance at the Chaplains School was delayed, as the school was in the process of moving from Fort

Benjamin Harrison, Indiana, to its new location at Harvard University in Cambridge, Massachusetts and did not offer classes for two months due to the move.

After his graduation from the Chaplains School, Chaplain Poling was assigned to Camp Miles Standish in Taunton, Massachusetts, where troops were gathered before being assigned to transport ships to be sent overseas. From there, Chaplain Goode was assigned to the SS Dorchester, along with 3 other chaplains and 901 sailors and soldiers.

JOHN P WASHINGTON, BA, Four Chaplains Medal, Distinguished Service Cross, Purple Heart. Service no. O-463529. Age 35. 1st Lieutenant, United States Army Chaplain Corps. Commemorated on the Tablets of the Missing, Cambridge American Cemetery, Cambridge, UK and commemorated in the Chapel of the Four Chaplains, Philadelphia, PA.

John P. Washington was born in Newark, New Jersey, on 18 July 1908 to Frank and Mary Washington. John had two sisters, Mary and Anna, and four brothers, Thomas, Francis, Leo and Edmund.

In 1914, John enrolled at St. Rose of Lima Catholic Elementary School. While in school, he enjoyed playing baseball with his friends. However, his family was not well off, and John also had a newspaper route to help with the family finances. As a boy, John turned out to have musical talents and was enrolled in piano lessons and sang in his church choir. John began middle school (grade 7) and felt a call to ordained ministry. At this time, he also began serving as an altar boy at his local parish church.

John was an excellent student, and for his final high school years, he was enrolled at Seton Hall Preparatory School in South Orange, New Jersey. Seton Hall was noted as a place of preparation for young men considering ordination to the priesthood of the Roman Catholic Church. John graduated from Seton Hall and entered Seton Hall University's Immaculate Conception Seminary, where he graduated in May 1933 with a Bachelor of Arts degree. He was ordained a deacon on Christmas Day, 25 December 1934. John was ordained a priest on 15 June 1935.

Upon ordination, Father Washington's first parish was at St. Genevieve's Roman Catholic church in Elizabeth, New Jersey, where he served for a year, and then he was moved to St. Venantius Roman Catholic Church for another year. In 1938 he was assigned as the priest at St. Stephen's Roman Catholic Church in Arlington, New Jersey, where he served until April 1941. As so many clergy in America did, Father Washington, with his bishop's permission, volunteered for duty as an Army Chaplain shortly after the attack on Pearl Harbour on 7 December 1941,

Chaplain Washington was commissioned in the Chaplain Corps on 9 May 1942 and was assigned to the first Chaplain training school at Fort Benjamin Harrison, Indiana. In June 1942, Chaplain Washington was assigned to the 76th Infantry Division at Ft. George Meade, Maryland. In late November 1942, Chaplain Washington was assigned to Camp Miles Standish in Taunton, Massachusetts, where troops were gathered before being assigned to transport ships to be sent overseas. From there, Chaplain Washington was assigned to the SS Dorchester, along with 3 other chaplains and 901 sailors and soldiers.

3 February 1943 – Sinking of the SS Dorchester

The SS Dorchester was chartered by the United States Army in February 1942, and as many of her peacetime crew remained at their posts, she was never officially commissioned as a United States Army Transport (USAT). Her crew complement was enhanced by the assigning of a contingent of Naval Armed Guards to man the 3"/50 calibre gun on the foredeck and a 4"/50 calibre gun on the stern of the ship, as well as four 20 mm guns for air defence. The Naval Armed Guard also was responsible for operating the ship's radio.

On 23 January 1943, the SS Dorchester left New York harbour, bound for the top secret army base at Narsarsuaq in southern Greenland. This site was to become a major airbase on the route from Maine to Gander, Newfoundland, to Blue Two (Narsarsuaq, Greenland) to Keflavik, Iceland and on to Stornoway or Prestwick airbases in Scotland, where so many aircraft went from manufacture in North

America to the battlefields of Europe. The convoy (codenamed SG-19) consisted of six ships: SS Dorchester, two merchant ships (SS Lutz and SS Biscaya) leased by the United States from the Norwegian government-in-exile, and their escorts, the small United States Coast Guard cutters Comanche and Escanaba, and the larger cutter, Tampa.

As convoy SG-19 slowly made its way towards its destination in Greenland at 00:55 hours on 3 February 1943, the SS Dorchester was torpedoed by the German U-boat U-223. The SS Dorchester was severely damaged on her left (port) side, and her boilers lost all the steam pressure they had, which meant that the 6-whistle signal to abandon ship could not be sounded. The SS Dorchester sank bow first in about 20 minutes. As water rushed in through the huge hole on its port side, the vessel began to tilt in such an extreme manner that many of the port-side lifeboats could not be launched. This led to overcrowding of other lifeboats, and some capsized, tossing the men into the almost freezing water from where the men chilled so rapidly they were unable to clamber into the remaining lifeboats or up the cargo nets on rescue vessels, and they drowned.

Chaplains Goode, Washington, Fox and Poling arrived on deck shortly after the torpedo hit the side of the SS Dorchester. As there had been no warning of the U-boat attack, many of the soldiers on the SS Dorchester had been sleeping, and as the lights below deck had gone out when the torpedo hit, the men arrived on deck without their lifejackets. The four chaplains were seen helping soldiers into the lifeboats and also gave up their own life jackets when they encountered soldiers without one. Petty Officer John J. Mahoney, one of the crews of the SS Dorchester, tried to re-enter the ship to retrieve some gloves but was stopped by Rabbi Goode. "Never mind," smiled Goode, "I have two pairs." and he gave the petty officer his own gloves. Afterwards, Mahoney realized that Rabbi Goode was not carrying two pairs of gloves, and the rabbi knew he was not going to survive the sinking of the SS Dorchester. There was much panic during the 20 minutes it took the ship to sink, but the four chaplains became a beacon of calm when they were seen linking arms and praying together.

The USCG cutters who were escorting the SS Dorchester were able to rescue 230 of 904 troops and crew of the ship, both from the water and in the few lifeboats that were upright. However, the remaining 674 men on the SS Dorchester either went down with the ship or froze to death in the water within an hour of the ship's sinking. The SS Dorchester sinking was the largest loss of life of Americans in any convoy of World War Two. The heroic actions of the four chaplains, related by so many of the survivors, touched a nerve with the American public. Each of the chaplains was posthumously awarded the Distinguished Service Cross and the Purple Heart. The chaplains were also nominated for the Medal of Honor but were found ineligible as they had not been personally engaged in combat with the enemy. Due to this restriction, 17 years after the chaplains' deaths, the United States Congress created a special medal for them, the Chaplains Medal for Heroism, which had the same weight and importance as the Medal of Honor.

7 February 1942

First Lieutenant **HORACE E. GRAVELY, Purple Heart.** Service no. O-238342. Age 42. United States Army Chaplain Corps. Commemorated on the Tablets of the Missing, Cambridge American Cemetery, Cambridge, UK.

Horace Gravely was the son of Alvin (Will) Willoughby and Hannah Elizabeth (Betty) Gravely (nee McKinney) and was born on 10 October 1901 in Pickens, South Carolina. Within two weeks of Horace's birth, his older brother, George, died of diphtheria and scarlet fever. In November of that year, another brother, Rufus, also died of the same diseases. Horace had two other younger brothers, Marven and Tom, and a sister Eula.

Horace's father, Will, was a lay minister for the Old Salem Methodist Church in Pickens. Will was killed in a wagon accident in 1918, and his mother was left to care for 4 children aged 4 to 17. His father's death meant that Will had to withdraw from high school to work and help provide for his family. However, Horace was able to finish his high school and entered university in 1922 with the goal of becoming an ordained Methodist minister.

In 1923, while in his first year as a student at Wofford College, he received his license to preach. While at Wofford, he also enrolled in the Reserve Officers Training Corps (ROTC) to help finance his college education.

In 1925 he met his wife, Katherine (Kate) Carter, and they were engaged to be married 3 weeks after their first meeting. In 1925, he began his trial ministry as a Methodist minister, meaning he could preach and lead services, but could not perform marriages or celebrate the sacrament of Holy Communion. In November 1928, he began his formal ministry in the Upper South Carolina Methodist Conference, and two years later, he was ordained deacon and then, in 1932, he became an ordained elder.

Reverend Gravely served in six different congregation appointments in his 12 years in ministry. In his first charge, he and Kate had two children, Martha, born in March 1929 and Horace Jr. in October 1931. Horace and his family moved around South Carolina during his pastorates. He and Kate had a second son, John, born in 1936. In late 1936, Horace became the minister of the Walhalla Methodist Circuit centred on Walhalla, South Carolina, initially involving four churches (located at Bethel, Double Springs, Monaghan, and Zion), with a fifth church at Fairview being added a year or so later. The relationships that Horace and his family had in Walhalla were so good that Kate and her family ended up settling there after Horace's death. In November 1940, Horace's final congregational appointment sent him to Latimer Memorial Church in Belton, South Carolina, and two rural congregations, Ebenezer and Oak Hill.

While serving as a minister in a variety of congregations, Rev Gravely maintained his status as a member of the US Army Officers' Reserve Corps as well as being a chaplain for the Civilian Conservation Corps (CCC) during the Great Depression. With the rapid expansion of the US

Army, Rev Gravely was called to active duty on 7 March 1942.

Chaplain Gravely was initially assigned to Camp Robinson, near Little Rock, Arkansas. While there, Chaplain Gravely ministered to over 2000 men, which required that he hold three services each Sunday. At Camp Robinson, the chaplain had some unusual and sad experiences. For example, Chaplain Gravely married a couple while using a telephone to talk with the bride so that they could be married before her new husband was shipped overseas. On another occasion, Chaplain Gravely had to perform the burial of a soldier who committed suicide in the base chapel by drinking iodine.

In November 1942, Chaplain Gravely, even with his Reserve Officer experience as a chaplain, was transferred to the Chaplain School at Harvard University, and he graduated on 8 December 1942. He was then assigned to assist the US Army that had occupied Iceland to prevent a German takeover of what was then Danish territory. He and 6 other chaplains were assigned to the SS Mallory for the journey to Iceland in January 1943. Only 2 chaplains survived the journey. One of the two chaplains who survived, Chaplain Gerald Whelan, wrote, "The last time I saw Horace was when he was heading for a lifeboat. Due to the roughness of the sea and a storm on the black night, only two boats got away without being overturned. He Chaplain Gravely) was not in either of these two boats." Chaplain Whelan added about Horace, "He was a good man and fine Christian gentleman, and I say this with all my heart and soul."

Chaplain Gravely's wife, Kate had trouble accepting her husband's death and wrote the US War Department a number of letters in the spring of 1943 inquiring if her husband might still be alive, as he was initially only listed as missing. Six months after the sinking of the Mallory, Chaplain Gravely was officially listed as killed in action on 7 February 1943.

As the money a war widow, even with children, received was not enough, Kate Gravely took a job as a switchboard operator for Wesleyan College in Macon, Georgia, for a year. Kate then moved her family back to Walhalla, South Carolina, where she and Horace had such an enjoyable time when he was the Methodist minister there. Kate took a position teaching typing, shorthand and other business-related courses at Walhalla High School, where she taught until 1968.

An interesting note about the Gravely family is that on the day that Chaplain Gravely died, his mother, Betty, had a dream that "she was reaching her hand out for him before he went under the water." Her grip was so strong that she broke her second finger on the headboard of her bed.

Besides being commemorated in Battery Park in New York City, Chaplain Horace Gravely is commemorated in a window donated by his family in 1948 to Grace United Methodist Church in Pickens, South Carolina, where he was born. A United Methodist Church formed in a suburb of Spartanburg, South Carolina, was formed in 1948 and named Gravely Memorial in 1950 in his memory.

DAVID H YOUNGDAHL, BTH, Purple Heart. Service no O-448376. Age 38. Captain, United States Army Chaplain Corps. Commemorated on the Tablets of the Missing, Cambridge American Cemetery, Cambridge, UK.

In Swanville, Minnesota, on 16 February 1905, two Swedish immigrants, Joel and Huldah Youngdahl, had a baby named David, who was followed by a sister named Judith and a brother named Warren. David Youngdahl grew up to graduate in 1930 with a Bachelor of Theology degree from the Bethel Theological Seminary in St. Paul, Minnesota. In April of 1930, David became assistant pastor of the First Baptist Church (Northern Baptist Conference) in New Richmond, Wisconsin.

Later in 1930, Pastor Youngdahl moved to Washington State, where he went on to earn a Bachelor of Arts Degree from Seattle Pacific College. The following year he again moved, this time to Berkeley, California, where he attended the Berkeley Baptist Divinity School, earning a Bachelor of Divinity degree. Pastor Youngdahl then became the minister of Temple Baptist Church in San Francisco, California. While at Temple Baptist Church, Pastor Youngdahl married Charlotte Youngdahl (nee Bridge) in Seattle in August 1935. In January 1937, the Youngdahl's had a son they named Samuel.

After Pearl Harbour, Pastor Youngdahl felt called to serve as a military chaplain and was commissioned into the Chaplain Corps in April 1942. His wife and young son moved to Santa Barbara, California, while Pastor

Youngdahl was in the army, possibly to be with Charlotte's family.

In the Spring of 1942, Chaplain Youngdahl trained at the Chaplain School at Fort Benjamin Harrison, Indiana and then was assigned to the 53rd Field Artillery Regiment at Camp Myles Standish in Taunton, Massachusetts. While at Camp Myles Standish, Chaplain Youngdahl was promoted to the rank of Captain.

As Camp Myles Standish was also the major army base where various units of the American Army were assembled before being sent overseas, it was here Chaplain Youngdahl met the 7 other chaplains who would be travelling overseas with him. They were all assigned to assist the US Army that had occupied Iceland to prevent a German takeover of what was then Danish territory. He and 6 other chaplains were assigned to the SS Mallory for the journey to Iceland in January 1943.

Since her husband was lost at sea, Mrs Youngdahl was notified only that he was missing at sea shortly after the sinking of the SS Mallory. It was only in August 1943 that Charlotte received official notice that her husband David had been declared killed in action at sea, and his body was not recovered.

VALMORE "BUD" G SAVIGNAC, Purple Heart. Service no. O-477261. Age 32. 1st Lieutenant, United States Army Chaplain Corps. Commemorated on the Tablets of the Missing, Cambridge American Cemetery, Cambridge, UK.

Valmore (Vud) G. Valmore's father was a French-Canadian who had immigrated to Rhode Island in about 1890. His father's full name was John Valmore Savignac, and young Valmore took his first name from his father's middle name. In Providence, Valmore's father, John, became a policeman with the Providence Police Department.

Valmore had an older sister named Mary, who was born in 1908. Another sister named Anna was born in 1909, followed by Valmore (who was known as Bud). Lastly, another sister named Rita was born in 1915. Bud's mother, Annie, died in January 1921. Sometime after Annie died, Bud's father, John remarried a woman named Mary. However, their marriage was not long, as John died in November 1928. After John's death, his widow Mary was left with 3 of her 4 stepchildren to care for. Bud's oldest sister, Mary, had moved out of the family home before her father died, but her stepmother Mary supported her remaining three stepchildren, Anna, Bud and Rita, by working as a department store bookkeeper. Anna, Bud's second eldest sister, was living at home but had found employment as a nurse in a local Providence hospital.

At the age of 17, shortly before his father's death in 1928, Bud enrolled in the LaSalle Academy in Providence. This was an all-boys college preparatory school that served the Providence Cathedral and Saint John parishes. Besides preparing young men for college, the LaSalle Academy also prepared them to enter seminary to become Catholic priests. After his graduation from LaSalle Academy, Bud attended Providence College for two more years of studies before going on to earn his Bachelor of Arts degree in Philosophy in 1932. Bud then went to the Grand Seminary in Montreal, Canada, where he graduated in 1936 with a Bachelor of Sacred Theology degree and a Licentiate of Sacred Theology (a graduate degree).

Upon his graduation from the Grand Seminary, Bud returned to Rhode Island and was ordained in the Roman Catholic Church in his home Diocese of Providence. In the spring of 1942, Father Savignac sought permission from his bishop to leave his parish and volunteer as an Army Chaplain. His request was granted, and Bud was commissioned on 9 June 1942. Two weeks later, Father Savignac was assigned to Fort Eustis, Virginia, as the Chaplain School was in the process of moving from Indiana to Cambridge, Massachusetts. Later in the summer of 1942, Chaplain Savignac was assigned to the Chaplain School at Harvard University. Upon completion of his 5-week course, Chaplain Savignac was assigned to Camp Myles Standish in Massachusetts.

In mid-January, Chaplain Savignac received orders to board the SS Henry R. Mallory, along with 7 other chaplains from his class at Harvard. Their ship was to join a convoy taking supplies and troops to serve on the island of Iceland.

JAMES M LISTON, STB, Purple Heart. Service no O-462733. Age 38. 1st Lieutenant, United States Army Chaplain Corps. Commemorated on the Tablets of the Missing, Cambridge American Cemetery, Cambridge, UK.

James M. Liston was a native of the Chicago area and was born on 16 September 1905. James was a first-generation Irish Catholic and the eldest son of James and Margaret Liston (nee Noonan), who had married in Ireland in 1901 and immigrated to the United States in 1902 and became an American citizen in November 1907. James' father worked as a streetcar conductor in Chicago. The Liston family grew quickly, with James as the oldest, a second son, John, born in 1908 and a third son, William, born in 1909, a daughter Anna in 1911 and another son, Thomas, in 1914.

The Liston family home was also the home of James' uncles, 26-year-old Dennis and 22-year-old Patrick, who had immigrated to America in 1909. As well, James' mother's sister, Ellen Noonan, also resided in the large household.

As a teenager, James attended the Quigley Preparatory Seminary (High School) for young men considering becoming priests, and he graduated from it in 1925. James went on to attend and graduate from St. Mary of the Lake

Seminary in 1931 with a Bachelor of Sacred Theology. Now called the University of Saint Mary of the Lake but also known as Mundelein Seminary (after Cardinal Mundelein), this institution is the principal seminary of the Roman Catholic Archdiocese of Chicago. Upon his graduation, James was ordained a Roman Catholic priest. Following ordination, Father James M. Liston began his ministry, serving in various parishes in the Chicago Archdiocese until he was granted permission from his bishop to join the Army Chaplain Corps. Chaplain Liston was commissioned in early 1942. His first assignment after graduating from the Chaplains School at Fort Benjamin Harrison, Indiana, was to Camp Croft, an infantry basic training base near Spartanburg, South Carolina.

With the increased American deployment of troops overseas, Chaplain Liston was assigned to duty in Iceland in late 1942 and travelled to the Army Transit Camp Myles Standish in Massachusetts. In mid-January 1943, Chaplain Liston received orders to board the SS Henry R. Mallory, along with 7 other chaplains. Their ship was joining a convoy taking supplies and troops to serve on the island of Iceland.

Chaplain Liston was not among the men rescued from the sinking of the Mallory, but his body was identified along by a survivor who knew Chaplain Liston and saw his body floating on the waves, already dead from the effects of the icy water.

ERNEST "PAT" WARBURTON MACDONALD, Purple Heart. Service no. O-449888. Age 32. Captain, United States Army Chaplain Corps. Commemorated on the Tablets of the Missing, Cambridge American Cemetery, Cambridge, UK.

Ernest (Pat) MacDonald was born on 25 December 1911 to John Ernest and Patience (nee Stewart) MacDonald in Quincy, Massachusetts. He also had an older sister, Catherine, who died in 1917 of tuberculosis, and a younger sister named Mabel.

Ernest attended elementary school in Quincy and then high school at Thayer Academy in Braintree, Massachusetts. While in high school, he was very active in the Order of DeMolay (a part of Freemasonry for teenage boys). Upon graduation from Thayer Academy, Pat enrolled at Dalhousie University in Halifax, Nova Scotia, Canada, where he earned a Bachelor of Arts degree in 1938. While at Dalhousie, he met his wife, Kathryn MacDonald. They were married in 1938 and had a son, Gregory, and a daughter, Heather. When Pat was studying at Dalhousie, he felt the call to ordained ministry and took some theology classes at the Pine Hill Divinity School, run by the United Church of Canada. After graduation, Pat entered the Andover Newton School of Theology and graduated with a Bachelor of Divinity degree in 1939. Pat was called to the Newington, Connecticut, Church of Christ, where he was ordained and began his ministry as assistant pastor to Rev. Harold Burdon. In 1940, Pat and his family accepted a call for him to be the new pastor at the Community Congregationalist Church in Garden City, Kansas, to replace the existing minister who had volunteered for the Chaplain Corps. While serving in the congregation, Pat was very popular with the young people's group, which took the name of "The MacDonald Club" in honour of Pat after his death.

In April of 1942, Reverend MacDonald also felt the call to Army Chaplaincy and volunteered for active service. Mrs MacDonald and the two children left Garden City and returned to Wollaston, Massachusetts. Chaplain MacDonald was in the first few classes that trained at Fort Benjamin Harrison in Indiana, and after graduation, was assigned to minister to the 9th Service Command to minister to the troops in the state of Oregon. However, shortly after beginning this assignment, Chaplain MacDonald was transferred from the west coast of America to the east coast in preparation for overseas service. While waiting to be assigned a ship to travel overseas, Chaplain MacDonald was promoted to the rank of Captain. In mid-January, Chaplain MacDonald, along with 7 other chaplains, received orders to board the SS Henry R. Mallory. Their ship was joining a convoy taking supplies and troops to serve on the island of Iceland.

Chaplain MacDonald died in the sinking of the Mallory. Later in World War Two, one of the survivors of the sinking, specifically one of the ship's cooks named George Dunningham, visited Captain MacDonald's parents. He told them of his having begged their Chaplain MacDonald, whom he met in a companionway in the sinking ship, to accompany him to a lifeboat. However, Chaplain MacDonald refused. Instead, Chaplain MacDonald headed down the steeply listing stairs into the bowels of the ship to try and help wounded and disoriented soldiers to the deck. Pat's mother after his death, as she was having a great deal of difficulty accepting his death. In fact, her doubts were so strong that she wrote to the President of Iceland, asking if her son might have made it to that country in one of the rescue ships. Chaplain Whelan, who survived the Mallory sinking and was serving on the island of Iceland, was tasked with writing to Mrs MacDonald Sr. He wrote to her, "I got to know Chaplain MacDonald fairly well en route to Iceland. He took turns with the other Protestant chaplains in holding services for the men of the Protestant Faith. On the day before the fatal disaster, as the weather was clear, we had boxing matches on the quarter deck in which Chaplain MacDonald took an active part. He was a likeable chap." He also told Pat's mother about the night the ship was torpedoed, "There was confusion down there in the hold and much running down along the companionways. The last I saw of Chaplain MacDonald was when he left his stateroom, which was adjoining mine and the other chaplains." From accounts with other men who were saved with me, I learned that he was washed off a raft by the heavy seas that night. He had done heroic work in calming the men, as did the other chaplains."

Due to Chaplain MacDonald's body not being recovered, it was not until the end of July 1943 that his wife was notified that he had been presumed dead in the sinking of the SS Mallory. Chaplain MacDonald's mother had a great deal of difficulty in accepting her son's death in action and wrote to the President of Iceland seeking more information and to inquire if a mistake in reporting his death had been made.

Chaplain MacDonald is commemorated In the chapel at Andover Newton Theological School on a bronze memorial plaque placed there in 1946 by the members of his class. Also, a student's reading room in the school is named for him.

After the war, and Captain MacDonald had been declared dead, his widow Katherine and their children moved to England, where Katherine remarried a former British Royal Navy Lieutenant-Commander, Robert J. Barcham and lived the rest of her life in England.

7 February 1943 – The Sinking of the SS Henry J Mallory

This ship is common to the stories of these chaplains: First Lieutenant Horace Gravely, First Lieutenant James Liston, First Lieutenant Valmore "Bud" Savignac, Captain Ernest "Pat" MacDonald, and Captain David Youngdahl.

In late January 1943, seven chaplains, all commissioned or called to active service in the spring of 1942, were assigned berths on the SS Henry Mallory, as it was forming up as part of Convoy SC-118 that would be heading for Iceland to bring fresh troops to relieve those already stationed there. The Mallory set sail from New York City on 24 January 1943. The vessel was a small combined cargo and passenger ship that had been converted into a troop transport. It had a crew of 76 and a gun crew of 34 men of the Naval Armed Guard, as well as 72 Marines, 173 other naval personnel, 2 civilians and 136 US Army troops.

On the evening of 6 February, the evening of the disaster, the Chaplains aboard the Mallory held a service for the men. About the service that evening, one of the Mallory survivors relates, "Word was passed that there would be a prayer meeting in the mess hall at 1900 hrs. Several of us decided to attend. The leader of the meeting was a chaplain, denomination unknown. His sermon was on the Lord's Prayer. He took the prayer phrase by phrase and explained its meaning. The phrase 'Thy will be done' made a particularly strong impression on me. After the meeting, we went below to our quarters. It was soon time to turn in."[2]

The Mallory had an inexperienced captain and was assigned to a slow convoy, which moved at a speed of 7 knots even though the SS Mallory was capable of a sustained speed of over 14 knots. The fate of the SS Mallory was sealed when a survivor of an earlier convoy, HX-224, was rescued from the icy North Atlantic south of Greenland by a German U-boat after his ship was torpedoed on 2 February. This survivor inadvertently gave the captain the news that a slower convoy was a few days behind his convoy. Additionally, the Mallory convoy's location was divulged by two incidents on merchant's vessels: one during the day 3 February and another later that night, when careless seamen, by mistake, fired some very bright illuminating rockets whose lighted displays were visible as far as twenty miles away. They were spotted by another U-boat, U-187, which reported the sighting to the German U-Boat Command, which in turn passed it on to a variety of U-Boats stationed in the North Atlantic. As well, Mallory's captain, either due to inexperience, or sheer incompetence, seemed to keep putting his ship in danger. Other ships in convoy SC-118 noted that the Mallory was straggling behind the convoy, especially when the group executed a course change and when it failed to execute a zigzag pattern, of course-changes to help put off the aim of a U-boat that might be stalking the ship.

On 7 February 1943, at 2:13 (GMT), the German U-402 found SC-118 with no warships defending its starboard (right) side. The U-boat, Captain Forstner, fired at the undefended convoy and hit a small freighter named the SS Toward, which had been tasked with being a rescue ship for other ships that might be torpedoed. Another torpedo hit the American tanker, the SS R.E. Hopkins. Shortly after 3:00 am, U-boat Captain Forstner torpedoed another ship, the large tanker SS Daghild. Two hours later, the U-402 torpedoed the freighter SS Afrika. While all this action was going on, the SS Mallory had continued to dawdle behind the convoy, and it became U-402's next victim.

While the crew and passengers of the SS Mallory had been alerted at 3:30 am to dress and put on their life jackets, they never were given a specific warning of an impending attack. In the half darkness of an early February morning, the lookouts on the SS Mallory were changed at 6:00 am and due to just coming on duty from the lighted interior of the ship, the watch crew's eyes had not adjusted to the semi-darkness, and no one saw the torpedo fired at the Mallory from 900 yards away by U-402. While the SS Mallory was hit squarely by the torpedo, initially, it did not seem a major problem as the ship stayed upright, although its engines had been stopped. However, a hole big enough "to drive a truck through," as it was described by survivors, had been blown in the side of the vessel. Lifeboats were lowered, but only a few got away with passengers on board, with many capsized due to the heavy seas that early morning and the inexperience of the SS Mallory's crew in handling the lifeboats and their inability to release the life rafts fitted around the ship's sides as well. The SS Mallory crew was so unprepared for the ship sinking that they did not even realize they had to cut the ropes attaching the lifeboats to the slowly sinking SS Mallory, and a number of lifeboats were pulled under as the SS Mallory sank. Only 227 of the 498 aboard got away from the sinking ship in lifeboats, and a few others on rafts. But being on a raft was almost the same as floating in the sea, and very few men survived their almost 4 hours on a lift raft before being rescued.

Unfortunately, as the SS Mallory had been straggling behind the convoy and had not sent out a distress call using its radio, the convoy commander did not fully realize that the SS Mallory had been hit and was actually sinking. One of the escorting destroyers closed to within 2 miles of the SS Mallory and radioed the convoy commander for permission to pick up survivors. However, the convoy commander expected the SS Lobelia, tasked with shadowing the convoy from a distance of 30 miles behind it, to be able to pick up any survivors. What the convoy commander did not know was that the SS Lobelia was fully engaged in picking up survivors from the earlier sinkings and was in no position to help those in the water from the Mallory.

A survivor of the SS Mallory sinking had stayed aboard the sinking ship until the railing had almost touched the water. He tells how one of the chaplains, who was still on the ship's deck as it sank, came over to him and offered him a chocolate bar saying, "You might need this." This survivor was eventually able to just walk over the side of the ship into the water, which meant he was in the water for a shorter time than many of the others who had jumped in as soon as the ship was torpedoed. He swam to a life raft that was floating in the water and clung to it until he was rescued by the USCGC Bibb, almost dead from being partly submerged in the icy waters for almost 4 hours.[3]

Almost four hours after the sinking, the United States Coast Guard Cutter Bibb, one of the SC-118 escorts, sighted some of the SS Mallory's survivors in the water and was able to report to the convoy Commander that the SS Mallory had been sunk. The USCGC Bibb rescued 205 men from the SS Mallory's few lifeboats and rafts still afloat, and at 12 noon, the USS Ingham, another convoy escort, also rescued a further 22 survivors from lifeboats. The next day, the convoy made the turn north towards Iceland and dropped anchor there on 15 February after surviving a horrific winter hurricane that engulfed the convoy after the devastating U-boat attack. Two chaplains were saved from the sinking Mallory and continued on the rescue ships to Iceland, where they took up their ministry as Chaplains to the American troops stationed there.

Sudden Death on the British Home Front

5 June 1944

DERRICK LOVELL WILLIAMS, MA. Service number 297476. Age 30. Chaplain 4th Class, Royal Army Chaplains' Department. Attached to 45 Commando, Royal Marines. Buried in Section M, row 12, grave 79 Southampton (Hollybrook) Cemetery, Southampton, England.

One of the saddest stories of a chaplain who died in World War Two is that of Rev Derrick L Williams.

Derrick Williams was born 14 April, 1914, to Hal and Cecil Margaret Williams of Hampstead, London. He was married to Rosalind Anne Williams, and they had two sons.

Derrick Williams studied at Marlborough College and at Jesus College, both part of the University of Cambridge, and Wycliffe Hall, the University of Oxford. However, before enrolling in Wycliffe Hall, Derrick Williams visited New Zealand, where his parents had immigrated. As a young man, he had also visited Germany, Eastern Europe and the Balkans.

After graduation from Wycliffe Hall, Reverend Williams was ordained on 6 October 1939 by the Bishop of London. His initial curacy was in Hayes, Middlesex, where he served as curate at the Church of Saint Peter and Saint

Paul in Harlington, an affluent suburb of London, very close to the location of the modern Heathrow Airport. In 1940 Reverend Williams transferred to be the curate of Saint George-in-the-East on Cannon Row in Stepney, London, due to it being a busy parish near the docks in east London and in subsequent need of more assistant priests.

This parish was a stark contrast to the suburban parish he first started his ministry in! St George's-the-East was the same parish that, in 1936, British Fascist leader Oswald Mosley and his British Union of Fascists marched through to try and intimidate its large Jewish community. This was the catalyst for what became known as the Battle of Cable Street, in which a crowd of local people stood side by side, Jews and Church of England members, to prevent the fascists from marching into the parish. The Rector of the parish, Reverend Jack Boggis, stood at the heart of the crowd and had his nose broken while resisting Mosley's fascists. It also was a Church that was in the centre of the London Blitz, and Reverend Williams is reported to have spent every night during Blitz in the fall and winter of 1940-41 putting out fires, rescuing people, and comforting the bereaved. Reverend John B. Groser, the vicar of the neighbouring Christ Church (which was grouped with St Georges due to a shortage of clergy) who had supervised Reverend Williams, noted about him: "He was the sort of young man who was always in the middle of it, and would either get the Victoria Cross or be killed." Rev Williams was credited with saving the Stepney Public Library's collection of books when German incendiary bombs had set it alight fire during a bombing raid.

In late 1942 Reverend Williams left his parish work and was commissioned as a Royal Navy chaplain, but transferred to the army on 6 November 1943, as he learned there was a shortage of army chaplains. After training at the Chaplain School at Tidworth, he was attached to

Number 4 Infantry Training Centre. On 6 January 1944, he was transferred to the Headquarters of 16 Army Group Royal Artillery, 557th Heavy Artillery Regiment in Northern England. However, Padre Williams appears to have wanted more action and volunteered for commando training, which began on 11 March 1944 and lasted until 24 March 1944. After completing the two-week intensive and strenuous commando course, Padre Williams received his green beret and was assigned to Lord Lovat's No 1 Special Service Brigade, 45 Royal Marine Commando, where he served until 5 June 1944. It should be noted that the two-week Commando course was much shorter than that of the regular RM Commandos. It was designed to ensure those attached to the Commandos, such as chaplains, quartermasters, and other ancillary staff, had an understanding of what Commando training and battle was like, but they were not expected to be in the frontline of Commando units.

On Sunday, 4 June, the final denomination-specific church services were held before the Commandos were to be marched onto the ships taking them to Normandy for the D-Day landings. These services were then followed by an interdenominational Church Parade that all ranks of 45 Commando were required to attend. The commander of the 1st Special Service Brigade, Lord Lovat, noted that the hymn "Eternal Father Strong to Save" (which has become the hymn of the Royal Marines) was sung heartily by the men. However, he also noted that Padre Williams, who had only been with 45 Commando for two months, preached a horrible sermon full of death and destruction to the assembled troops preparing to go into battle.

Brigadier Lord Lovat later gave this account: *"On Sunday René de Naurois, his decorations a splash of colour on a white surplice, said Mass for three hundred men kneeling on the grass. At the Interdenominational Church Parade later that evening, a favourite hymn, that has since become our own, was sung with feeling: "Eternal Father, strong to save, O hear us when we cry to thee, For those in peril on the sea." It goes well with male voices, but the new padre preached a rotten sermon about death and destruction which caused surprise. There are few atheists to be found before a battle, or later in shell-holes. Tension was building up, and charity perhaps a trifle thin on the ground. There were a number of complaints; the cleric was suspended and told to return from whence he came. Poor fellow! A spark can cause the prairie fire! It was mistaken zeal from a man, lacking combat experience, who did not know his congregation, and doubly unfortunate in that it conflicted with my own "Godspeed" before departure. The incident was forgotten but the dismissal was taken badly. On the last day in camp the unfortunate man took his own life. A sad business, with barely time for regrets, for troops were belting up amid the dust and shouting as embarkation transport came grinding into Southampton to take us away. Max, a most humane officer and the soundest of administrators, cleared up the pitiful remains. The padre was put down as a "battle casualty".* This account by Lord Lovat clarifies the inaccurate accounts of Padre Williams being killed in the 45 Commando attack on Ouistreham in Normandy.[4]

At that time, suicide was still regarded in the Church of England as not fit for a regular church funeral, and there were even some church cemeteries which would not permit the remains of someone who committed suicide to be buried there, the 45 Commando adjutant listed Padre Williams as "killed on active service", and he was buried in a War Grave in the Southhampton Cemetery.

Being listed as a war casualty also meant that Padre Williams' wife was spared the shame, at that time, of her husband's suicide, and also that she and their two sons would receive any pension and insurance due for someone who was killed on active service. With Padre Williams being listed as a "battle casualty", it could mean that he is the first recorded British casualty of the D-Day invasion.

18 JUNE, 1944

RALPH HENRY WHITROW, MA. Service number 40452. Chaplain 2nd Class, Royal Army Chaplains' Department, Age 47. Officiating in the Guards Chapel, Wellington Barracks, London. Buried in Winchester (West Hill) Old Cemetery, Square 27, grave 3963.

Ralph Whitrow was the son of Benjamin and Mary Whitrow and was born on 20 December, 1896 in Tunbridge Hill, Kent. His father was a chemist and druggist in Tunbridge Hill. Ralph had an older brother named Philip, who was born in 1894.

Ralph was educated at the Tonbridge School from 1910-1916 and won the school prize at his graduation in 1916. Ralph then enlisted in the Royal Artillery on 28 August 1916 and was sent to an Officer Training Unit before being commissioned as a 2nd Lieutenant in the Royal Field Artillery on 13 January 1917. He was then sent to France to serve at the front. While in France in 1918 took part in the final advance through Wulverghem, Messines, Houthem and Menin. In late 1918, he was made an acting Captain and Adjutant of his brigade, which was based at Aisne, a village in Belgium.

Upon returning to England from France in 1919, he was demobilized and enrolled in Worcester College, a part of the University of Oxford, where he was a member of the Rowing Club. He graduated with a degree in Modern History in 1922. In the fall of that year, Ralph enrolled in Cuddesdon Theological College at the University of Oxford and was ordained in 1923. Ralph continued to serve in a battery of the Royal Artillery while at university in the Territorial Army (Reserves). He resigned his commission in the Territorial Army upon his ordination. In 1928 Ralph rejoined the Army, only this time in the Royal Army Chaplains' Department, where he became a chaplain 4th class serving with the Territorial Army.

After his ordination, Rev Whitrow was the assistant curate of St Luke's Anglican Church in Balham, in Battersea, London. He served there until 1930. In 1930 he was assigned his own parish and became vicar of St Paul's Anglican Church in the parish of Putney, Streatham, just a short journey further up the Thames River from Balham.

While serving as the assistant curate of St Luke's, Ralph met a young woman named Brenda Muriel Bent, and they fell in love. They were married in St Luke's Anglican Church, Battersea, on 7 June 1932. They had three children, William, born in 1933, and twins John and Lucy in 1936.

In 1937, Rev Whitrow and his family moved to St Matthew's Church in Weeke, Winchester, where he became the rector of the parish. He continued as Rector of this parish, even while serving in the Chaplains' Department, until his death. While at St Matthew's, he was made a Canon of Winchester Cathedral.

Padre Whitrow was called from the Territorial Army to active service on 5 September 1939, and on the following day, he marched with the men of his Territorial Army unit to Southampton for embarkation for France. However, later in September 1939, Padre Whitrow was promoted to the rank of Chaplain Third Class and was posted as Senior Chaplain to the 45th Division Headquarters in England. He took up the appointment in Exeter on 27 September, twenty-three years after his Army career had begun there in 1916. Padre Whitrow had noted in letters to his wife that he did not like Headquarters life, as it was too administratively based. As the 45th Division was dispersed over a wide area of Southern England, Padre Whitrow travelled between the various subunits of the Division located near important buildings and structures they were guarding. In October 1941, Padre Whitrow was posted to another unit in Northern England for much the same duties as he had with the 45th Division. In 1943 Padre Whitrow was then transferred again to southern England again, this time as Deputy Assistant Chaplain General for the London District, and Chaplain of the Guards Division Regimental Chapel in London.

At 11.20 am, on Sunday, 18 June 1944, a V1 flying bomb hit the Guards Chapel that faced onto Birdcage Walk, London, SW1, not far from Buckingham Palace, while a service to commemorate the Battle of Waterloo in 1815 and the success of the Normandy landings was taking place.

The congregation that morning was a mixed military and civilian group and had gathered for a service of Matins (Morning Prayer) with the Bishop of Maidstone scheduled to offer the sermon. Just as the choir had started to sing the Te Deum, a V1 Flying Bomb's engine cut out, and it nosedived onto the Guards Chapel roof. The direct hit completely destroyed the roof, and the blast blew out its supporting walls and concrete pillars, as well as the portico of the chapel's western door.

Tons of rubble fell onto the congregation. 121 soldiers and civilians were killed, and 141 others were seriously injured.

The high death toll included the officiating chaplain, Padre Ralph Whitrow, several senior British Army officers, two Canadian Officers, and a US Army Colonel, as well as many lesser-ranked men and women. Included in the dead was Major Windham, the director of Music of the Coldstream Guards. This service was to be his last official function before his retirement. Many of the well-known regiments and units of the armed forces of the United Kingdom had casualties in the bombing of the Guards Chapel, including the Coldstream Guards, the Grenadier Guards, the Scots Guards, the Irish Guards, and the Welsh Guards, as well as the Auxiliary Territorial Service, and the Women's Royal Naval Service, to name but a few. The Bishop of Maidstone, who was to preach the sermon that day, was one of the few left uninjured by the blast.

Within 10 minutes of the V1 bomb going off, as the clouds of dust were dissipating, first aid teams and heavy rescue crews arrived to find a scene of utter devastation. An initial City of Westminster Air Raid Precautions organization assessment put the number of casualties at 400-500. At first, the debris appeared impenetrable; the smashed remains of walls and the collapsed roof had trapped dozens. The doors to the Chapel were blocked; the only access point for the rescue teams lay in a single door behind the altar. Doctors and nurses were obliged to scramble in between the fallen concrete walls to administer morphine and first aid to the wounded. Several rescuers and survivors later recalled that the silver altar cross had been untouched by the blast and that candles continued to burn. The rescue services and Guardsmen from Wellington Barracks nearby immediately began freeing survivors from the wreckage and carrying them to safety and medical treatment. The operation to free the trapped and recover the dead took 48 hours. The chapel itself was almost completely ruined, and in rubble were the remnants of over two thousand small memorial plaques dedicated to the service of various men of the Guards Division since 1660.

The Guards Chapel incident was the most deadly V1 attack on London of the war. The flying bomb left only the apse (the curved area with the altar in the centre) of the chapel intact. This horrendous attack, as part of the V1 campaign against London, shocked the British and the rest of the world, who thought bombing attacks on London had ended. The Guards Chapel bombing received much publicity in the international press and was highlighted by journalists and in government statements as a particular atrocity aimed at a chapel of the military on a Sunday morning. However, this was just Allied propaganda, as the V1 flying bombs were not accurate enough to even target specific areas of a city.

Despite the very serious damage, part of the Chapel was reopened for services in time for Christmas 1944. In 1962-1963 the chapel was rebuilt, and, just inside the Chapel's west entrance, a large engraved wall memorial and book of remembrance record the soldiers and civilians who died in the 1944 attack. The original altar cross and six silver candlesticks still adorn the Chapel's altar.

A Funeral Requiem (Memorial service) was held for Padre Whitrow in Winchester Cathedral on 23 June 1944, followed by a funeral service in his parish church St. Paul's Church, Weeke. Padre Whitrow is commemorated on the Memorial in St Luke's Church, Battersea, the church where he began his ministry and he and his wife were married.

Death amongst the Hedgerows and Apple Orchards of Normandy

6 June 1944

GEORGE ALEXANDER HARRIS, BA, LTh. Age 34. Chaplain 4th Class, Canadian Chaplain Service. Attached to the 1st Canadian Parachute Battalion, Royal Canadian Infantry Corps, 6th British Airborne Division. Buried in Ranville Commonwealth War Graves Cemetery, grave VA C 6, Ranville, France.

George Alexander Harris was born in 1910 to Alfred and Blanche Clarinda Harris of Solihull, Warwickshire. As a young man, he had immigrated to the province of Manitoba in Canada, where he worked for a few years to save enough money for studies at the University of Manitoba. George finally had saved enough money to enter the University of Manitoba in Winnipeg and earned a Bachelor of Arts degree, and then a Licentiate of Theology from St John's and St Chad's Theological College (an Anglican seminary affiliated with the University of Manitoba). After graduation, he was ordained in the Diocese of Rupert's Land and was appointed the curate at All Saints Anglican Church in Winnipeg, Manitoba.

When war was declared, Rev Harris initially joined the Royal Canadian Navy as a chaplain. However, learning of a shortage of chaplains in the Canadian Army, he requested a transfer to the Canadian Chaplains Service and this request was granted by the Chaplain-General, Bishop George Wells. Once he was serving in the army, Chaplain Harris also volunteered for the 1st Canadian Parachute Battalion that was training at Camp Shilo, located just a couple of hours by train west of Winnipeg. At Camp Shilo, Chaplain Harris became the first Canadian chaplain to become a qualified parachutist.

In his work Airborne: The Heroic Story of the 1st Canadian Parachute Battalion in the Second World War, Brian Nolan describes Chaplain Harris' selfless devotion to the men he served. He writes, "The plane bearing a stick composed of many of the battalion's headquarters people, including Regimental Sergeant Major W.J. Clark, Padre George Harris, and Private Tom O'Connell took a direct hit in its left-wing engine. As flames started engulfing the wing and the plane nosed towards the ground, the paratroops took to the silk. O'Connell and Harris jumped so close together that their parachutes tangled, and the two men plunged towards the earth under largely collapsed canopies. Panicked, O'Connell thrashed wildly about in an effort to pay his field kit out below him so that he would not be crushed by it when they hit the ground. Speaking almost into his ear, a voice calmly said," Take it easy, old man. Whatever you do, take it easy." O'Connell calmed instantly at the padre's softly spoken advice, and even as the two men crashed down through some trees managed, he managed to assume the correct landing position. The force of the impact knocked the private unconscious, and he did not awaken until about noon on 6 June and was saddened to find Padre Harris lying dead beside him. Their two parachutes were twined together like a rope, and it was a wonder they had managed to slow the men's descent at all. Had it not been for Harris's calming counsel, O'Connell believed he would surely have died."

Mr. David Blake, curator of the Royal Army Chaplains' Department Museum, has confirmed that two of Padre Harris' older brothers were killed in action during WWI, as is noted on his headstone. Lance Corporal Joseph Edgar Harris, who was with the Royal Warwickshire Regiment, 1st/ 5th Battalion. and died on 18 July 1916 and Lance Corporal Charles Rudolph Harris with the Coldstream Guards, 2nd Battalion, who died on 27 August 1918.

GEORGE EDWARD MAULE PARRY, AKC, Service no. 173033. Age 29. Chaplain 4th Class, Royal Army Chaplains' Department. Attached to 7th Battalion (Light Infantry) The Parachute Regiment, Army Air Corps. Buried in Benouville Church Cemetery, grave 21, Benouville, France.

George Parry was born in Hornchurch, Essex. He was one of the four sons of Muriel Constance St. J. Parry and the Rev Canon Allen James Parry of Leytonstone, Essex. Parry's three brothers also entered military service during World War Two. His brother Peter was killed in action in North Africa in 1942. One of his other brothers, Allan, also served with 6th Airborne Division in the 9th (Essex) Parachute Battalion. After the war, a third brother of Padre Parry ended up commanding the 16th Parachute Brigade in 1953.

George Parry was educated at Farnfield's Preparatory School, Bickley and then attended Weymouth College; and studied for his undergraduate degree at King's College, London. He trained for Holy Orders at Bishop's College, Cheshunt. After ordination, Rev Parry began his ministry under the supervision of Canon Brown, the Vicar of St. John's, Leytonstone, in the Diocese of Chelmsford in 1938. This was the same church that he had been brought up in as a boy. Canon Brown died on 3 September 1939, the day that World War Two began, and Rev Parry had to take charge of an important parish while still an inexperienced priest. Rev Parry was up to the challenge, though, and was well regarded by the congregation of St John's. In early 1940, Rev Parry was assigned as the Vicar of a Forest Gate parish after the previous vicar had been commissioned as a chaplain to the forces.

In February of 1941, Rev Parry volunteered as a chaplain. After initial service in England, Chaplain Parry was sent overseas to the Gold Coast (now Ghana) in West Africa. He served there as a chaplain until March 1943, and then, after over a month of travelling back to the UK by sea, he was posted to Bicester. In September 1943, Padre Parry volunteered for parachute training and completed his training with Training Course Number 78 at RAF Ringway (now Manchester International Airport), in September 1943. Padre Parry's training report stated that he was cheerful and enthusiastic and an asset to his training stick, as a group of parachutists in training or in a plane is called. After completing training, he was assigned to the 7th Parachute Battalion, 5th Parachute Brigade, 6th Airborne Division.

In June 1944, Padre Parry parachuted into Normandy during Operation Overlord. Before the men left, Padre Parry led a service described this way: "As the shadows lengthened on Monday, 5 June, the stand-to order was given. The last ceremony that day was a drumhead service in a meadow near Fairford Airfield by our popular padre, Captain Parry, known to us all as "Pissy Parry the Parachuting Padre". Parry was a wiry little Welshman with a nature as fiery as his red hair and a heart and courage to match. Drawn up in a semi-circle, 610 men faced inwards towards the padre who stood on an ammunition box. A more unlikely or piratical congregation could not be imagined, every man a bristle with weapons, his face and hands besmirched with black cream, his helmet on the ground before him, his rifle or Sten gun laid across it. Onward Christian Soldiers went well. Abide With Me was rather more ragged. It was not easy to sing that in such a setting and at such a moment."

Chaplain Parry was described by the commanding officer of his battalion as a keen and enthusiastic member of the battalion and took with good nature the ribbing and teasing by the other officers of the unit, including his alliterated nickname" of "Pissy Parry the Parachuting Padre."

Padre Parry parachuted into Normandy from a Short Stirling bomber, modified for dropping parachutists, at about 1 am on 6 June to reinforce the glider-borne troops who had captured the bridges over the Canal de Caen and the Orne River by a coup-de-main. One of these bridges is referred to now as Pegasus Bridge.

Benouville Church

There is much confusion about Padre Parry's death, as there are no surviving eyewitness accounts. It is noted that he was killed in a confused melee around the Regimental Aid Post located in the Benouville Church. One account held at the Armed Forces Chaplains Centre and originally provided to the British Chaplain General's Office in 1944 indicates Chaplain Parry and the men of the RAP heard a German patrol, including a former French tank impressed into German service, approaching their location, and crept out of the Benouville Church through a side door to climb over the wall at the rear of the churchyard to hide from the Germans. After a period of time, Padre Parry and the other men thought the German patrol had continued on, and Padre Parry emerged from cover and clambered back over the churchyard wall and went to check on two wounded paratroopers laying on stretchers outside the door of the church. However, the German patrol had not moved as far as Padre Parry thought, and he was seen by the German troops. Padre Parry leapt up to run back to the churchyard wall and leap over it. A German soldier, not seeing the Red Cross armband that Padre Parry wore, opened fire on the running figure in a paratroop uniform and killed him. Other airborne troops opened fire on the patrol, and the German who had shot Padre Parry was killed. The two bodies of Padre Parry and the German soldier who had killed him were reportedly found separated by only a few metres in the churchyard. It has been suggested that Padre Parry's body fell on top of the two wounded men on the stretchers he had been checking on, but there is no proof of this story.

A second account indicates Chaplain Parry died trying to defend wounded soldiers as the Regimental Aid Post was overrun by the German forces. This implies that Chaplain Parry's death was against the Rules of War in the way other paratroops who had not been at the RAP in the Church had written home about it. This news, from the letters home, led to an inquiry in the House of Commons with the Secretary for War, Sir James Grieg, being asked by Sir Herbert Williams "whether any statement would be made on the murder of the Rev George Parry by the Germans in Normandy. Sir James Grieg replied that the matter would be Investigated." However, no records of an investigation being conducted exist.

A further account that was reported in the Australian *Sydney Morning Herald* noted that "A war correspondent reported that:" *"Chaplain Parry was killed by a knife or bayonet while defending helpless wounded men in a German raid on a Medical Aid Post. The Germans are reported to have been bayoneting and shooting the wounded when Parry threw himself In front of them."*

A final account by Lt Richard Todd, courtesy of "The Pegasus Archive" stated: "... Padre Parry had learned that A Company of his battalion had many wounded, and he set off through the darkness of the early morning of 6 June to reach the Regimental Aid Post. However, there was no solid frontline yet, and the paratroops were under attack from all directions. They were able to fend off many of the attacks, but one German attack broke through the Para's lines and reached the Regimental Aid Post located in the Benouville Church, where Chaplain Parry was assisting the medical troops. The German troops seemed crazed with bloodlust and set about shooting and bayoneting the wounded paratroops. Parry immediately confronted the German troops and tried to stop the killing. When they did not listen to his entreaties, it is believed Chaplain Parry tried a physical intervention, putting himself between the Germans and the wounded British paratroops. The German soldiers charged him, and following a struggle, Chaplain Parry was bayoneted to death. When the British recaptured the area, the bodies were found of all the wounded killed in the Aid Post, along with Chaplain Parry's body lying on top of "his men."

The differing accounts of Chaplain Parry's death, especially as there are no written first-person accounts of it, serve to illustrate the "fog of war" as well as Allied propaganda designed to discredit the Germans, especially as a chaplain, who was a non-combatant, appeared to have been killed in cold blood. As so often happened with battlefield accounts, Padre Parry's death in the churchyard has probably been mixed up and confused by 2nd and 3rd hand accounts of his death. Since he was a well-liked and respected Chaplain, the men of his battalion would have been very affected by his death.

Seventy years after Padre Parry's death, in 2014, British TV presenter Jenni Crane purchased a suitcase at a used goods shop that had the name Rev GEM Parry painted on it. As Chaplain Parry never married, the suitcase had been given away by a relative to the shop shortly before, who was not aware of the controversy of his death on D-Day. However, the purchase of the case led to a renewed interest in  the death of Chaplain Parry in action. A radio program about Padre Parry on the radio show Object Trouvé (The Chaplain's Suitcase), broadcast on 27 December 2016 by BBC Radio 4.

IGNATIUS MATERNOWSKI, FFC, Purple Heart. Service no:0-480972. Age 31. 1st Lieutenant, United States Army Chaplain Corps. Attached to the 508th Parachute Infantry Regiment, 82nd Airborne Division. Buried in South Hadley, Massachusetts Mater Dolorosa Cemetery plot: Section B, South Hadley, Massachusetts, USA.

Ignatius Maternowski was born in Holyoke, Massachusetts, on 28 March 1912. After graduating from Mater Dolorosa Parochial School in 1927, he attended St. Francis High School in Athol Springs, NY, where he was a member of that school's first graduating class in 1931. He entered the religious order of the Franciscan Friars Conventual and became a professed friar in 1932. After pursuing further studies, he was ordained a priest by Bishop Thomas O'Leary of Springfield, Massachusetts on 3 July 1938, in the chapel of Saint Hyacinth College and Seminary in Granby, Connecticut.

After the outbreak of World War II, Chaplain Maternowski and several other members of the community of Franciscans of St. Anthony Province responded to the urgent call for Roman Catholic military chaplains. In July 1942, he joined the Army Chaplain Corps and later volunteered to become a member of the 508th Parachute Infantry Regiment of the 82nd Airborne Division. After rigorous training with fellow troops, he attained the rank of captain and served for 23 months before his death. Reflecting on the D-Day anniversary in his book, *Serving God and Country: United States Military Chaplains in World War II*, Professor Lyle Dorsett indicated that other chaplains he interviewed for his book described Chaplain Maternowski as "a tough, energetic Pole, and who was extremely liked by the men of his regiment. He was a man's man." Chaplain Maternowski didn't find it amusing when men were telling filthy jokes, speaking crudely, or taking the Lord's name in vain. More than once, he would say, "Put on boxing gloves" and offer to have a boxing match with anyone who made disparaging remarks about the Church or Confession."

Chaplain Maternowski jumped into Normandy at about 1:30 am on D-Day and landed near Guetteville, and immediately began ministering to the wounded and dead in heavy fighting in the hedgerows near the town of Picauville in Normandy. His ministry was to both paratroopers, who jumped onto the battlefield, as well as to those who landed by glider shortly after daylight on 6 June.

Chaplain Maternowski was killed after attempting to negotiate with German medical officers for a common field hospital. In the mid-morning of 6 June, Chaplain Maternowski removed his helmet and displayed, as best he could, both his uniform's chaplain insignia and his Red Cross armband. He approached German lines to seek out the German medical staff, with the hope of negotiating for this joint aid station, where the wounded of both armies could be treated with dignity. As Chaplain Maternowski was returning to American positions (it is not clear if he was able to contact members of the German Army to negotiate the hospital), he was shot in the back by a German soldier who was not aware of his mission and probably did not see his Red Cross armband indicating his non-combatant status. Chaplain Maternowski's body remained lying in no man's land between the American and German positions for three days before Allied forces were able to advance into the area near Guetteville. Chaplain Maternowski's remains were discovered by troops of the American 90th Infantry Division. He was initially buried in the large American cemetery near Utah Beach. However, in 1948, at the request of the Franciscan Order, his remains were returned to the U.S. and buried at the Franciscans' Mater Dolorosa Cemetery in South Hadley, Massachusetts.

WALTER LESLIE BROWN, BA, LTh. Age 33. Chaplain 4th Class, Canadian Chaplain Service. Attached to the Headquarters, 2nd Canadian Armoured Brigade (27th Armoured Regiment, Sherbrooke Fusiliers). Buried in the Beny-sur-Mer Commonwealth War Graves Cemetery, grave 13 C 1, Rivieres, France.

Walter Leslie Brown was the son of George C. Brown and Florence Brown and was born on 13 August 1910 in Peterborough, Ontario. Walter Brown was ordained a deacon in the Diocese of Huron (centred on London, Ontario) on 6 June 1937 after graduating with a Licentiate of Theology from Huron College (now Huron University College, a part of the University of Western Ontario, now known as Western University in London, Ontario). He was made a priest on 5 June 1938 by Bishop Charles Seger of the Diocese of Huron. He served his assistant curacy at St James' Westminster Anglican Church in London, Ontario. However, on 6 June 1938, Rev Brown was appointed curate at All Saints Anglican Church in Windsor, Ontario. Father Brown served in this role until going on leave from the parish on 9 April 1941, when he joined the Canadian Army to serve in the Canadian Chaplains Service.

On 19 June 1941, after his initial training at the Canadian Army Chaplains' School located at Camp Borden near Barrie, Ontario, Chaplain Brown was assigned as the padre of the Grey and Simcoe Foresters, a training regiment of the Canadian Army. As was common for most officers, including chaplains, Walter Brown passed his military driving test on 19 September 1942. The Grey and Simcoe Foresters Regiment had companies scattered across southern Ontario, and Chaplain Brown provided ministry in various locations in Ontario.

On 16 June 1943, Chaplain Brown was assigned to the Canadian Army (Overseas) in the United Kingdom. After moving by train to Halifax, Padre Brown, like so many other Canadian soldiers, boarded a troop ship and made the perilous journey across the Atlantic to the UK. Upon disembarking, Chaplain Brown waited at a Canadian Army replacement depot for a week before being assigned to the Canadian 2nd Armoured Brigade, where he served in a general capacity, without being assigned to a specific regiment until 15 May 1944. On that date, he was assigned to the Headquarters of the 27th Armoured Regiment (the Sherbrooke Fusiliers, whose origins were in two militia regiments located in Sherbrooke in the Eastern Townships of the province of Quebec).

Chaplain Brown landed on Juno Beach on the Nan White sector in Bernieres-sur-Mer around noon on D-Day with the majority of the Sherbrooke Fusiliers men and equipment. Padre Brown immediately began to minister to the Canadian soldiers along the roads leading inland from the invasion beach as the vehicles of his regiment moved towards the front line. Almost from the beginning, Padre Brown was separated from his regiment's troops as he lagged behind the advancing tanks, half-tracks, jeeps and trucks, helping the wounded and dying. Chaplain Brown is known to have officiated at the brief graveside funerals of a number of Canadian soldiers whom he buried in the temporary cemetery on the edge of the village of Beny-sur-Mer (not to be confused with the current Commonwealth War Graves Cemetery, also named Beny-sur-Mer).

In the late evening of D-Day, as the sun began to sink in the west, Padre Brown was walking towards the frontline and the location of the Headquarters of the Sherbrooke Fusiliers. As he walked along the road, a jeep belonging to the Sherbrooke's, driven by Corporal John Greenwood and carrying Lieutenant W.J. Grainger, the Sherbrooke Fusilier's assistant Tank Unit Landing Officer, stopped and offered him a ride. Due to an accident on the LST (Landing Ship, Tank) of the primary Tank Landing Officer, this officer had not been able to disembark, so Lieutenant Grainger became responsible for ensuring all the vehicles and men of the Sherbrooke's unloaded properly and were directed to the assembly areas inland from the beaches. As one can imagine, disembarking dozens of tanks, as well as hundreds of half-tracks, trucks, jeeps, trailers, etc, takes a long time. By late in the day, sometime after 9:00 pm (Central European Summer Time), Lieutenant Grainger had finished his unloading supervision, and Padre Brown had finished burying the dead and caring for the wounded. There was still quite a bit of light in the sky at that time of the year in Northern Europe, with sunset much later in the evening due to wartime adjustments to daylight saving time.

The 3 men in the jeep began to make their way southeast away from the invasion beaches, towards the 9th Canadian Infantry Brigade Headquarters, whom the Sherbrooke Fusilier tankers were supporting in their nighttime defensive position. The German forces, as an anti-invasion tactic, had removed many of the road signs, and Walter Brown and his party missed the turn to the night position of their regiment. They stopped to get their bearings, and Lieutenant Grainger consulted his map in the growing twilight in what was actually the middle of no man's land. After the war, Lieutenant Granger's testimony at 12th SS Panzer Division commander Kurt Meyer's trial for war crimes indicates Chaplain Brown was heading towards the regimental aid post of the Sherbrooke Fusiliers. However, this RAP would have been located near the 9th Infantry Brigade headquarters, where the medical officer would have his vehicle, often within a few hundred meters of the front lines but protected by a screen of tanks and infantrymen. The war diary of the Sherbrooke Fusiliers indicates that the regiment, along with the North Nova Scotia Highlanders Infantry Regiment, had bivouacked in what was described as a "fortress" or "British square" type of encampment between Les Buissons and Anisy with the tanks in the centre being resupplied with fuel and ammunition, and the infantry in trenches in front of the tanks protecting them from German infantry attack. It must be remembered that the front line at the end of the day on 6 June was not continuous, so it would be easy to miss the turn between Les Buissons and Anisy, especially in the twilight, with the three men in the jeep being very tired after a hectic, and horror filled day, as well as not being familiar with the road network of the Norman countryside. While trying to determine their location, the 3 men in the jeep came under submachine gun and rifle fire. Lieutenant Grainger subsequently reported that the troops that ambushed the jeep were wearing uniforms of a German Waffen SS Unit.

Part of the mystery around Chaplain Brown's death is that official Allied records show that the 12th SS Panzer Division, the first Waffen-SS unit to enter the fighting in Normandy, only began moving into the Canadian sector late in the morning of the 7 June and that they were not where Chaplain Brown died on the evening of 6 June. However, according to the Divisional History for the 12th SS Panzer Division, its 12th SS Reconnaissance Battalion, commanded by Sturmbannführer Gerhard Bremer, was already in action and had armoured car patrols scouting as far west as Arromanches (Gold Beach) and on towards the American Omaha Beach, as well as on the heights overlooking the Canadian Juno Beach and the British Sword Beach. In fact, the Divisional History of the 12th SS indicates that this reconnaissance battalion had been ready for action since the first reports of Allied paratroop landings just after midnight on 6 June. It is recorded that the 12th SS Reconnaissance Battalion troops had, by 1:30 am in the early morning of 6 June, already captured some British paratroopers who had missed their drop zones near the Orne River, west of Caen. This was almost 24 hours before Walter Brown's encounter with them, even though the 12th SS troops were not on the front lines at that time, as the majority of the division was located southeast of Caen, near Lisieux.

The road where Chaplain Brown's party was ambushed (now the D79) leads directly from the roads that parallel the Normandy Coast to Caen. This is where the rest of the 12th SS Panzer Division was moving towards, in preparation for its initial attack on the Canadians on the afternoon of 7 June. A 12th SS reconnaissance unit was most likely the one Padre Brown and his companions encountered, as they would have been in the process of returning to the 12th SS divisional headquarters, moving away from the Allied landing beaches, and most certainly would have been low on fuel for their armoured cars and other vehicles, and seeking a hot meal and rest after a day avoiding Allied air and ground attacks.

In the gunfire of the ambush, the SS troops aimed at the driver of the jeep, perhaps hoping to take the other occupants prisoner for the information they might provide on Allied troop dispositions. Corporal Greenwood, at the steering wheel of the Jeep, was killed immediately. Lieutenant Grainger, in the front passenger seat, was seriously wounded in the left shoulder. Only Padre Brown, in the backseat of the jeep, was not hit. The German troops gestured to Padre Brown with their weapons and would have issued terse commands in German, or rudimentary English, for him to get out of the jeep. He was seen, by the badly wounded Lieutenant Grainger, clambering out of the vehicle with his small suitcase containing the tools of his vocation (communion kit, stole, service booklets, etc.). Lieutenant Granger, fading in and out of consciousness due to his severe shoulder wound, last saw Chaplain Brown being marched away by the German troops, with his arms raised, holding his small suitcase above his head.

When the SS reconnaissance troops had moved away from the ambush, they left Lieutenant Grainger alone, believing that he was dead or about to die. In fact, Lieutenant Grainger, through great personal fortitude, was able to revive himself after the SS troops had disappeared and was able to push the body of Corporal Greenwood out of the jeep's driver's seat so he could get behind the steering wheel himself. Luckily for him, the jeep's engine had not been damaged in the ambush, and he was able to start the vehicle up and turn it around, and drive back towards Les Buissons, where he encountered the forward positions of the North Nova Scotia Highlanders. He was immediately taken to the Regimental Aid Post, where his wounds were bandaged, and he was evacuated the next day to hospital in England. While in hospital, he was visited, later that month, by the Canadian High Commissioner to Great Britain (Ambassador), Vincent Massey (who later became the first Canadian-born Governor-General of Canada), with whom he had his picture taken on 18 June.

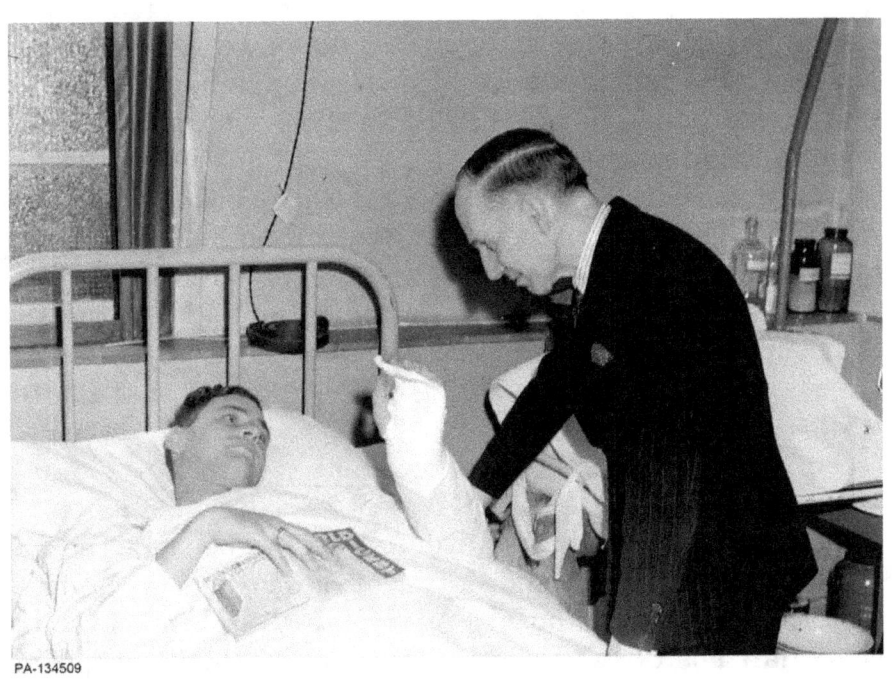

On 7 June, Chaplain Brown was listed as missing in action by the Sherbrooke Fusiliers, based on Lieutenant Grainger's report. His mother, who was living in Orillia, Ontario, was notified, but nothing more was heard of Padre Brown, with no reports from the Red Cross regarding his being a POW, etc., until 11 July. On that day, a British tank regiment, moving forward towards the fighting around Caen, was bivouacked in a field near Galmanche, the hamlet where Padre Brown and the others had been ambushed the month before. Members of the tank unit came across the solitary body wearing the uniform of a Canadian officer, and they realized he was a chaplain due to the Canadian Chaplain Service flashes on the shoulders and possible clergy shirt he wore. After Padre Brown's body was recovered, since it was found without any other bodies or signs of fighting nearby, it was subject to a thorough examination, as it was known by that time that other Canadian prisoners of war had been murdered after

surrendering in June to 12th SS Panzer Division troops. The examination of Padre Brown's body indicated that there were no bullet holes in Padre Brown's uniform, and upon closer inspection, it was noted that there was only one wound in his chest, and it appeared to have been made with a knife or bayonet. If Chaplain Brown had been wounded by gunfire in the ambush and subsequently died of his wounds, there would have been indications of this on his uniform. But, as Lieutenant Grainger had seen Padre Brown being marched away alive, the reality is that Padre Brown was murdered by the 12th SS Panzer Division reconnaissance troops in cold blood.

Padre Brown was quietly murdered, firstly, because the SS reconnaissance troops did not want to deal with a captive who could provide no useful military information on Canadian positions, as chaplains did not lead troops in battle; secondly, because of the inability of reconnaissance troops to carry prisoners easily in, or on, their small vehicles; and finally and most notably; the 12th SS Panzer Division had, as its officers and non-commissioned officers, men who had been brutalized by service on the Russian Front and had been taught there to regard clergy just as they had communist political commissars, namely that were to be executed immediately, rather than being taken as prisoners of war, because they could organize and inspire troops, even in captivity.

Chaplain Walter Brown is the only chaplain known to have been murdered in cold blood in the North West European Campaign. Many other chaplains were killed in the heat of battle, including one attached to the 6th Airborne Division near Ranville in Normandy, who was reported to have been bayoneted on the 7 June when the Aid Station he was ministering in was overrun by German forces. However, the evidence strongly indicates that Rev Walter Brown was the only chaplain to have been actually murdered in truly cold blood.

There is an amazing postscript to the Walter Brown story. An undergraduate student at Huron University College in the late 1990s, Chris McCreery, as part of his penultimate project for the conclusion of his undergraduate degree in history, had been researching graduates of Huron College who had been killed in World War Two. He had discovered that there were a number who had been missed from the memorial plaque placed in the foyer of the main College entrance. As Mr McCreery had researched each name on the memorial plaque, including Walter Brown's, Mr McCreery was familiar with who he was and the basics of his story.

In 1999, after his graduation from Huron College the year before, Mr McCreery, who was now working on a Master of Arts degree (he would later earn a PhD in history and became a famous expert on Canadian Honours and Awards). While visiting family in Windsor, Ontario, he wandered into a Salvation Army charity shop. He saw a tarnished silver cup with a small plate fitted into the rim of the cup on display. Mr McCreery is an active Anglican, so he recognized a Communion chalice and paten, and upon picking it up, he noticed it had a Broad Arrow engraved in its base, surrounded by a large C, indicating it was a Canadian military issue item. Mr McCreery asked the staff if there were any other pieces that went with the cup and plate (the staff had no idea what the cup and plate actually were), and they went and hunted in the store's storage room and returned with a battered suitcase and indicated the cup had come in with the suitcase. Mr McCreery, upon seeing the small bottles, box and priestly vestments, immediately realized the suitcase was a chaplain's kit from World War Two and offered the employees $50 (£30) for the lot, and they agreed.

When Mr McCreery got to his car and began examining his find in more detail, as he wiped the grime off the side case, he saw the name W. Brown stencilled on it. He realized that by some twist of fate, he had bought Walter Brown's communion kit – the one that had been found beside his body all those years before in Normandy. No one can explain how Rev Brown's communion kit ended up in a charity shop in Windsor, Ontario, thousands of miles from Normandy. It is presumed that as Rev Brown's last parish, before his enlisting in the Chaplain Service, had been in Windsor; the kit had been sent there, even though his service records list his next of kin as his mother living in Barrie, Ontario, north of Toronto and at least 200 miles from Windsor. Perhaps Mrs Brown had donated it to the Windsor congregation, but this is not known. It is also unknown why if this was the case, a church would have disposed of a communion set in this way.

Mr McCreery donated Walter Brown's Communion kit to the chapel at Huron University College, and it is used each Remembrance Day at a Communion Service held to commemorate those who served and those who fell during the wars that Canadians were involved in during the 20th and 21st centuries.

JUNK STORE FIND REMEMBRANCE TREASURE

A banged-up suitcase and some well-worn pieces of silver hardly catch the eye. But this particular suitcase is different. It holds the account of a sacrifice made more than 60 years ago by a young Canadian doing what many his age were doing at the time—defending their country. The story of the return of the field communion kit of Captain the Rev. Walter L. Brown to Huron University College is providing an opportunity to shake the complacency of a new generation and to better understand and honour the deeds of those who fought for Canada.

The Rev. Canon William Cliff, Chaplain at Huron University College, says with a number of reservists studying at Huron - - officers and enlisted soldiers working towards degrees and some wanting to serve in the military as chaplains—the field communion kit of Brown, who graduated from Western in 1937 and Huron in 1938, makes them stop, think and remember. "He has come alive for the students," says Cliff. "Though he died 61 years ago, because of his old suitcase, it gives students the rare chance to touch history made by one of their own." Commissioned as a Captain in 1941, Brown was the first Canadian chaplain to land at Juno Beach on D-Day, June 6, 1944.

He served his men and even buried some fellow soldiers at Beny-sur-Mer, now a Canadian war cemetery. Within days, he was captured by an SS unit led by the notorious Kurt Meyer and listed as a prisoner of war and then missing in action. The truth, however, was far darker. Brown was summarily executed by his captors—the only Allied chaplain killed in such fashion during the war. His body, found five weeks later by the side of the road, was buried at Beny-sur-Mer on July 11. He rests there still, but his kit has come home to be used regularly for worship and display in the Huron chapel and, says Cliff, to teach about "the demands of sacrifice and the necessity of the willingness to serve." Yet how the kit got to Huron was through a bit of serendipity.

The gift of Huron graduate Chris McCreery (BA '98), the kit contains the tools of Brown's trade: a chalice, a paten (small silver plate to hold the bread), a silver hip flask for a small supply of wine, small wooden box of bread and a brocade stole, crushed and folded into the case with some tattered old linens used in worship. McCreery came across the kit in a Windsor junk store in 1999. A collector of military medals, McCreery recognized the kit as a military field communion set. "I bought it purely on a whim, more interested in the chalice and the fact it was a field communion set than anything else," says McCreery. When he got back to his car and emptied the contents, he found a small wooden box for communion wafers. "But it has the name Walter L. Brown on the bottom with Canadian Army Chaplain Service written below," says McCreery, which jogged his memory back to his work on a plaque at Huron two years earlier.

McCreery had researched and raised funds for the plaque in the Memorial Tower while a student at Huron. He continues to research the lives of students and graduates who fought and died in both World Wars. "So, at that point, I made the connection and could hardly believe it." Brown is one of 18 members of the Huron community who died in the two World Wars. He carried only his dusty kit. "This is what Brown faced war with," says Cliff. "He carried no gun. He carried kind words comforting presence, and in times of need, he carried the sacraments to dying and frightened men with this kit. He and all who served will be remembered."5

6/7 June 1944

JOHN R. STEEL, Purple Heart. Service no: O-435366. Age 32. Captain, United States Army Chaplain Corps. Attached to the 1st Battalion, 401st Glider Infantry Regiment (operating as a 3rd Battalion of the 327th Glider Infantry Regiment), 101st Airborne Division. Buried in Rose Hill Cemetery in Ardmore, Carter County, Oklahoma.

John Steel was born in 1912 in the state of Oklahoma. Chaplain Steel was married to Hazel Frances Steel (nee Balch). After his ordination, he ministered to the Baptist congregations of Soper and Boswell, Oklahoma, until he was commissioned into the United States Army Chaplain Corps in February 1942.

After Chaplains School at Fort Benjamin Harrison, in Indiana, Chaplain Steel joined the 401st Glider Infantry Regiment (GIR) for training as part of the 101st Airborne Division at Camp Claiborne, Louisiana, and then Fort Bragg, North Carolina, until it went overseas to the United Kingdom in September 1943. In March 1944, the 401st GIR component battalions were separated, and most of its battalions were attached to other GIRs. The 1st Battalion 401st GIR would stay with the 101st Airborne Division but would be attached to the 327th GIR as its 3rd battalion. The 2nd Battalion of the 401st GIR would go to the 82nd Airborne Division's 325th GIR as its 3rd battalion.[6]

The 1st Battalion of the 401st GIR (327th GIR) arrived in Normandy, not by air in gliders but landed as regular infantry over Utah Beach in the Uncle Red sector after the noon hour on 6 June. Officially it was the Division reserve of the 101st Airborne Division but was immediately sent into action to link up with the widely scattered paratroopers and glider-borne infantry of the 101st AB division that had landed in the early morning darkness, as well as landing by gilder shortly after dawn earlier that day.[7]

The 327th GIR, including Chaplain Steel's battalion, immediately after landing on Utah beach, began to move towards the town of St Come-Du-Mont. Just before midnight, at last light, on 6 June, the battalion contacted forward elements of the 506th Parachute Infantry Regiment (PIR) near Angoville-au-Plain. While in the assembly area with the 506th PIR, preparing for the attack on St. Come-Du-Mont, Chaplain Steel, is reported to have commented to the commander of the 1st Battalion, 401st GIR (3rd Battalion 327th GIR), Colonel Allen, that so far, his battalion's role had been the same as it was on training exercises in the USA and England, with the exception of being issued live ammunition.[8] Sometime during the night of 6/7 June, Captain Steel was killed by a single gunshot to his chest. Due to the confused frontline situation, which was really only groupings of isolated companies, platoons and squads, and not a continuous frontline, there is some uncertainty as to the circumstances surrounding his death.

One account suggests that Chaplain Steel was moving between foxholes bringing comfort and support to the nervous and fearful troops, and he was mistaken for a German infiltrator by a soldier, hearing the rustling of Chaplain Steel approaching the soldier's location. The soldier shot at the sound without issuing the proper challenge and waiting for the response from Chaplain

Steel. The other account of his death has Chaplain Steel being shot and killed by a German soldier, as the Germans were reported as trying to infiltrate into the American positions. Whatever happened, Chaplain Steel was out of his own foxhole, moving amongst the skittish troops in his battalion's position and this lack of understanding of how confused a battlefield is for airborne troops led to Chaplain Steel's death on the night of 6/7 June, within hours of his landing in Normandy.

Chaplain Steel was temporarily interred in the American cemetery near Utah Beach. After the end of World War Two, Chaplain Steel's wife exercised her right to have his body returned to the United States for permanent burial. His body was returned to a grave site close to his former Oklahoma home in 1947 or 1948.

7 June 1944

PETER FRANCIS FIRTH, MA, Croix de Guerre. Service no. 257744. Age 33. Chaplain 4th Class, Royal Army Chaplains' Department. Attached to the 8th Field Ambulance, 21st Army Group. Buried in Hermanville Commonwealth War Graves Cemetery, grave 1 J 15, Hermanville, France.

Peter Firth was the son of Ernest Cecil Clark Firth and Agnes St. John Firth (nee Abdy) of Scorton, Lancashire. He was born in Preston and ordained in the Roman Catholic Diocese of Lancaster. Reverend Firth joined the Royal Army Chaplains' Department on 3 February 1943. He was originally assigned to the 20th Anti-tank Regiment of the 3rd Division. He was then transferred to the 8th Field Ambulance, 21st Army Group, for embarkation to the Normandy beaches. In the account of the Roman Catholic chaplaincy in the British Army, "The Cross on the Sword", it is noted that as Padre Firth was landing on the beaches of Normandy on 7 June, he waved a cheery hello to a soldier he knew, and was shot and instantly killed by a German sniper, still active in the beach area. Padre Firth was originally buried in the orchard beside the Hermanville-sur-Mer parish church before being exhumed and reinterred in the Hermanville Commonwealth War Graves Cemetery after the war.

GEORGE ALEXANDER "ALEC" KAY, MA. Service no. 150817. Chaplain 4th Class, Royal Army Chaplains' Department, Age 36. Attached to the 8th Battalion (Midlands), The Parachute Regiment, 716th Light Company RASC, 6th Airborne Division. Buried in Ranville Commonwealth War Graves Cemetery, grave 1A M 2, Ranville, France.

Alec Kay was born on 19 November 1907 in Wellington, New Zealand. His father was the Rev Thomas George Brierley Kay, who was Irish, and his mother, Fanny Kay, who was Scottish. At the time of George Kay's birth, his father was serving in a Church of England (in the Province of New Zealand) parish. In the early days of World War Two, Alec Kay's parents returned to the United Kingdom and his father was appointed the vicar of St Bartholomew Parish Church in Shapwick, Dorset.

Alec Kay attended Harrow School and later the University of Oxford at Brasenose College. He earned a Bachelor of Arts in 1929 and returned in 1937 to earn a Master of Arts. After completing his undergraduate degree, Alec Kay gained experience as a social worker in the slums of the East End of London and then went to teach at a missionary school in Agra, India, for three years. In the early 1930s, Alec Kay returned to England and became a teacher at Aysgarth School, Bedale, North Yorkshire. He was a recipient of the George V Jubilee Medal while serving at Aysgarth. After finishing his Master of Arts degree in Theology from Cuddesdon College, Oxford, Alec Kay was ordained a deacon in 1938 and a priest in 1939. In 1938 Rev Kay was appointed a curate at St Matthew's Church, Wood Lane, Chapel Allerton, Leeds, in West Yorkshire 1938. While at St Matthew's, he was married to Janet Evelyn Kay (nee Lucas).

In early October 1940, Rev Kay joined the Royal Army Chaplains' Department and was sent for initial training to the Chaplains School at Tidworth. After completing his training, Padre Kay was transferred to the large army camp at Aldershot, where he served with the 7th Hampshire Regiment of the 43rd Division's 130th Infantry Brigade. During this time, Padre Kay also served with the 5th Dorset Regiment, also a part of the 43rd Division. In late 1943, Padre Kay applied for parachute training, and his commanding officer from the 43rd Infantry Division indicated in a letter that Chaplain Kay was "of the type and possesses ~~possessed~~ the manner and qualifications which should serve him well in the Parachute Regiment".

In August 1943, Padre Kay qualified as a parachutist on course 91 at RAF Ringway. In November 1943, Padre Kay was assigned to the 8th Parachute Battalion, 3rd Parachute Brigade of the 6th Airborne Division, where Padre Kay was highly regarded by the men of his division. Padre Kay had been originally assigned to the 224th Parachute Field Ambulance of the 3rd Parachute Brigade, but the Division senior chaplain switched Padre Kay from landing with this Field Ambulance unit to parachuting with the Headquarters of the 8th Parachute Battalion for the Normandy landings.

Chaplain Kay was killed on 7 June 1944, the day following his parachuting into Normandy with his battalion. Accounts vary as to how Chaplain Kay was killed. One account says he was driving a jeep clearly marked with Red Cross flags to collect wounded personnel when he was shot and severely wounded by German machine gun fire. However, another account says that he was killed by mortar or shellfire while walking along a road seeking out injured paratroops. I would suggest that the second account is more accurate, as airborne chaplains normally did not have jeeps assigned to them, as generally speaking, there were limited numbers of vehicles that could be brought into the battle zone by glider for the airborne troops.

According to another airborne chaplain, Padre A. L. Beckingham, Chaplain Kay was brought to the airborne Regimental Aid Post but died upon arrival. He was buried by Padre John Gwinnett at Le Mesnil, France. After the war ended, a memorial stone to Padre Kay was placed in the Parish Church of St Bartholomew, Shapwick, Dorset, his father's church during the war. It reads: "In Grateful Memory of Rev. George Alexander Kay C.F. M.A., Airborne Chaplain killed while tending the wounded in Normandy D Day 1944."

10 June 1944

PHILIP EDELEN, Purple Heart. Service no: O-513674. Age 31. Captain, United States Army Chaplain Corps. Attached to the 9th Infantry Regiment, 2nd Infantry Division. Buried in the Normandy American Cemetery, plot I, row 13, grave 28, Colleville-sur-Mer, France.

Philip Edelen was born in Raleigh, North Carolina, on 29 June 1913 to Mr & Mrs Philip B. Edelen.

Philip attended grammar and high school at Sacred Heart Cathedral School in Raleigh. After finishing high school, he enrolled at the seminary at Mount St Mary's University in Emmitsburg, Maryland, and immediately following his graduation, was ordained on 2 May 1940. He served as Assistant Priest of St Anthony's Church and Chaplain to Notre Dame Academy in Southern Pines, North Carolina. He was then assigned as the Parish Administrator of Blessed Sacrament Church, Raleigh, North Carolina.

In March 1943, Rev Edelen joined the US Army Chaplain Corps. He was sent to the Army Chaplains School at Harvard University. After graduating from the Chaplains School, he was assigned to the 9th Infantry Regiment of the 2nd Infantry Division and, in October 1943, proceeded overseas with his regiment to their initial deployment in Northern Ireland.

On 8 June 1944, Chaplain Edelen and the men of his Regiment landed on Omaha Beach. The next day, the 2nd

Infantry Division went into action by attacking across the Aure River. On 9 June, Chaplain Edelen was seriously wounded in the head by shrapnel from an exploding German mortar shell as he was bent over a wounded soldier giving him first aid. He died in a field hospital on 10 June. Chaplain Edelen's records indicate that his younger brother Neil was also killed in the war.

Chaplain Edelen was interred in a temporary grave on the battlefield, where one source indicates his grave was tended by the Contesse d'Ursely with the help of her daughters. Moreover, this lady kept in touch with Chaplain Edelen's mother in America for many years. Chaplain Edelen's remains were later permanently interred in the Normandy American Cemetery.

11 June 1944

RAYMOND J HANSEN, Purple Heart. Service no: O-464313. Age 32. Captain, United States Army Chaplain Corps. Attached to the 8th Infantry Regiment, 4th Infantry Division. Buried Normandy American Cemetery, plot F, row 1, grave 30, Colleville-sur-Mer, France.

Raymond Hansen was born on 15 July 1912 to Peter A Hansen and his wife in Eau Claire County, Wisconsin. He had two sisters and three brothers. Raymond graduated from high school in Denmark, Wisconsin, in 1930. As with many in Wisconsin, he was fluent in German and Danish, as well as English. He enrolled in North Central College in Napierville, Wisconsin and graduated in 1933. Raymond then entered Evangelical Theological Seminary in Napierville and graduated in 1936. Upon graduation, he was called to be the pastor of Grace Evangelical Lutheran Church in Webster, Wisconsin (where he had been the student pastor while attending seminary). In 1938, Rev Hansen was appointed pastor of United Brethren Emmanuel Evangelical Lutheran Church in Augusta, Wisconsin, where he also served as the town's Scoutmaster. Rev Hansen married Leona A. Hansen (nee Marks) in Clintonville, Wisconsin, on 14 April 1941.

When America entered World War Two in December 1941, Rev Hansen resigned from his parish and was commissioned in the US Army Chaplain Corps. He received no formal training, as most other chaplains did at the US Army Chaplain School, and upon his enlistment and was initially assigned to the Chaplain Reserve Pool at the Storage Area at Fort Indiantown Gap, Pennsylvania, on 21 May 1942. On 12 June 1942, Chaplain Hansen was transferred to the 4th Motorized Division at Camp Gordon, Georgia, as part of the Special Troops (Medical/Engineer, MP). After serving for almost eight months in Georgia, he finally was sent to the Harvard Chaplain School on 7 March 1943 from which he graduated on 4 April 1943. Chaplain Hansen then returned to the 4th Motorized Division in Georgia, which had, while he was being trained, been renamed the 4th Infantry Division. The 4th Division then moved to Fort Dix in New Jersey, and Chaplain Hansen was assigned to the division's Artillery Battalion. He accompanied his Battalion to Camp Gordon Johnson in Florida in September 1943 for manoeuvres, and then when these were completed, moved in November 1943 to Fort Jackson in South Carolina. After arriving at Fort Jackson, Chaplain Hansen was transferred to the 8th Infantry Regiment of the 4th Infantry Division and went overseas with his new unit to England in early January 1944. Chaplain Hansen was described by members of his Regiment as: "... *as a fun-loving person, not an old sour puss. He was a fairly well-built man; a little taller than average, stocky, but not heavy set.*" Chaplain Hansen's battalion is noted to have been with the first seaborne troops to land in France on Utah Beach on D-Day.

Chaplain Hansen was killed in action on 11 June while the 4th Infantry Division was beginning to clear the Cotentin Peninsula between Fresville and Magneville.

In a quirk of history, Chaplain Hansen's empty storage box for his chaplain's supplies was found in a barn in Normandy 62 years after his death. However, the US Army list of Chaplain Hansen's personal effects, which would have been in this storage box, listed: 11 books, all sorts of miscellaneous and assorted uniform and related things, a communion set,  "chaplain garments", etc. So it is unclear how his personal effects were separated from this storage box.

19 June 1944

DOMINIC TERNAN, OFM, Silver Star, Purple Heart, Service no: O-442928. Age 42. Captain, United States Army Chaplain Corps. Attached to the 315th Infantry Regiment, 79th Infantry Division. He was buried in the cemetery of St. Bonaventure Friary in Paterson, N.J. (although his original grave at the entrance to the Chateau Servigny near Cherbourg is still maintained as a memorial to him.)

Dominic Ternan was born in Brooklyn, N.Y., on Nov. 8, 1902, and grew up in that part of New York City. He graduated from Fordham University in New York City and went to work for the New York Telephone Company before joining the Order of Friars Minor at St. Bonaventure Friary in Paterson, New Jersey, on 26 August 1933. Brother Dominic professed temporary vows 27 August 1934, and made his profession of solemn vows 17 September 1937. While a member of the community of St Bonaventure Friary, Brother Dominic studied to become a Roman Catholic priest and was ordained a priest in the Paulist Chapel in Washington, DC, on 30 September 1937. Upon his ordination, Rev Ternan was assigned to the monastery of St. Francis of Assisi in Manhattan, New York City. Rev Ternan was especially active in visiting the sick in hospitals and seeking out the less fortunate in the area around the monastery. Rev Ternan was known for his quiet and gentle ways and was popular in hearing confessions due to his kindness, but was also regarded as insightful and firm in the penance he assigned.

In April 1942, Father Dominic was commissioned in the U.S. Army Chaplain Corps and received initial training at Fort Benjamin Harrison, Indiana, before being assigned as headquarters chaplain of the 79th Infantry Division at Camp Pickett, Virginia. He subsequently moved with the division as it received additional training in various military bases around the country. Padre Ternan went overseas with the Division in April 1944 and landed in Liverpool, England, on 17 April. Shortly after arriving at their quarters in England, his unit began training in amphibious operations. Chaplain Ternan was noted for his rugged constitution and his ability to endure all the physical hardships that his men did, and that to them, he was really a padre and regarded with affection by the men he served.

The 79th Infantry Division landed on Utah Beach, in Normandy, between 12 and 14 June. The Division entered combat on 19 June with an attack on the high ground west and northwest of Valognes and south of Cherbourg. It was this initial combat, perhaps as newly arrived troops with no battle experience, that led to Chaplain Ternan's death. Chaplain Ternan's regiment ran into heavy German machine gun fire, causing many casualties, but he was not hit. The machine gun fire stopped for a moment (probably as the machine gunner changed his gun barrel that would have been red hot), and Chaplain Ternan, thinking that the firing was over, ran to help a wounded sergeant lying in a ditch at the side of the road. A German soldier saw Chaplain Ternan moving about the battlefield and, not seeing his Red Cross armband, shot him while he was administering the last rites to the wounded soldier. Chaplain Ternan was killed immediately. He was awarded the Silver Star posthumously for immediately seeking to minister to the wounded of his unit, with no thought for his own safety.

Chaplain Ternan was originally buried at the gates of the Château de Servigny at Yvetot-Bocage, within yards of where he was killed, but according to the Register of World War II Dead compiled by the War Department, his remains were returned to the USA after the war in 1947 or 1948, and he is buried in the cemetery of St. Bonaventure Friary in Paterson, New Jersey.

25 JUNE, 1944

ROBERT EDWARD CAPE, MA. Service no. 260316. Age 30. Chaplain 4th Class, Royal Army Chaplains' Department. Attached to the 7th Battalion, the Black Watch Regiment, 51st Highland Division. Buried in Ranville Commonwealth War Graves Cemetery, grave 3 F 25, Ranville, France.

Robert Cape was born in France in 1914. He was the son of Rev Herbert Taylor Cape (minister of Knightswood United Free Church, Glasgow) and Alice Mildred (Thorp) Cape. Robert Cape was educated at Ruthin College, Eckington, Derbyshire and Glasgow University, where he earned a Master of Arts in Philosophy. After graduation from university, he worked for the firm of William C. Jones in Manchester, and Felber Jucker & Co, also in Manchester. Both of these firms had diversified interests, including engineering, shipping and importation of raw materials.

In 1940 Robert Cape enrolled in the United Free Church of Scotland College in Edinburgh. In late 1942 he graduated from the college and was ordained at the North Woodside Free Church, Glasgow, on 1 January 1943. He entered the Royal Army Chaplains' Department on 5 February 1943. While serving in the army, he married Catherine "Lena" Buchanan Cape (nee Bowie) on 1 May 1943. Upon being commissioned into the Royal Army Chaplains' Department, he was sent to the Chaplain Training Centre at Tidworth for his initial 3 weeks of chaplaincy training. He was then transferred back to Scotland to serve in a holding and training unit for soldiers awaiting assignment to a permanent unit. During this time, though, he was hospitalized for appendicitis, which he recovered from with no lasting effects on his ministry with the British Army. At the beginning of January 1944, Padre Cape was assigned to the 1st Battalion (the Gordons) 7th Black Watch Regiment, 154th Infantry Brigade of the 51st Highland Division.

While in Normandy, Padre Cape was ministering to the wounded in the Regimental Aid Post of the 1st Battalion, the Black Watch, when the RAP came under German mortar attack. Chaplain Cape was killed instantly by an exploding mortar bomb.

30 JUNE, 1944

CYRIL MINTON-SENHOUSE, MA. Service no. 133104. Chaplain 4th Class, Royal Army Chaplains' Department, aged 35. 151st (The Ayrshire Yeomanry) Field Regiment, Royal Artillery, 11th Armoured Division. Buried in Ryes Commonwealth War Graves Cemetery, grave 5 D 3, Ryes, France.

Cyril Minton-Senhouse was born in Newcastle, Staffordshire, on 19 November 1909. He was the son of Herbert Hoskins, Darby Minton-Senhouse, and Emily Hilda Minton-Senhouse. Cyril attended Pembroke Lodge Preparatory School and then Worcester College, Oxford, where he earned a Bachelor of Arts in 1932 and a Master of Arts in 1935. He had, concurrently with his Master of Arts at Worcester College, also undertaken his theological training at Wells Theological College beginning in 1932 and was ordained a deacon in 1934. He was ordained a priest in 1935 by the Bishop of Portsmouth. Rev Minton-Senhouse served as curate of Petersfield at Saint Peter's Church, Hampstead, until 1938, and then moved to the Diocese of Winchester at Burghclere in 1938. According to his military records, as a young man, Cyril travelled extensively and had visited France, Belgium, Holland, Germany, Switzerland, Italy, Yugoslavia and Denmark. He married his wife Kathleen in Haslemere, Surrey.

Rev Minton-Senhouse joined the Royal Army Chaplaincy Department on 11 June 1940 and was posted to the Chaplain Department Training School at Chester. After the obligatory three-week training course, he was transferred to the 2nd Rangers of the King's Royal Rifle Corps at the beginning of July 1940. In October, he was transferred to the 4th Battalion Grenadier Guards Regiment in London, where he served with them until January 1944, when he was transferred to the 151st Field

Artillery Regiment (The Ayrshire Yeomanry) of the 11th Armoured Division. He attended the Chaplains Battle Course (Refresher Training) at Stone Weedon at the end of January 1944.

The 11th Armoured Division, as part of the VIII Corps, which the 151st Artillery Regiment was supporting, was committed to action in Normandy on 26 June as part of Operation Epsom. The 11th Armoured Division managed to seize Hill 112 (a dominant feature in the Normandy landscape near the village of Baron) and succeeded in capturing and holding this high ground against increasingly intense German counter-attacks. On 30 June, Lieutenant-General Sir Miles Dempsey, commanding the British Second Army, fearing a general counter-offensive, ordered the 11th Armoured to withdraw from Hill 112, and it was during this withdrawal that Padre Minton-Senhouse was killed by a fragment from an artillery shell which hit him in the head beneath the brim of his helmet as his regiment was retreating under heavy enemy fire.

JAMES SHEPHERD TAYLOR, MA. Service no. 95734. Age 43. Chaplain 4th Class, Royal Army Chaplains' Department. Attached to the 2nd Battalion, Highland Light Infantry (Glasgow Highlanders), 15th Scottish Division, Buried in St Manvieu Commonwealth War Graves Cemetery, grave 2 D 1, Choux, France.

James Taylor was born 3 December 1900 in Perth, Scotland. His parents were Peter Chalmers Taylor, a writer, and Helen Shepherd Taylor, after graduating from the University of Glasgow with a Master of Arts in 1922. James Taylor served as a Lay missionary in Argentina until 1925. He then returned to Scotland and was licensed by the Perth Presbytery in 1925 at New Kilpatrick to officiate in services at the Church of Scotland there. He was ordained in November 1926 and returned to Argentina after ordination and served as an assistant Presbyterian minister in Buenos Aires. He married Evelyn Ramsay Taylor (nee Darbyshire) in Argentina on 10 June 1931. Rev Taylor and his wife returned to Scotland in 1933, and he became minister of Stevenson Memorial Kirk in Glasgow.

Rev Taylor joined the Royal Army Chaplains' Department on 27 June 1939. He was appointed to the 2nd Battalion of the South Wales Borders in mid-December 1939 and then transferred to the 5th Battalion of the Scots Guards in March 1940. Only a couple of weeks later, he was transferred again to the 2nd Battalion (the Glasgow Highlanders) of the Highland Light Infantry Regiment.

In March 1942, Padre Taylor was attached to the 9th Battalion (Gordon Highlanders) but was, after only a few months, transferred back to the 2nd Battalion (the Glasgow Highlanders) of the Highland Light Infantry Regiment. On 16 June 1944, Padre Shepherd landed in Normandy with his battalion as part of the 46th Infantry brigade. Within two weeks of his battalion landing, Padre Shepherd had been severely wounded in a mortar attack on his battalion position and according to the official records of his unit, died of his wounds on 29 June 1944, although the Medical Officer of the field hospital recorded his date of death as 30 June, which is what is recorded on his gravestone.

5 July 1944

A. J. Dieffenbacher

ARTHUR J DIEFFENBACHER, BA, MA, Purple Heart, Service no: O-525647. Age 35. 1st Lieutenant, United States Army Chaplain Corps. Attached to the 330th Infantry Regiment, 83rd Infantry Division. Buried in the Normandy American Cemetery, plot D, row 17, grave 44, Colleville-sur-Mer, France.

Arthur Dieffenbacher was born in Titusville, Pennsylvania, on 29 April 1909. His parents were Lloyd E Dieffenbacher and Mildred J. Dieffenbacher. His early years were spent in Erie, Pennsylvania. where he graduated from high school at the age of fifteen. Arthur enrolled in Grove City College in Erie and graduated in 1927 with a Bachelor of Arts degree. Arthur then enrolled as a student at the Dallas Theological Seminary in Texas. Arthur graduated from the seminary in 1931 with a Master of Arts degree and some credits toward a doctoral degree as well. He was ordained in the Presbyterian Church of the United States.

In September 1932, Rev Dieffenbacher was appointed a missionary of the China Inland Mission in Changteh, Hunan Province, China, where he studied the Chinese language. While there, in 1934, he met Junia White, daughter of Dr. Hugh W. White, editor of *The China Fundamentalist* newspaper. Arthur and Junia were soon engaged, but due to illness, and other causes, they were not married until June 1938. The same year they were married, they joined the Presbyterian Foreign Missions Board.

Mr and Mrs Dieffenbacher

The years of being a missionary in China provided all sorts of adventure for Rev Dieffenbacher, including a flight on foot from advancing Chinese communist forces in 1935. In the summer of 1938, just after Rev Dieffenbacher and his wife were married in Kuling, China, there was fighting all around the city. On their way from Kuling, Rev Dieffenbacher and his wife had to pass through the front lines. The Dieffenbachers moved on to Harbin, Manchuria, then under the control of the Japanese army. Rev Dieffenbacher continued his ministry there until the summer of 1940. After eight years in China, Mr Dieffenbacher and his wife returned to America on leave. On 19 June 1941, their daughter, Sara Junia, was born. The situation with the Japanese forces in Manchuria was deteriorating, and his superiors felt that Rev Dieffenbacher should return to his mission there while leaving his wife and infant daughter safely in America.

Rev Dieffenbacher had obtained a visa to return to Manchuria from the Japanese and had booked his passage on a ship travelling there, but his plans were permanently interrupted by the 7 December 1941 Japanese attack on Pearl Harbour.

Rev Dieffenbacher remained in America and proved to be a good and effective missionary speaker. He held a brief pastorate in the Bible Presbyterian Church in Cincinnati, Ohio. But when the American Council of Christian Churches was asked to provide chaplains for the Army, Rev Dieffenbacher volunteered and joined the Army Chaplain Corps on 18 July 1943. He entered the Harvard Chaplain School that same month and graduated in August 1943.

After his training, Chaplain Dieffenbacher was assigned to the 330th Infantry Regiment of the 83rd Infantry Division and went overseas to England with them, arriving on 16 April 1944. During his regiment's training, Chaplain Dieffenbacher won recognition for demonstrating his faith in the men of his regiment by participating in training courses, including the dangerous and difficult "infiltration" course and doing other things which were not required of chaplains but which he did. Chaplain Dieffenbacher remained with the 330th Regiment and landed with them on Omaha Beach on 18 June 1944.

His regiment went into combat southeast of Carentan, Normandy, on 27 June 1944 and moved slowly through the bocage (hedgerow country) of Normandy. Records show Chaplain Dieffenbacher was with the men of his regiment when it attacked on 4 July but were in turn counter-attacked by German forces and driven back. On the morning of 5 July, they again attacked against stiff resistance. The 330th Regiment suffered many casualties from German artillery and mortar fire as they battled through the dense vegetation of the hedgerows surrounding the fields.

Chaplain Dieffenbacher was noted for always being amongst the front-line troops while they were in combat, providing aid and comfort to them. Chaplain Dieffenbacher was killed with his regiment's front-line troops by German artillery fire in the attacks of 5 July. His body was recovered by his Division's senior chaplain, and it was reported that an impressive funeral service was held with attendance by all the chaplains of his division, as well as the senior officers of the 83rd Division.

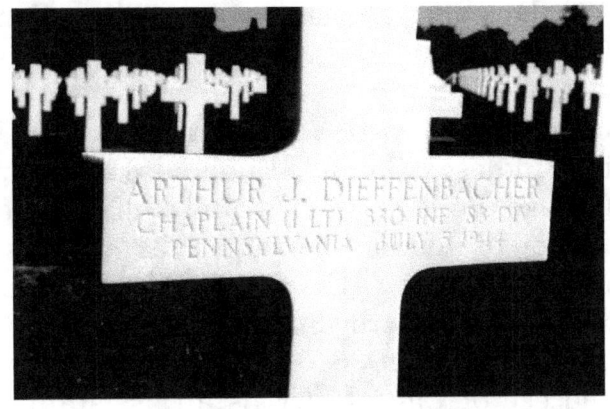

7 July 1944

CECIL JAMES HAWKSWORTH, AKC, Mentioned in Dispatches. Service no. 90874. Age 35. Chaplain 4th Class, Royal Army Chaplains' Department. Attached to the 6th Battalion, Durham Light Infantry, 151st Infantry Brigade, 50th Division, Buried in Jerusalem Commonwealth War Graves Cemetery, grave B 2, Chouain, France.

Cecil Hawksworth was born on 17 May 1909 in Willesden in Middlesex County, England. He graduated from King's College, London, in 1933 and was ordained a deacon by the Bishop of London the same year. He was ordained a priest in 1934. He served as curate of St John the Evangelist with St Saviour, Fitzroy Square in London until the end of 1935. On 1 January 1936, he moved to St Peter's, Croydon, in the Diocese of Canterbury as an assistant curate, and while there, he married his wife Diana, who came from Kingsclere, Hampshire. While at St Peter's, Rev Hawksworth joined the Territorial Army as a chaplain in June of 1939. His specific ministry, while at St Peter's, was ministering in the Mission to Seamen organization that provided pastoral care to merchant seamen while in port.

Upon being called to active service after the outbreak of war, Padre Hawksworth was initially assigned to 63rd Searchlight Regiment, 46th Anti-Aircraft Brigade, a part of the 5th AA Division, and he served with this regiment until April 1941. He was then transferred to the Middle East, where he served in Sudan and Eritrea until October 1942. He was then transferred to H Force, where he was assigned to the British North African Forces taking part in the invasion of North Africa. At the end of August 1943, he was assigned to the 6th Durham Light Infantry Battalion of the 151st Infantry Brigade, part of the 50th (Northumbrian) Infantry Division. This battalion had just completed its role in the invasion of Sicily. The 6th Battalion was then returned, along with Padre Hawksworth, to the UK to prepare for the invasion of Europe. It was felt that the invasion force would benefit from having some of its units with battle experience, as many of the assigned units had not seen combat. Like most of the other British Chaplains, Padre Hawksworth completed a two-week refresher course for combat chaplains in the spring of 1944.

An article in the parish magazine of St Peter's Church, Croydon, from August 1944 mentions that the parish had kept Rev Hawksworth's assistant curacy unfilled in the hope that he would return from his time of service with the Army Chaplains Department.

In **The Faithful 6th**, *a history of the 6th Battalion of the Durham Light Infantry*, it was recorded:

"On the 6 July, the 6th Battalion the DLI suffered a real loss with the tragic death of Padre Hawksworth, the Church of England padre. He was seriously injured whilst riding a motorcycle in a collision with a Bren Gun Carrier. He was taken to 149th Advanced Dressing Station and then on to 3rd Casualty Clearing Station, but died of his injuries. He had been with the Battalion since the end of the Sicilian Campaign and his loss was felt deeply by all officers and other ranks. His funeral was held later in the 50th Divisional cemetery.... As Chaplain Hawksworth was being buried by fellow Durham Light Infantry Chaplain Gerard Nesbitt, the burial party came under bombardment and Chaplain Nesbitt was killed by an exploding shell....

Chaplain Hawksworth, a Protestant, is buried beside Chaplain Nesbitt, a Roman Catholic, in the appropriately named Jerusalem Commonwealth War Graves Cemetery, perhaps reminding everyone of how the ecumenical movements of the post-war era began. Chaplain Hawksworth is remembered in St Peter's Church, Croydon, on their memorial altar, and a flag that hangs beside it was donated in his memory. It is noted in the parish magazine of February 1945 that Rev Hawksworth's wife was most appreciative of this effort to remember her husband.

GERARD NESBITT, DPhil, Mentioned in Dispatches, Croix de Guerre. Service no. 163330. Age 33. Chaplain 4th Class, Royal Army Chaplains' Department. Attached to the 8th Battalion Durham Light Infantry. Buried in Jerusalem Commonwealth War Graves Cemetery, grave B 1, Chouain, France.

Gerard Nesbitt was the son of Stephen and Jane Nesbitt of Felling-on-Tyne, County Durham and was born on 22 January 1911. He was educated at St Cuthbert's Grammar School in Newcastle and then at Ushaw College at Durham University and The Venerable English College (Roman Catholic) in Rome. He was ordained in the mid-1930's and returned to teach at his former grammar school, St Cuthbert's in Newcastle. While teaching at St Cuthbert's, he was also appointed curate at St Roberts in Morpeth, Northumberland. Rev Nesbitt joined the Royal Army Chaplains' Department on 30 December 1940, where he was assigned to the 50th Division.

In the history of the 8th Battalion of the Durham Light Infantry, it was noted:

"Padre Nesbitt was killed today by a stray artillery shell whilst burying the dead just behind the 9th DLI positions including Chaplain James Hawkworth, who had died the previous day.

Padre Nesbitt had been with the 8th DLI since the end of 1940 and was well loved by all ranks whether of Roman Catholic faith or not his quiet manner yet very strong personality impressed all those who came in contact with him. Always cheerful and willing to help anyone in trouble, he was regarded as a personal friend by many. He was a great example of courage and fortitude and his death deeply affected all members of the Battalion. All the old officers of the 8th DLI headed by the CO went back to attend the funeral at 149th Field Ambulance..."

Chaplain Gerard Nesbitt's obituary in the Catholic Herald states:

"Few Army Chaplains in this war have experienced so exhausting a time or witnessed so much active fighting as did Father Gerard Nesbitt whose death in action was announced last week in the Catholic Herald. He was Chaplain to the Durham Light Infantry in the famous 50th Division and within a few weeks of joining the Army he accompanied his regiment to Cyprus, then Palestine, Iraq and he was present with his soldiers in every battle from El Alamein to the Invasion of Sicily.

More perhaps than the fighting soldier Padre Nesbitt was brought face to face continually with the tragedies of battle, in the burial grounds among the minefields at the casualty clearing stations and at the base hospitals. The experience made him seem older, and more serious and it was only with difficulty that one could get him to talk about Egypt, Africa or Sicily. He was endowed with great personal courage and his esteem for the men of The 50th Division and especially the DLI was second to none, not even to that of General Montgomery.

Once when things were quiet in North Africa Padre Nesbitt took the opportunity of going to a base hospital to have an injury to his knee attended to. He was there only a day or two when he heard that his regiment was to take part in an Invasion of Sicily. He got up from bed and went straight back to his beloved DLI.

He had many narrow escapes from German shells and small arms fire in the Middle East and Sicily but in England whilst awaiting the opening of the second front he expressed his presentment that he would not return home alive. He set out for France with a profound sense of loyalty to his men and a high sense of duty.

Padre Nesbitt was twice recommended for the Military Cross and he was Mentioned in Dispatches in the London Gazette on 12 January, 1944 for his service in North Africa and Sicily. Padre Nesbitt was awarded after his death, the French Croix de Guerre also in recognition of his ministry to both the British troops under his care, but also for his providing priestly services to the French civilians in the areas where his battalion was located in Normandy.

Padre George Markham who was posted to the 8th Durham Light Infantry after Padre Nesbitt was killed stated: *"My first job with the Durham Light Infantry was to bury my predecessor Padre Nesbitt who was killed by a shell whilst conducting the funeral service of another Padre (James Hawksworth) who had been accidentally killed a day or so before!"*

11 July 1944

DAVID DANIEL THOMAS, BA Hon. Service no. 305657. Age 32. Chaplain 4th Class, Royal Army Chaplains' Department. Attached to the 2nd Devonshire Regiment, 231st Brigade, 50th Division. Buried in Bayeux Commonwealth War Graves Cemetery, grave 21 E 19, Bayeux, France.

David Thomas was born in Tonypandy, Rhondda, Wales, on 13 March 1912 to Samuel and Anna Maria Thomas. David studied at the University of Wales and earned a Bachelor of Arts degree in Economics in 1933, then became a high school teacher for 2½ years before entering training to become an ordained minister. In 1936 Rev Thomas trained for ordination into Anglican priesthood in the Church of Wales at Clifton Theological College in Bristol and was ordained a deacon in 1937 by the Bishop of Swansea. Rev Thomas was appointed the curate of Gellygaer in the Diocese of Llandaff from 1937 until 1941 and then was appointed the curate of Risca in the Diocese of Monmouth. While in Risca, Rev Thomas married his wife Esther in Pen-Y-Graig, Glamorgan.

Rev Thomas joined the Royal Army Chaplains' Department on 1 January 1944. After his 3 weeks of training at the Army Chaplain's School, he was posted to the 12th Primary

Training Centre at Bulford, Salisbury, where potential non-commissioned officers and cooks were trained for assignment throughout the army. On 11 May 1944, Padre Thomas was transferred to the HQ of the 50th Division of 21st Army Group.

Chaplain Thomas was severely wounded in the back by a mortar barrage on 7 July 1944 while he and the regiment's Medical Officer were visiting a battalion on the front lines. Chaplain Thomas died of his wounds on 11 July in a field hospital.

16 July 1944

CAMERON DUNDAS CARNEGIE, MA, Royal Academician. Service no. 301343. Age 28. Chaplain 4th Class, Royal Army Chaplains' Department. Attached to the 31st Transport Column, Royal Army Service Corps, 11th Line of Communication Area. Buried in Douvres-La-Delivrande Commonwealth War Graves Cemetery, grave 6 L 1, Douvres-La-Delivrande, France.

Cameron Carnegie was the son of John Clarke Carnegie and Mary Denoon Carnegie of Edinburgh. He was born on 1 January 1916. He was educated at Clayesmore Preparatory School in Iwerne Minster, Blandford, Dorset. His secondary education was at George Watson College in Edinburgh in 1934. He went to Edinburgh University and graduated with a Master of Arts degree in 1939. After graduation, he entered New College at Edinburgh University, studying Divinity. While there, he was a student assistant at St. George's Church of Scotland Parish Church, Edinburgh. On the outbreak of war, Cameron Carnegie was eager to enlist as a combatant but was persuaded to finish his Divinity course with a view to a Chaplaincy.

He graduated from New College and joined the Royal Army Chaplains' Department on 26 November 1943, after being ordained on 21 November the previous week. Padre

Carnegie was initially assigned to the 196th Heavy Anti-Aircraft Regiment on the Island of Orkney. However, within 6 months, Padre Carnegie was posted in May 1944 to 31st Transport Column of the Royal Army Service Corps 11th Line of Communication Area, whom he accompanied to Normandy on 8 June 1944. Chaplain Carnegie was killed in  a fatal motorcycle accident (non-combat) on 16 July. As 4-wheeled motor transport in the summer of 1944 in Normandy was at a premium, Chaplains often unofficially "acquired" motorcycles that permitted them to travel quickly and easily to the various scattered parts of the units they ministered to, as well as often providing ministry to other battalions nearby as well.

19 July 1944

HENRY THURLOW WAGG, Mentioned in Dispatches. Service no. 294758. Age 35. Chaplain 4th Class, Royal Army Chaplains' Department. Attached to the 7th Field Dressing Station, 11th Armoured Division. Buried in Hermanville Commonwealth War Graves Cemetery, grave 3 C 9, Hermanville, France.

Henry Wagg was born in Docking, Norfolk, to James Henry and Eva Wagg. Rev Wagg and his wife Kathleen Wagg lived in North Lancing, Sussex, with their son Michael, who was born in 1942. Rev Wagg studied at the Lincoln Theological College beginning in 1931 and was ordained a deacon in 1934 and ordained a priest by the Bishop of London in 1935. He began his ministry as the curate of All Saints Hillingdon in 1934 and remained there until 1937. He then transferred to the Diocese of Chichester to the parish of St James the Less at Lansing from 1937 until 1943.

Chaplain Wagg joined the Royal Army Chaplains' Department on 9 October 1943. He was originally assigned to the 8th AA Regiment but was transferred to the 7th Field Dressing Station of the 11th Armoured Division, Headquarters Squadron, with whom he embarked for Normandy on 11 June 1944. On the night of 18 July, Padre Wagg was just south of Amfreville with the 7th Field Dressing Station. The Dressing Station was in the process of setting up in a new location and had not yet dug foxholes for the protection of its members from shells and bombs. The German Luftwaffe bombed the location of the Dressing Station, and Padre Wagg was killed by a bomb fragment. He was buried on 19 July by Chaplain E.T. Lang.

20 July 1944

JOHN ARTHUR NEWSON, BA. Service no. 191487. Age 38. Chaplain 4th Class, Royal Army Chaplains' Department. Attached to the 5th Dragoon Guards, 28th Brigade, 9th Armoured Division. Buried in Bayeux Commonwealth War Graves Cemetery, grave 2 F 9, Bayeux, France.

John Newson was born on 5 August 1905 in London. He was the son of John Newson MBE and Ada Emily Newson. He was educated at Norbury College, City of London School. In 1933 he began training at the Sarum Theological College and was ordained a deacon in 1935 and a priest in 1936 by the Bishop of Newcastle. He was initially a curate of St Peter's Church, Wallsend, until the end of 1936. He then became curate at Seaton Delaval from 1936 to 1938 and then curate in charge of St John's Church, Bury St Edmonds, in 1938. He was then transferred to the Diocese of St Edmundsbury of Acton, Waldingfield, from 1940 to 1941.

Rev Newson was married to Sophie Newson of Norbury, Surrey and was the father of Helen Margaret Newson, who died the same year as he did. Rev Newson and his wife lived in Holbrook Hall, Little Waldingfield, Sudbury. For some reason, his application to be a wartime chaplain does not note that he was married.

At university, Rev Newson is reported to have excelled in boxing and cross-country running. He was also a licensed referee for amateur boxing. Rev. Newson joined the Royal Army Chaplains' Department on 25 June 1941. He served with the Royal Norfolk Regiment from July 1941 to March 1942. He was then assigned to the 5th Dragoon Guards, 28th Brigade of the 9th Armoured Division. In June 1943, he transferred within the same division to the 15th Inniskilling Dragoon Guards for a brief period of time and then transferred back to the 5th Dragoon Guards in September 1943.

Padre Newson's older brother, Flying Officer Edward Ranald Newson, had joined the RAF and was killed in a training accident on the night of 16/17 November 1942 while training with 25 Operational Training Unit. He was the bomb aimer when the plane he was flying in had fuel problems over Yorkshire, and the crew abandoned it before it crashed. It is not known if F/O Newson was unable to parachute to safety in time or became trapped in the plane, but he was the only one killed in the crash.

There are two different accounts of Chaplain Newson's death by drowning in the Baie de Seine off the Normandy invasion beaches. One account says he drowned while leading a human chain in rough seas to try and rescue Canadian soldiers from a Landing Ship Tank (LST 689) that was sinking in rough seas just offshore of the invasion beaches. While records don't indicate what sank LST 689, it is likely the LST hit a mine that had been missed when the area off the landing beaches had been swept by minesweepers. The second account indicates that Chaplain Newson was leading a bathing party of his unit, as they had been behind the lines for two weeks, preparing for the next Allied offensive to break out of Normandy, and the troops were getting bored. A rip current had developed along the coast opposite Arromanches, where the troops were swimming, and a number began to experience difficulty in returning to the shore. Chaplain Newsom, who was fully clothed, helped to form a human chain to try and rescue these men and was successful in bringing some to shore. However, the wind had come up even more, and the waves had become larger. A man standing next to Padre Newson in the human chain is reported to have seen a large wave approaching and jumped up to ride it out, but Padre Newsom had not seen it and was wearing his full uniform, including his boots and was swept under, and not seen again. It is possible the two accounts have been mixed together over the past 74 years. All that can be accurately known is that Padre Newson drowned while trying to save another man's life.

Author's Note: Chaplain Newson's records, specifically his AF B199 record of postings, promotions and appointments, has been lost by the MOD records office. Many of the officers' records were maintained on paper until the computerization of military records in the 1970s and due to records offices being moved around at various times between the end of World War Two and the 1970s. Some records have gone missing. Interestingly, one of the few records remaining for Padre Newson is the list of his personal effects that were gathered by the Regimental Personal Effects Officer upon his death, who recorded in great detail all that was recovered from his personal kit, down to things such as bottles of tablets and pen nibs.

21 July 1944

WILLIAM ALFRED SEAMAN, BA. Chaplain 4th Class, Canadian Chaplain Service, aged 34. Attached to the 3rd Light Anti-Aircraft Regiment and the 5th Field Regiment, Royal Canadian Artillery, 2nd Canadian Infantry Division. Buried in Beny-Sur-Mer Commonwealth War Graves Cemetery, grave 16 B 14, Rivieres, France.

William Seaman was born on 14 June 1910 in Springfield Township, Prince Edward Island, Canada. He was the son of William James Seaman and Sophia Seaman. He was married to Louise Seaman (nee Van Duyn) of Sackville, New Brunswick. Chaplain Seaman was a graduate of Mount Allison University, New Brunswick. In 1939 Rev Seaman and his wife moved to the parish of River John and West Branch, United Churches and lived in the manse located in Salem, Nova Scotia.

Shortly after Canada declared war on Germany on 10 September 1939, Rev Seaman volunteered to serve in the Canadian Chaplain Service and, after a period of waiting, joined the 2nd Battalion of the Pictou Highlanders Regiment at the beginning of August 1940. However, Chaplain Seaman was assigned duties across all of Military District 6, in which the 2nd Battalion of the Pictou Highlanders was located. Military District 6 encompassed all of the province of Nova Scotia. It is interesting to note that Chaplain Seaman has no records indicating he attended any sort of Chaplain training in Canada or in the United Kingdom. He seemed to have learned his work as a military chaplain "on the job".

There was a shortage of chaplains serving with the Canadian Army in the United Kingdom, and on 15 May 1943, Chaplain Seaman was ordered overseas and, after a period in a transit camp in New Brunswick, and a time on a troop ship crossing the North Atlantic, Chaplain Seaman arrived in the UK on 7 July 1943. He was initially assigned to two different Canadian Reinforcement Units, providing chaplain services while waiting for a permanent posting. On 14 September 1943, Padre Seaman was assigned as chaplain to the 5th Field Regiment Royal Canadian Artillery, 2nd Canadian Infantry Division. As chaplains were always in short supply, Chaplain Seaman would also minister to troops in neighbouring units, and Chaplain Seaman is noted as also ministering with the 3rd Light Anti-Aircraft Regiment that was also assigned to the 5th Field Regiment to provide anti-aircraft protection for the 25 pounder guns of the Field Regiment.

Chaplain Seaman was badly wounded by enemy mortar fire on 14 July 1944 northwest of Verson, Normandy, between Saint Manvieu-Norrey and

Carpiquet Airport. His records indicate he was hit by enemy shell fire with wounds to his head, right thigh and left knee. Chaplain Seaman was evacuated from the battlefield to a field hospital behind the lines in Normandy, but his wounds were too severe, and Chaplain Seaman died of wounds on 21 July 1944.

24 July 1944

PETER E BONNER, Purple Heart. Service no.: O-471750, aged 40. Captain, United States Army Chaplain Corps. Attached to the 86th Replacement Battalion. Buried in the Normandy American Cemetery, plot J, row 16, grave 15, Colleville-sur-mer.

Peter E. Bonner was born in Philadelphia, Pennsylvania, on 10 January 1904. He was a Roman Catholic and a gifted linguist who spoke French, Latin, and Italian. Rev Bonner was ordained on 31 March 1931. He had served as Assistant Rector of Our Lady of Rosary Church, Philadelphia until he joined the Army Chaplain Corps in the fall of 1942. Chaplain Bonner graduated from the Chaplain School at Harvard University in November of 1942.

Chaplain Bonner arrived in Normandy in July 1944 and was assigned to the 86th Replacement Battalion at Vouilly, France, inland from Omaha Beach. Chaplain Bonner, while waiting to be assigned to a Regiment, ministered to the soldiers of the replacement Battalion. Although the Replacement Battalion was behind the front lines, it still came under fire by hit-and-run attacks by the German Air Force. Chaplain Bonner, during a German air attack, while crouched in a protective trench, heard wounded men calling for help. He left the safety of his trench and began ministering to, and praying over, the wounded men.

Chaplain Bonner was killed instantly by shrapnel from another bomb landing close to where he was kneeling over a wounded soldier.

A sad postscript to Chaplain Bonner's death was that the Archbishop of Philadelphia, Dennis Cardinal Dougherty, where Chaplain Bonner had ministered before joining the Army, made no mention of his death in the *Catholic Standard and Times* newspaper of the Diocese and was noted for showing no care at all for the chaplains serving in the American Armed Forces from his diocese, as he did not like them leaving their parishes to serve their country It is known that Cardinal Dougherty had experienced difficulties 30 years before with an Army Chaplain while serving in a parish in Manila, Philippines, and held nothing but contempt for the military chaplaincy. There was hardly a mention in the whole Diocese of Philadelphia of Chaplain Bonner's memorial mass in late August 1944 due to this animosity to military chaplaincy.

25 July 1944

DIETRICH FELIX EBERHARD RASETZKI, Purple Heart. Service no. O-525810. Age 29. 1st Lieutenant, United States Army Chaplain Corps. Attached to the 119th Infantry Regiment, 30th Infantry Division. Buried in the Long Island National Cemetery, section H, site 8673 East Farmingdale, New York.

Dietrich Rasetski was born in Austria on 11 March 1915 but immigrated to the United States in 1924 at the age of 9 with his parents, Alfred and Margaret Rasetzki. He grew up in Canton, Massachusetts and graduated from Canton High School in 1932. He then attended Hobart College, The Episcopal Theological School in Cambridge, Massachusetts, from which he graduated. He then entered Andover-Newton Theological School in Newton, Maryland, where he completed his graduate studies in 1941. While he was still studying at Andover-Newton, he took on the leadership of The Congregational Church Of Chester, New Hampshire and was ordained on 1 October 1941. Pastor Rasetski married Frances Elizabeth Griffin Rasetzki (née Knott) while ministering in Chester, and they had a baby girl who was stillborn in 1943 while Chaplain Rasetzki was away from home serving his country.

On 23 February 1943, Pastor Rasetzki resigned from the Chester Church and joined the US Army Chaplain Corps, and attended the Harvard Chaplains School. Following training, he joined the 199th Infantry Regiment of the 30th Infantry Division in July 1943. Chaplain Rasetski trained with his regiment in Tennessee and Indiana and went overseas with his Regiment on 12 February 1944. They arrived in Liverpool, England, on 25 February. While with the 119th Regiment, Chaplain Rasetzki was revered by the men of his regiment. One of Chaplain Rasetzki's innovations in his regiment was distributing small cards to the men, which he called "The Ticket of Sympathy", for those who got into trouble or needed support. The card contained a bible verse on the back for the men to think about.

Chaplain Rasetzki landed with his regiment on Omaha Beach on 11 June 1944 and moved to a holding area near Isigny-sur-Mer. His regiment fought in the bocage (hedgerows), taking numerous casualties due to the confined and difficult fighting that these hedgerows created. The continuous casualties in these small battles kept Chaplain Rasetzki busy with burials and pastoral support.

On 25 July, Operation Cobra began the breakout of American forces from Normandy. However, this attack was preceded by an intensive bombing raid on the German front lines facing the Americans.
Unfortunately, some of the bombers dropped their bombs short of the German lines, and some fell on the Regimental HQ of the 119th Regiment, where Chaplain Rasetzki was stationed. Chaplain Rasetski was killed immediately by a bomb blast, along with numerous other soldiers, and many others were wounded. Included in this "short bombing" was Lieutenant-General Leslie McNair.

Chaplain Rasetzki was initially buried in the American cemetery at La Cambe (which has become the main German cemetery in Normandy), and then his remains were repatriated in the spring of 1948 to his final resting place in the Long Island National Cemetery, East Farmingdale, New York. It is interesting that his obituary in his hometown notes he was killed by a sniper's bullet on the streets of Paris in June of 1944, but this is incorrect, as Paris was not liberated until 25 August 1944.

27 July 1944

WALTER HENRY ARTHUR BERRY, AKC, MA, Mentioned in Dispatches. Service no. 291270. Age 40. Chaplain 4th Class, Royal Army Chaplains' Department, Attached to the 2nd Battalion Grenadier Guards, 5th Guards Armoured Brigade, Guards Armoured Division. Buried in Ranville Commonwealth War Graves Cemetery, grave 3 C 15, Ranville, France.

Walter Berry was born in London on 25 May 1904 and was the son of Walter Joseph and Mary Selena Eleanor (Smith) Berry. He studied at Gonville Caius College, Cambridge, where he obtained his BA in Modern Languages and Economics. In 1923, prior to being ordained, Walter worked in the business world for 12 years in the wholesale stationery and paper industry, where he was an assistant manager. The firm's name was Berry & Roberts of London, which indicates he was employed in a family business in London. He married his wife Kathleen from Keston, Kent, in September 1929 and had three children who were aged 14, 11, and 6 when he was killed.

In 1939 he obtained an MA from Kings College, London and was ordained a deacon in 1939 and a priest by the Bishop of Rochester in 1940.

His first appointment was a curacy at Bexley Heath. A year and a half later, he was appointed Vicar of Horton Kirby in 1941. He lived with his wife and family in the vicarage of Horton Kirby. His records indicate he could speak French and German at the basic level but was fluent in his reading of these languages.

Rev Berry served two years in the Home Guard, which included serving as an Officiating Chaplain for the same period. (An Officiating Chaplain was a civilian minister who performed religious duties for the military on an occasional basis.)

Rev Berry joined the Royal Army Chaplains' Department on 21 August 1943. After the obligatory 3 weeks of training at the Chaplains School, he was assigned to the 2nd Battalion of the Grenadier Guards of the 5th Guards Armoured Brigade.

In late July of 1944, Padre Berry was with his unit in the Colombelles area of Caen, supporting the Canadian Army in its advance. Padre Berry was talking to some wounded men who had bailed out of their disabled tanks on the battlefield and were taken to the Regimental Aid Station when it came under German shellfire, and he was killed by the first shell.

It is interesting to note that he is listed as the vicar of his last parish from the beginning of his service with the Home Guard until his death in 1944. This is due to the fact that British clergy volunteers for the forces were guaranteed their civilian ministries after the war had ended.

43rd Wessex Division Chaplains

The Division had come out of the front line on 23 July from the Maltot—Hill 112 sector of the Allied front. As the Division was regrouping, all the chaplains were called to the 21 Army Group HQ for a day. They were provided with a bath, fresh uniforms, as well as a good rest.

The photo below (taken on 24 July) includes 3 Chaplains who would be dead within the next 18 days. It also includes 3 more chaplains who would be wounded in action out of a total of the 12 chaplains pictured serving with front-line battalions.

Front Row: Ivor Richards, John Wilson, Ivan D Neill (Senior 43rd Division Chap); Alfred Thomas Arthur Naylor, the Deputy Chaplain General; Geoff Druitt (Deputy Assistant Chaplain General, 12 Corps); J. Eric Gethyn-Jones; Lieut. Gwen; unknown, Bernard Hadelsey.

Back Row: Willie Speirs; J. Talfryn Davis+; A.E. Gibbins; Bob Lehey; James Douglas+; Francis Musgrave+; Hugh Etherington

+ indicates died in Normandy.

2 August 1944

FRANCIS WILLIAM MUSGRAVE, BA. Service no. 147348. Age 39. Chaplain 4th Class, Royal Army Chaplains' Department. Attached to the 5th Battalion, The Dorsetshire Regiment, 130th Infantry Brigade, 43rd Wessex Division. Buried in Hottot-les-Bagues Commonwealth War Graves Cemetery, grave 10 C 1, Hottot-les-Bagues.

Francis Musgrave was the son of William Gummow Musgrave and Mary Musgrave and born on 24 December 1904. He was the husband of Alma Grace Musgrave of Hove, Sussex. He attended Bancroft's School in Woodford, Essex and graduated from St Deiniol's College, Lampeter, University of Wales, where he obtained a BA in 1926. He was ordained a deacon in 1928 and ordained a priest by the Bishop of Asaph in 1929. He was the curate of Hop from 1928 to 1930 and moved to Seaford, where he was curate from 1930 to 1935. He then took up a position at St Barnabas in Hove from 1935 to 1937, where he met and married his wife. He then was the Vicar of St. Cushman's Church, Whitehawk, in East Brighton, in 1938, when the church was being built, until he entered the Army in 1940.

In September 1940, Rev Musgrave joined the Royal Army Chaplains' Department. He was initially assigned to the Gordon Barracks in Bulford, Salisbury. He then transferred to the 1st Battalion of the Berkshire Regiment in Northern Ireland. In mid-1942, he transferred to the 148th Independent Infantry Brigade. He then served for short periods of time in a variety of units before being assigned to the 7th Survey Regiment of the 21st Army Group, with whom he embarked for Normandy. He was transferred to the 5th battalion of The Dorset Regiment, 130th Infantry Brigade, 43rd Wessex Division, on 20 July 1944.

Chaplain Musgrave was killed by a shell burst during his battalion's attack at Mount Pinçon on 2 August 1944. As a new chaplain with a battalion in combat, Padre Musgrave had not learned to recognize the sound of incoming mortar shells and did not take cover in time. A member of the 10th Medium Artillery Regiment mentioned seeing the body of a Padre with his hands covering his ears while trying to move a Half-Track vehicle that was on fire away from the ammunition stacked nearby for an artillery gun.

3 August 1944

ARCHIBALD SELWYN PRYOR, MA. Service no. 26457. Age 41. Chaplain 4th Class, Royal Army Chaplains' Department. Attached to the 153rd (Leicestershire Yeomanry) Royal Artillery Regiment, Guards Armoured Division. Buried in St Charles de Percy Commonwealth War Graves Cemetery, grave 1 C 8, Valdallière, France.

Archibald Pryor was born in London on 7 December 1902 and was the son of Margaret and Selwyn Pryor. He was educated at Eton College, where he was a member of the Officer Training Corps from 1918-1921. He then entered Cambridge University, where he served in the Officer Training Corps. While studying, he joined the Territorial Army with the 85th Brigade, where he served from 1923-1927. Upon completion of his theological studies at Westcott College, Cambridge, he was ordained and then appointed as a curate in a church in Hackney, London. In 1930 he was appointed Chaplain 4th class with the 56th (1st London) Division of the Territorial Army. In 1933 he transferred to the 46th (North Midland) Division, most likely due to his being called to be the Rector of the parish of St Luke's Upper Broughton after marrying his wife Elizabeth Gulielma Pryor (nee Lister), originally of Purley, Berkshire. His youngest son, Hugh, was born on 24 July 1944, just two weeks before his father was killed.

Rev Pryor was well known in his parish at Upper Broughton for going sledding with his children in the garden of the rectory and also down Muxlow Hill. He was fond of riding horses and often would arrange to officiate at the early morning service each day in his parish, so he could go riding following, while his curates looked after the later services and pastoral duties.

In September 1939, as a member of the Territorial Army, he was called to active service with the 153rd Leicestershire Yeomanry (which became a Royal Artillery Regiment) as part of the 2nd Armoured Division. He served continuously with the 153rd Field Regiment, which was eventually attached to the Guards Armoured Division during the Normandy campaign.

On 3 August 1944, Padre Pryor was travelling in a jeep near the village of Le Tourner along a paved road when it came under German shellfire. Padre Pryor's jeep took a direct hit, and he was killed. He was originally buried on a hill near Le Tourner on 4 August, overlooking the road where he was killed.

Padre Pryor is now buried in St Charles de Percy War Cemetery, which is the southernmost of the Normandy cemeteries. The majority of those buried in this cemetery died in late July and early August 1944 in the major thrust made from Caumont l'Éventé towards Vire, whose goal was to drive a wedge between the German 7th Army and Panzer Group West

5 August 1944

JAMES DOUGLAS, Mentioned in Dispatches. Service no. 244123. Age 34. Chaplain 4th Class, Royal Army Chaplains' Department. Attached to the 5th Battalion Wiltshire Regiment, 129th Infantry Brigade, 43rd Wessex Division.

Buried in Tilly sur-Seulles Commonwealth War Graves Cemetery, grave 7 C 3, Tilly-sur-Seulles, France.

James "Jimmy" Douglas was the son of John and Kathleen Douglas and the husband of Annie Hildegarde Douglas of Dunmurry, Co. Antrim, Northern Ireland. He was born in Waterford and educated at Wesley College and Trinity College, Dublin.

He earned a BA in 1932. He was ordained a deacon in 1933 and a priest by the Bishop of Down in 1934. He was appointed curate of Magheralin (Maralin) Parish in August 1933 and remained there until 1938. While in this parish, he married his wife Annie in 1935. In 1938 he moved to be curate in charge of Aghalurcher in the Diocese of Clogher until joining the Royal Army Chaplains' Department In 1942.

Padre Douglas was killed at about 6 pm on 5 August 1944. His unit was taking up a position to attack Mont Pinçon, and Padre Douglas was climbing out of a truck with other men at the new location of the Regimental Aid Post when the truck sustained a direct hit by a German shell. Padre Douglas was killed instantly, but none of the other men were even scratched. Just a few days earlier, Padre Douglas had reviewed news of his father's death and was worried about his mother's financial situation but had not shared his worries with any of the men of the RAP.

10 August 1944

JOHN MACDOUGALL, MA. Service no. 279927. Age 33. Chaplain 4th Class, Royal Army Chaplains' Department. Attached to the 2nd Battalion, Seaforth Highlanders, 152nd Infantry Brigade, 51st (Scottish) Division. Buried in Ranville Commonwealth War Graves Cemetery, grave 9 B 20, Ranville, France.

John MacDougall was born on the Isle of Skye on 15 March 1911 and was the son of Daniel and Flora Macdougall. He attended Portre Secondary School and Glasgow University, where he earned a Master of Arts degree. He was ordained in the Church of Scotland in 1936. Rev MacDougall was married to Donaldina "Dolly" Macdougall (nee Gunn) of Durness, Lairg, Sutherlandshire. He served in the Home Guard in Tongue, Durness, from July 1940 to July 1942. He also acted as an unofficial chaplain to members of the armed forces in Durness, Lairg during this time, as well as being the leader of the Church of Scotland Hut and Canteen for the military posted at Durness.

Rev MacDougall joined the Army Chaplains Department on 6 August 1943. After a few weeks of training at Chaplains School, he was returned to Scotland to the Stranraer Transit Camp. In early January 1944, he was transferred to the 2nd Battalion, The Seaforth Highlanders Regiment, 154th Infantry Brigade, 51st Scottish Division. Subsequently, the 2nd Seaforth were transferred to the 152nd Infantry Brigade.

Padre MacDougall was killed on 10 August at 8 am when visiting the wounded at the Regimental Aid Post, which received a direct hit by a large calibre German shell. Four other men were also killed by the shell, and the Senior Chaplain of the 51st Division performed the funerals for all 5 men that afternoon at Conteville.

11 August 1944

JOHN TALFRYN (OR TIMOTHY) DAVIES, BA, BD. Service no: 250524. Chaplain 4th Class, Royal Army Chaplains' Department. Age 38. Attached to the 4th Battalion, Somerset Regiment, 129th Infantry Brigade, 43rd Wessex Division. Buried in Tilly-sur-Seulles Commonwealth War Graves Cemetery (grave 6 E 7).

John Davies was born in Swansea, Wales and was the son of Daniel and Sarah Davies of Brynhyfryd, Swansea. He and his wife, Phyllis Elizabeth Davies of Brynhyfryd, lived in Caernarvonshire. Padre Davies was educated at the Bangor Baptist College, University of Bangor, Wales. He earned Bachelor of Arts and Bachelor of Divinity degrees and was ordained in 1938. He was called to the English Baptist Church, Bangor, and ministered there until joining the Royal Army Chaplains' Department in May 1943.

After Chaplain Davies completed his initial training at the Chaplain School, he was assigned to the 141st Field Artillery Regiment of the 9th Armoured Division. However, Padre Davies was then transferred to the 4th Battalion Somerset Light Infantry of the 129th Infantry Brigade of the 43rd Wessex Division upon its being sent into action in Normandy. According to records held by the British Armed Forces Chaplains Centre, Padre Davies was *"leaning on the tail-board of his battalion's Regimental Aid Post truck when he sustained a serious injury in his back from a*

German artillery or mortar shell. The Medical Officer had just walked around the other side of the truck and was not injured by the shell, but he was unable to say what type of shell had hit Padre Davies." Due to the Medical Officer being immediately available, Padre Davies was stabilized and evacuated to 3rd Casualty Clearing Station near Aunay Sur Orne. However, the surgeon who operated on Padre Davies to try to save his life indicated he was not optimistic about Padre Davies' chances, and Padre Davies died later that day.

Padre Davies was noted by the commanding officer of the Somerset Regiment that *"while he was a new addition to the Battalion, but was noted for his fitting in quickly and was becoming a valued member of the Division."*

13 August 1944

JOHN WILLIAM SCHWER, Purple Heart. Service no. O-529000. Age 37. Captain, United States Army Chaplain Corps. Attached to the 6th Armoured Division. Buried in Brittany American Cemetery, plot J, row 12, grave 5 Saint-James, France.

John Schwer was born in Los Angeles, California, on 23 June 1907. He was the son of Dr JL Schwer and Georgia Schwer of Pueblo, Colorado. After high school, he attended the University of Colorado and then switched to Carleton College in Minnesota, from which he graduated in 1935. He then attended Seabury-Western Theological Seminary and was ordained a priest in the Episcopal Church of the United States on 7 December 1936. Rev Schwer was married to Dorothy Gail Schwer (nee Smith).

Rev Schwer served as the priest-in-charge of St Matthews and St Timothy's Episcopal Church in Minneapolis from 1937-1939. In 1939 he moved to a parish with two congregations, St. Barnabas Episcopal Church, Denton and St Paul's Episcopal Church, Gainesville, Texas. Rev Schwer also served on the faculty of the Texas State College for Women. In 1942, Rev Schwer became the Assistant Rector of the Church of the Good Shepherd in Corpus Christi, Texas.

Chaplain Schwer entered the Army Chaplain Corps in 1943. He attended the Harvard Chaplains School. Following completion of this school, Chaplain Schwer was assigned to a "commando school" in California before being reassigned to the 6th Armoured Division.

Chaplain Schwer and his division left America on a troopship for England on 11 February 1944 and arrived in England on 23 February 1944. The 6th Armoured continued to train in England until landing in Normandy on 19 July on Utah Beach. The 6th Armoured assembled at Le Mesnil on 25 July 1944. and then went into combat to clear the heights near Le Bingard on 27 July 1944. The division then turned south towards the Bay of Biscay and liberated the French port of Granville on 31 July 1944. The 6th advanced to Avranches and provided security in holding open the hole that the American forces in Operation Cobra had forced in German lines. The 6th Armoured then relieved the 4th Armoured Division and secured the area bridges.

The 6th Armoured Division was moving from positions behind the lines at Precey towards Medreac in the Brittany Peninsula and striving to take the German submarine bases on the coast of the Peninsula. Chaplain Schwer moved forward with his division. The front line in Brittany was very fluid at this time, and there were large groups of German soldiers, moving both east, towards the Seine River, due to General George Patton's 3rd Army breaking out of Normandy, but also others moving westwards towards the fortress ports of Lorient, St Nazaire, and Brest.

Chaplain Schwer and his assistant, Technical Specialist 5 (TS5) Forest Nelson, were both reported missing on 3 August. It was later learned that they had become lost and ended up driving in no man's land and had been ambushed by retreating German forces. Chaplain Schwer was killed in the ambush, and TS5 Nelson was taken prisoner. This information was not discovered until the 6th Armoured besieged the German Fortress of Lorient in mid-August 1944. Specialist Nelson was released from captivity in a prisoner exchange later in the fall of 1944 due to the German forces at Lorient being unable to care for Prisoners of War during the siege that was to last until the end of the war on 8 May 1945.

14 August 1944

PATRICK JOSEPH MCMAHON, SSH, Mentioned in Dispatches. Service no. 218709. Age 28. Chaplain 4th Class, Royal Army Chaplains' Department. Attached to the 9th Regiment Royal Tank Corps, 3rd Tank Brigade. Buried in Ussy churchyard (not a Commonwealth War Graves Cemetery), grave 6 E 7, Ussy, France.

Patrick McMahon was born in Dundalk, County Louth, Ireland, on 14 December 1916 in what became the Republic of Ireland. He was educated at Friary School, Dundalk, 1921 to 1924, the Christian Brothers School also in Dundalk, 1924 to 1926 and Oram Normal School in Castle Blayney, 1926 to 1929. He then attended the seminary of St. Macartan's College, Monaghan, 1929 to 1934. After graduating from St. Macartan's, he continued his studies at Dalgan College in 1934 and was ordained there in 1940. Rev McMahon was a member of the Roman Catholic Franciscan Servants of the Sacred Heart religious community.

Rev McMahon joined the Royal Army Chaplains' Department in late December 1941. He was initially assigned to the 20th General Hospital at Cambridge as an assistant chaplain. He served there until September 1942. Padre McMahon was then assigned to the 72nd Independent Infantry Brigade. From there, he was transferred to the 241st Light Anti-Aircraft Regiment for a few months. In November 1943, he was transferred to his final posting with the 9th Royal Tank Regiment, 3rd Tank Brigade of the British 2nd Army, with whom he landed in Normandy.

Chaplain McMahon was killed when he went out onto the battlefield under fire to rescue a wounded Canadian soldier of the infantry battalion that his tank regiment was supporting. There are two different accounts of Padre McMahon's death. One indicates he was in a jeep with a large Red Cross flag which was hit by a German anti-tank shell, and Chaplain McMahon was killed instantly. A second account is that Padre McMahon ventured onto the battlefield in the medical officer's half-track, clearly marked with the Red Cross on its sides, to rescue the wounded Canadian soldier. On the return journey to Allied lines, a German anti-tank shell destroyed the half-track. Chaplain McMahon was able to escape the destroyed vehicle but had been mortally wounded. This second report indicates that Padre McMahon was found sitting with his back against a wall with his breviary (a small book of prayers) in his hand, indicating he was probably saying prayers for the dying. Chaplain McMahon's Requiem Mass in the small parish church in Ussy, Lower Normandy, was attended by 50 other Commonwealth chaplains.

Chaplain McMahon is the only chaplain not resting in what is designated a Commonwealth War Graves Cemetery. Rather he is buried in the cemetery of the Ussy Roman Catholic Church. This has meant that his grave is much more like that of a French civilian, with a border delineating the edges of the plot, although it does have a Commonwealth War Graves Commission headstone.

15 August 1944

Rev Harry Smith, C.F., A.K.C.
Ordained 1934 Assistant Priest, Parish Church Ilkeston
Newbold 1936-38. S. Martin's 1938
Chaplain to Forces, September 6th, 1939
Killed in Action, Normandy August 15th, 1944.

HARRY SMITH, AKC. Service no. 95864. Age 37. Chaplain 4th Class Royal Army Chaplains' Department. Attached to the 53rd Regiment, Reconnaissance Corps, 53rd Division. Buried in Brouay Commonwealth War Graves Cemetery, grave 1 A 12, Thue et Mue, France. Harry Smith was born in Derby and was the son of Leonard and Cicely Smith of Littleover, Derby. Chaplain Smith was educated at King's College, London and ordained in 1934. He was then appointed assistant curate in the Parish of Ilkeston, Derbyshire, in 1934. From there, he moved in 1936 to the Parish of Newbold until 1938. Rev Smith then moved to St Martin's Church in Sherwood in the Diocese of Southwell until 1939. In September 1939, Rev Smith joined the Royal Army Chaplains' Department.

Padre Smith served in France in 1939-40 with the 14th Field Ambulance of the 2nd British Corps. On 28 May 1940, he entered the Dunkirk defensive perimeter. Padre Smith notes in an interview in the Nottingham Guardian on 3 June 1944 that:

"....he had to discard all his kit before being evacuated on a destroyer and that he had little sleep before being evacuated due to constant German bombing raids, although there was a reasonable amount of food on the Dunkirk beaches.

Padre Smith described the beaches at Dunkirk as "looking like an earthquake had hit the town, as it was all smashed up and burning." He went on to describe his escape on a British destroyer tying up along the jetty at Dunkirk, very early in the morning of Tuesday June 3, 1940, and the troops hurrying to board as quickly as possible, until every spot on the ship was occupied. The ship then cast off, but avoided German air attack, as Padre Smith notes, "due to the huge amount of smoke that hung in a pall over Dunkirk."

"Church Parade in the Desert."
(Is there any doubt as to the identity of the Padre?—E.L.
(By the courtesy of the Ministry of Information

After his return from the beaches of Dunkirk, Padre Smith was assigned to the 73rd Heavy Anti-Aircraft Battery and embarked for the Middle East in December 1941. Chaplain Smith served in Palestine and then was transferred to the 4th Parachute Brigade also in Palestine. He then served in North Africa with the 4th Para's in Tunisia. Padre Smith landed with the seaborne forces of the 4th Parachute Brigade in Sicily. In September 1943, Padre Smith also took part in the invasion of Italy with the 4th Para's, before he returned to Britain in December 1943.

As he was serving with a Parachute unit, Padre Smith had been trained as a parachutist while in the Middle East. When he returned to Britain, he was told that he was too old to parachute into Europe with the 1st Airborne Division (the cut-off age was 32). Chaplain Smith then transferred to the 81st Field Regiment of the Royal Artillery in April 1944 before being transferred shortly thereafter to the 53rd Regiment of the Reconnaissance Corps. It should be noted that the reconnaissance troops served in the vanguard of any Allied advance and was probably just as dangerous a place for a chaplain as being a parachutist. Padre Smith While serving with the Reconnaissance Corps, he also ministered to the 71st Brigade's 1st Battalion, Oxford and Buckinghamshire Infantry Regiment.

Mr. Smith's Grave in Normandy.

It was while serving at the front of the Allied breakout from Normandy that Padre Smith was killed by a German mine as he recovered the bodies of two officers of his regiment who had been killed when the armoured car they had been in was destroyed by a German shell. Padre Smith went out with a driver and another soldier in a Bren Gun Carrier to Martinville to recover and bring back for burial the bodies of the two officers. On the return trip, their Bren Carrier hit an anti-tank mine and was totally destroyed. The driver was killed instantaneously, and Padre Smith and the other soldier were seriously injured. They were taken to the 147th Field Ambulance for immediate treatment. Padre Smith was so seriously injured that he died in the ambulance before reaching the Casualty Clearing Station for further treatment. Padre Smith was reported to have been very calm and patient with the medical staff after his being so severely wounded. His Senior divisional Chaplain, in a letter to Padre Smith's father, *"he was not only my best padre, but also a pal and a brother."* His funeral was attended by all the 53rd Division Chaplains.

20 August 1944

WIKTOR FORTUNAT HUPA, OFM, Virtuti Militari. Service number 04559. Age 32. Major, Roman Catholic Chaplain. Attached to the 9th Rifle Battalion, 1st Polish Armoured Division. Buried in Polish Military Cemetery, grave V.B 2, Langannerie, France.

Wiktor Hupa was born on 19 October 1912 in Zawady, in the province of Rawicz, Poland. He had a standard upbringing for young Polish boys of the time. When he was 18 years old, Viktor began studying for the novitiate of the Assumption into Heaven of the Blessed Mary Province of the Order of Friars Minor (Franciscans) at Wieluń monastery. He made his first vows to the Franciscans on 27 October 1931. Brother Viktor was then sent to study at the Higher Theological Seminary at the Osieczna Monastery. Upon completion of his training there, he made his permanent vows to the Franciscans as a monk on 28 September 1934.

After becoming a monk, Wiktor began studying for the priesthood in the Roman Catholic Church at the Higher Theological Seminary in the Wronki Monastery. After his third year at the Wronki monastery, he was ordained a Roman Catholic priest on 26 September 1937. Father Hupa showed great promise as a priest and was sent for further studies at the Louvaine University in Belgium.

Father Hupa was still studying in Belgium when Germany and Russia invaded Poland in September 1939, and he was unable to return home. Like many Poles in Western Europe at the beginning of World War Two, the German invasion in May of 1940 of the low countries and then France drove him to travel further into France. Father Hupa officially joined the Polish Army in exile in France on 14 June 1940 and was immediately sent to the Polish Officer school in Coetquidan in, Brittany. However, some reports suggest he had already been attached to the officer training school in December 1939, where he acted as an unofficial chaplain until he was formally inducted into the Polish Army in exile in June 1940 with the rank of major.

As the Germans overran much of France and the French prepared for an Armistice with Germany, between the 19 and 22 June 1940, Father Hupa and the rest of the Polish Army in exile in France boarded ships at La Rochelle on the Bay of Biscay for England and landed in Plymouth. The Polish Army in exile was sent north to Scotland to regroup and continue training. Father Hupa was assigned as the chaplain to the 1st Reconnaissance Regiment of the 1st Polish Grenadier Division, as well as ministering to other Polish formations between the summer of 1940 and the spring of 1944. On 24 May 1944, Major Hupa was assigned as the chaplain of the 9th Polish Rifle Battalion in the 1st Polish Armoured Division, which landed in France on 29 July and was assigned to the First Canadian Army. The Polish Armoured Division, along with the other units of the First Canadian Army, was sent south along the highway from Caen to Falaise to try and encircle the German forces there as the American 3rd Army under General Patton pushed northwards from Argentan.

The fighting south of Falaise was very fierce as the German forces struggled to escape the closing ring around them.

The 1st Polish Armoured Division took a position on Hill 262(North) near Mont Ormel and fought off repeated German counterattacks to force them off this hill and open the way for the retreating Germans. Father Hupa was stationed at the BoisJos manor farm, where a Polish aid station had been set up. The manor was filled with wounded Polish and German soldiers and was well marked with large Red Crosses laid on the roof and hung from the buildings' high walls. However, these markings did not stop the desperate German attacks on the BoisJos manor, including one by a German Panther tank that almost got into the courtyard of the manor. Major Hupa personally led the attack on this tank, and it was destroyed before it could enter the courtyard of the farm.

As with so many battlefield stories, there are legends about the heroism of Father Hupa. One story says an already wounded Father Hupa marched towards well-marked ambulances filled with wounded soldiers and parked in the BoisJos courtyard. As he advanced with a wooden grave cross in one hand and a Red Cross flag on a pole in the other, he was shot and killed by the attacking

Germans. Another story of Father Hupa is that, according to the doctor who examined him, he was shot in the back three times, but he did not even realize he had been shot until someone commented on the blood on the back of his uniform. He was then treated by a doctor at the BoisJos aid station, but the shock had set in, and he died within an hour.

As with all stories, there is probably some truth in both. He assuredly did try to defend the BoisJos aid station from German assault and also would have been trying to indicate to attacking German forces that this was a non-combatant area and should not be attacked. There is no question that Father Hupa acted extremely bravely in trying to prevent the destruction of the BoisJos aid station, and for his extreme bravery, he was awarded the Virtuti Militari, the Polish Army in exile's highest award for gallantry in the face of the enemy.

The Pursuit North to Belgium and the Netherlands

2 September 1944

CHARLES S BLAKENEY, Purple Heart. Service no. O-521862. Age 40. Captain, United States Army Chaplain Corps. Attached to the 112th Infantry Regiment, 28th Infantry Division. Buried in the Epinal American Cemetery and Memorial, plot B, row 27, grave 15, Dinozé, France.

Charles Blakeney was born in Halifax, Canada in 1904. However, in 1930 he travelled to Boston to attend theological school. It appears that Rev Blakeney was ordained in the Methodist Church in the United States and remained there until going overseas after volunteering to be an Army chaplain. It is interesting to note that as of the 1940 American census, Rev Blakeney did not hold American citizenship, and so while serving in the American Army, he was still actually a Canadian.

Rev Blakeney was a Methodist Minister in Greenland, New Hampshire, from 1942-43. This ministry in Greenland was a somewhat unusual one, as the Congregationalist Church and the Methodist Church had started holding combined services in the 1920s after many years as separate congregations. Rev Blakeney resided in Greenland with his wife, Margaret E Blakeney, and their daughter, Ruth.

In 1939, when Germany invaded Poland and Europe went to war, Rev Blakeney volunteered to serve in the American Army but was turned down as he was still a Canadian citizen. After the attack at Pearl Harbour, when the US entered World War Two, Rev Blakeney again volunteered to serve as a chaplain in the American Army, and this time he was accepted. However, it was not all smooth sailing for Chaplain Blakeney, for at the time he volunteered in 1942, the American Army had set the upper age limit for Chaplains to join at 35, and Rev Blakeney was 37. He was also below the minimum weight requirement and had dental problems, although false teeth solved that. Lastly, his Canadian citizenship was still a problem until the American Government passed a law permitting foreign nationals to join the American Army. One of the requirements of the congregation in New Hampshire was that a replacement minister to preach on Sunday and to officiate at funerals be found before Charles could leave to join the army. A retired minister was found, and his wife Margaret took over much of the parish work to ensure that Charles would have a congregation to return to when the war ended. These duties included being a "surrogate pastor" as well as head of the Women's Alliance and Superintendent of the Sunday School and the Youth program. In almost all ways, she filled in for her husband's ministry.

After joining the US Army Chaplain Corps in early 1943, Rev Blakeney went to the chaplains' school at Harvard University and then was initially assigned to Camp Butner in North Carolina, which had become a major training base for the American Army. However, he was soon transferred to Camp Pickett, Virginia, where he became the chaplain of the 112th Infantry Regiment. Three weeks after joining the 112th, he accompanied it in October 1943 when it sailed for England. The 112th ended up being stationed in Wales for further training.

Chaplain Blakeney landed on Utah Beach in July 1944 with the rest of the 112th as part of the 28th Infantry Division. The 28th Infantry Division was involved in the breakout from Normandy and the advance to the Seine River. While serving with his regiment, as it took part in the liberation of Paris, Chaplain Blakeney was one of the thousands of 28th division soldiers who paraded down the Champs Elysees before turning north towards the Forest of Compiegne.

On 1 September 1944, during the fighting to clear the thick Compiègne Forest and capture the Mont du Tremble fortified radar station east of the village of Choisy-au-Bac, Chaplain Blakeney was moving forward on forest tracks with his driver that day, Private Joseph Mangini, as they had heard there were wounded men on the battlefield in the woods. Their jeep was ambushed by a German patrol at a crossroads in the forest. Private Mangini was killed in the ambush, and Chaplain Blakeney was severely wounded by a bullet in the abdomen. Medics on the scene tried to reach Chaplain Blakeney to tend to his wounds, but all were killed by the German snipers. Chaplain Blakeney's enlisted assistant, James Sullivan, heard that his boss had been hit and made his way to the scene of the ambush and was able to rescue Charles and drive him to the 28th Field Hospital in Raray.

After the war, Captain Minch, a dental officer at the 28th Field Hospital and a friend of Chaplain Blakeney, related to Mrs Blakeney the following about his being wounded and then arriving at the field hospital: *"The Germans were hiding in the woods protecting the ammunition dump. Charlie's outfit went in to flush them out. The aid station was up forward. Charlie and two other medics went forward to aid the wounded. Someone yelled, 'Get down!" but it was too late. He was shot through the belly, and men went to rescue him. Charlie and one other were wounded; the rest were killed. Charlie was recommended for the Silver Star. Charlie was admitted to our hospital about 4:30 pm, 1 September. When I saw him, he was drowsy from the opiate that had been given him for the pain. I spoke to him of the confidence I had in the surgical team, and he was confident they were doing their best, but he realized it was possible he would not live. He had been wounded by small arms fire. The bullet that struck him went through the abdominal area. He never regained consciousness after the operation, and it was about 2 o'clock on the afternoon of Sept. 2 that he died. I spoke to him a number of times during the night and the next morning. He was quiet most of the time but when he did speak, it was about his family and his wish to go home. He was buried Sept. 3. The men who carried him told me (Captain Minch) that the cemetery had a beautiful setting, and that the bodies were laid below a bank of flowers before internment."* The cemetery where Chaplain Blakeney was buried was about 15 miles from Paris, but, after the war, Chaplain Blakeney's remains were moved to the American Cemetery in Epinal.

Even though Chaplain Blakeney and his family had only resided in New Hampshire for two years before he volunteered to serve as an Army Chaplain, his wife, and daughter remained there after his death. Margaret Blakeney had become a teacher at the Greenland Public School, where she went on to teach grades 1 and 2 for many years. Chaplain Blakeney is remembered on a small memorial in Choisy-au-Bac park that adjoins the Town Hall.

14 September 1944

GERARD BARRY, BA. Service no. 244239. Age 33. Chaplain 4th Class, Royal Army Chaplains' Department. Attached to the 8th Battalion, Royal Scots Regiment. Buried in the Geel Commonwealth War Graves Cemetery, plot II, row A grave 25, Geel, Netherlands.

Gerard Barry and his twin brother Francis were born on 29 March 1911 to John and Bridget (née O'Keefe) Barry of Liverpool. Gerard had three elder brothers, Jack, Fred, and George, who were all born close together. Jack was the eldest and was only five years older than the twins. Gerard's mother and father had a total of 11 children, but three of his sisters died in childbirth or when they were very young. Their mother, Bridget, was described as a resolute Irish lady, and their father, John, a hardworking carpenter and joiner who set up his own business. Gerard and his younger brother Thomas both became priests. He attended St Michael & Sacred Heart Roman Catholic Church and graduated from St Michael's Roman Catholic School in Liverpool.

At the age of 13, Gerard began attending St Joseph's College, often called a "junior seminary", at Upholland near Wigan in Lancashire, and later enrolled in the main seminary, located in the same school, which prepared men for the priesthood of the Roman Catholic Church. Gerard played an active part in the life of the seminary during his training for the priesthood in what was then a thriving educational and religious community. He became editor of the school magazine, which provided him with an outlet for his witty sense of humour.

Gerard Barry was ordained a priest by Archbishop Downey on 22 May 1937. His first appointment as a curate was in North Lancashire, to the parish of St Mary Magdalen in the small town of Penwortham, just south of Preston, where he remained for two years. He was then assigned to the inner city parish of All Souls between Liverpool and Bootle, close to the docks, at the beginning of World War Two. At that time, during the Blitz, he was given a role for which he would have been eminently suited. As the German bombers were targeting the major British cities with factories and docks, it was decided that children, in particular, should be sent to the countryside to escape the threat of heavy bombing attacks. The Archbishop of Liverpool gave Father Gerard the task of providing counselling and practical guidance to help evacuees from displaced families. A familiar sight in railway stations were lines of children with their meagre possessions, leaving their distraught mothers as they boarded trains to get them to safety away from German bombs by moving them to rural areas. Father Gerard was ideally suited in his personality for this ministry as his jokes and sense of humour helped to calm frayed nerves and brought smiles to the faces of both the parents sending their children away and the anxious children, most likely travelling away from home for the first time.

All Souls Church was destroyed by German bombs, and Father Barry was then transferred to St Aloysius, Roby, Liverpool. St Aloysius Church was near the large housing estates built in Huyton-with-Roby to provide homes as the slums of Liverpool began to be cleared just prior to the start of World War Two. While the owners of these new homes were thrilled to be out of the squalor of inner-city Liverpool, these new housing estates meant a loss of the extended family units that had existed in the slums, and ties with the close-knit inner-city communities had been severed. Within a short time of the families moving to Roby, the children, teenagers, and young adults began to be involved in petty crime and vandalism, as there were no organized activities for them to take part in. This gap in services for young people was tailor-made for Father Barry to fill, and he became an organiser for the Young Christian Workers Association to work with the teenagers and provide activities for them. For the younger children, Father Barry became the Scoutmaster of the local troop based at St Aloysius.

By this time in the war, all of Gerard's older brothers were serving in the armed forces: Jack was a non-commissioned officer in the RAF, Fred was serving overseas in the Army, and George was in the Royal Navy. His twin brother Francis was also called up in the Army, and his youngest brother Bernard was called up for the Navy. Marie, his only surviving sister, went into nursing. It was in Gerard's nature to want to participate by following the example of his siblings, so he volunteered to serve with the Royal Army Chaplains' Department.

In late September 1943, he was posted to the South East Command in England and provided chaplaincy services there until 18 June 1944, when he was assigned to the Royal Artillery and landed in Normandy. Upon his arrival in Normandy, he was held in a replacement depot until 31 July 1944, when he was assigned to the 8th Battalion, The Royal Scots Regiment of the 44th Infantry Brigade, 43rd Division located near Caen. The fighting was heavy, and his division was unable to advance until there was a breakthrough and the enemy forces were driven back. Padre Barry became as closely involved with the spiritual welfare of the troops to whom he administered as he had been at St Aloysius. Many of the troops he was ministering to would have been Catholics from the city of Glasgow in Scotland. Moreover, at one stage, while serving with the Royal Scots in Northern France, Padre Barry had a chance to meet with his brother Francis who was also serving in the Army in Northwest Europe. However, the battle was soon rejoined, and Chaplain Barry and the Royal Scots were once more in the thick of things.

The town of Geel, just east of Antwerp, had been attacked by The Northumbrian Division on the 8 September 1944 and was finally captured with fierce fighting on the 10th. However, the next day, the Germans mounted a determined counter-attack which forced the Northumbrian Division to retreat. The British commander decided that the exhausted soldiers of the Northumbrian Division would be replaced by the Scots of the 43rd Division. Padre Barry's unit, the Royal Scots, was slowly moving towards the Geel town centre. The battalion medical officer told Father Gerard he would establish a regimental aid post in an old, abandoned white house near the canal and where Padre Barry could bring or direct stretcher bearers to bring the regiment's wounded.

The morning of 14 September was misty and overcast. The medical staff and Padre Barry were getting the wounded from the previous day's fighting ready to be loaded into ambulances to be taken to field hospitals further back from the front. However, later that day, in the afternoon, a British attack took place over the Albert Canal. As the attack was launched, the Germans opened fire with a massive barrage of rockets and artillery shells. The Royal Scots' forward aid station in the white house was hit by a barrage of mortar shells. They struck with devastating force: two stretcher bearers were killed outright, the medical officer was badly injured, and Padre Barry was mortally wounded by shrapnel that hit his chest, causing him to die a short while later.

Padre Barry was amongst over 200 casualties of the Royal Scots who were killed in action during the forming of the

Geel bridgehead. Following Padre Barry's tragic death, the pipe major of the Royal Scots called on the local Catholic priest to perform the funeral for Chaplain Barry, and he was temporarily buried on 15 September in the graveyard at St Dymphna Church in Geel before eventually being disinterred and reburied in the Commonwealth War Grave Cemetery in Geel.

14 September 1944

THOMAS EDMUND MOONEY, BA, Mention in Dispatches. Age 38. Chaplain 4th Class. Canadian Chaplains Service. Attached to the Algonquin Infantry Regiment, 4th Canadian Armoured Division. Buried in Adegem Commonwealth War Graves Cemetery, plot X row A grave 8, at Maldegem, Netherlands.

Thomas Mooney was born in Westport, Ontario, on 21 January 1906, to parents Michael Edmund and Anna Cecelia Mooney. Mooney's father, grandfather, and great-grandfather were lockmasters, as those that opened and closed the locks that permitted boats to travel up and down at the Rideau Canal leading from Lake Simcoe to Ottawa were called. Growing up on the Rideau Canal led Tom Mooney to have a love of fishing which he found a great stress reliever later in his life as a priest.

Thomas attended high school in Westport and, upon graduating, enrolled in the University of Toronto, from which he graduated with a Bachelor of Arts in Music in 1927. He also earned a diploma from Pope Pius X School of Music in New York State. Following his graduation, Tom Mooney was employed as the Director of Music at St. Mary's Roman Catholic Cathedral in Islington, Ontario (now a part of Toronto). However, Tom felt the call to ordained ministry and left his job as Director of Music and enrolled in St. Augustine's Seminary in Toronto and was ordained in the Cathedral of the Immaculate Conception, in Kingston, Ontario, on 21 May 1932. He served as Curate and Director of the Choir there until 10 January 1942, when he volunteered for the Canadian Chaplain Service.

After completing the Canadian Chaplain School, Padre Mooney was assigned to the Algonquin Regiment from Northeastern Ontario. After serving on guard duty in Newfoundland, the regiment was chosen in January 1943 for operations overseas. It landed at Liverpool and became part of the 10th Canadian Infantry Brigade of the 4th Canadian Armoured Division.

The division landed in Normandy on 18 July 1944 over Juno Beach. They were part of the Canadian effort to close the Falaise Gap. However, on 9 August 1944, the regiment, supporting the British Columbia Regiment (BCR), jointly forming "Worthington Force", was tasked with taking Hill 195, south of Caen. However, it took a wrong turn in the dark and ended up four miles east of the objective, deep in German territory. The regiment took heavy losses in this battle; however, Padre Mooney was not involved in the near destruction of this force as he had remained behind at the regimental aid station.

In late August 1944, after the Falaise Gap had been closed, the Algonquin Regiment, and the 4th Canadian Armoured

Division, moved quickly through Belgium and halted on 8 September at the Ghent-Brugge Canal. After heavy fighting, with Padre Money in the thick of it, supporting and encouraging the men, the regiment was able to establish a bridgehead across the canal on 10 September. A few days later, on 14 September, the attempt of the Algonquin Regiment to cross the next water obstacle, the Leopold Canal, was unsuccessful as they were repelled at Moerkerke by the German 245th Infantry Division.

Padre Mooney was killed by German shellfire on the attempt to cross the Leopold Canal while ministering to and tending the wounded of his regiment. His body was recovered, and, the next day, a Roman Catholic chaplain from a neighbouring unit held a requiem mass for Padre Mooney. As a tribute, the Protestant chaplains of the 4th Canadian Armoured Division served as pallbearers. Padre Mooney was the first Canadian Catholic Chaplain reported killed in action during World War II.

A Bridge Too Far – Operation Market Garden

20 – 25 (probably 23) September 1944

HENRY JAMES IRWIN, BA, Service number 270523. Age 28. Chaplain 4th Class Royal Army Chaplains' Department. Attached to 11th Battalion, 4th Parachute Brigade, The Parachute Regiment. Buried in the Arnhem Commonwealth War Graves Cemetery, plot 26 A grave 2, Oosterbeek, Netherlands.

Henry (known as Jim) Irwin was the son of James Thomas and Sarah Ann Irwin (nee Dennis) of Opawa, Christchurch, Canterbury, New Zealand, and born on 5 September 1906. He had a younger brother, Francis, also born in New Zealand. Jim Irwin attended the University of New Zealand, where he earned a Bachelor of Arts degree in 1938. He then travelled to Clifton, a suburb of Bristol in the United Kingdom, to attend the Bible Churchmen's Society College (BCM). He graduated from this college in 1939 and was ordained a deacon in 1939 in the Diocese of Chelmsford. In 1941 was made a priest and took up the post of Curate in one of the Anglican Churches in Dagenham in, an eastern suburb of greater London. However, Rev Irwin was not long in his ministry in

Dagenham, as he joined the Royal Army Chaplains' Department on 14 May 1941.

Padre Irwin jumped with the 11th Battalion, 4th Parachute Brigade, The Parachute Regiment, and some men of the South Staffords regiment on Monday, 18 September, onto the Ginkel Heath drop zone near Arnhem in the Netherlands. Padre Irwin's battalion was tasked with joining up with the 1st and 3rd Parachute Battalions and attempting to break through to the Arnhem Bridge. While the three battalions did link up, they did not attempt a joint attack to break through to the bridge, and each failed in their first attack on 18 September. They then attempted a more coordinated attack that began at 4 am on 19 September, and intense hand-to-hand combat occurred with the defending German forces. However, the Paras were unable to penetrate the German lines due to the Germans having Stugeschuetz III self-propelled assault guns in support of their defences, while the Paras had only infantry weapons. The command structure of the three parachute battalions fell apart as the commanding officer of the 3rd Para Battalion was killed in action, and the commander of the 11th Para and the commander of the South Staffords were both wounded and taken prisoner. Padre Irwin, along with the remaining men of the 11th Para Battalion, fought on but without their commanding officer. They were able to retreat in an orderly fashion to the Oosterbeek perimeter, where the majority of the 1st Airborne Division had formed a final defensive position.

Padre Irwin, Padre Benson, of the 181st Airlanding Field Hospital, and the 1st Glider Wing Chaplain, Rev Pare, ended up at the Schoonoord Hotel, which had been turned into an Aid Post. They remained there overnight, and in the morning, they went their separate ways. Padre Pare told Padre Irwin that he should wear a "dog collar" or priest's collar (as a low-church Anglican, Padre Irwin did not wear a clergy collar), so he could be more easily recognized by both fellow parachute troops, as well as the enemy. So they ended up making one out of white cardboard, and they fastened it around Padre Irwin's neck. Nonetheless, Padre Irwin was killed in this defensive position at Oosterbeek by an exploding mortar bomb on 20 September near the Hartenstein Hotel. There had been some confusion as to the date of Padre Irwin's death, as noted on his headstone sometime between 20 and 25 September 1944, but further research by author Chris van Roekel in the 1990s determined Padre Irwin was killed on 20 September and buried near where he died, close to the hotel. The uncertainty of his date of death, in the years following the end of World War Two, is a sign of the confusion of the close combat between the Germans and the British paratroops and the inability to keep accurate records of those killed in action.

23 September 1944

HENRY JEFFERYS LEIGH TAYLOR, Mentioned in Dispatches, Military Cross, Service no. 188501. Age 31. Chaplain 4th Class, Royal Army Chaplains' Department. Attached to the 8th Battalion, the Rifle Brigade, and the 23rd Hussars, as part of the 29th Armoured Brigade, 11th Armoured Division. Buried in the Mierlo Commonwealth War Graves Cemetery, plot V, row B, grave 7, Mierlo, Netherlands.

Henry Taylor was born in 1913 to Russell Leigh and Ethel May Taylor (nee Ackerley) of Clifton-on-Teme, Worcestershire. However, Henry was born in Maiden Bradley, Wiltshire. Henry was named after his uncle, Henry Jefferys Taylor. He had a younger sister named Ursula. As a boy, he attended Radley College, where his yearbook noted: "the things in his character chiefly remarkable were a deep, unaffected piety, sturdy moral courage often involving unpopularity and a very keen sense of humour. He graduated from Oxford University in 1935. He entered theological training at the Chichester

Theological College and, after graduation, was ordained a deacon in 1937 in the Diocese of Peterborough, where he served as curate of the parish of Oakham. Upon being made a priest, he moved to be the curate of Holy Cross Anglican Church in Daventry in 1938. After joining the Royal Army Chaplains' Department, he was assigned to the 8th Battalion of the Rifle Brigade, supporting the 29th British Armoured Brigade. Padre Taylor and his unit landed over Juno Beach on 13 June 1944. While officially assigned to the 8th Rifles, he ministered to all the units of the 29th Armoured Brigade through all the major British engagements in Normandy and during the breakout across the Seine and into Belgium.

Padre Taylor was awarded the Military Cross for his ministry with the 8th Rifles at his battalion's Regimental Aid Post during the battle of Normandy while it was under constant German shell-fire. This service also included his going out onto the battlefield with stretcher bearers to recover wounded men of his battalion and bring them back to the RAP. However, he did not live to receive it, as it was only announced in the spring of 1945, 6 months after his death. Padre Taylor was immortalized leading an outdoor service for men of the 23rd Hussars Tank Regiment, following Operation Epsom (to capture a bridgehead across the Odon River) at the end of June 1944 in a British short film of the time, held by the Imperial War Museum Archives. Records indicate that Padre Taylor was at the Regimental Aid Post of 23rd Hussars near the town of Ommel, Netherlands, as the 29th Brigade advanced northwards into Holland in trying to relieve the British and American paratroopers who had landed to try and take the bridges across the Rhine in Operation Market Garden.

The village where the RAP was located was under heavy German mortar and artillery fire. Word reached the RAP and Padre Taylor that a wounded soldier was trapped in a house, along with some wounded Dutch children. He set out to try and help these wounded, as there was a lull in the shelling. Records indicate he reached the house at 17:00, but as he entered, the shelling suddenly increased, and the house was subject to a direct hit that caused it to collapse upon Padre Taylor and those inside. Padre Taylor was rescued by other British troops and taken to the Advanced Dressing Station of the 8th Battalion at 18:00, but he had been severely wounded with head and chest injuries and died shortly after. He was initially buried locally by Padre E.T. Lang until he was disinterred and moved to his final resting place in the Mierlo Commonwealth War Graves Cemetery after the end of World War Two.

The history of the 8th Battalion and its fight in Northwest Europe from Normandy to the end of the war notes that Padre Taylor was one of the nicest men in the unit. He is described as having the nerve of a lion and a great wit, even though he was noted to have a pronounced stutter. His death was recorded as a major blow to his battalion's morale.

25 September 1944

HUBERT KS MISIUDA, OMI, Polish Cross of Valour. Age 35. Polish Roman Catholic Chaplain, attached to 3rd Casualty Parachute Battalion, 1st Polish Independent Parachute Brigade Group. Buried in the Arnhem Commonwealth War Graves Cemetery, plot XXIII, row C grave 6, Oosterbeek, Netherlands.

Hubert Misiuda was born to August and Emma Misiuda on September 23, 1909, in Nieborowice (Rybnik County), Poland. Hubert, as a young man, served as a missionary in Ceylon (now Sri Lanka) from 1927-1929. He then returned to Poland, where he entered the Theological Institute in Obra, Poland, and began studying to become a Roman Catholic Priest. While still in seminary in 1932, he joined the religious order of the Congregation of Missionary Oblates of Mary Immaculate (OMI). Hubert continued his studies until he graduated from seminary and was ordained a Roman Catholic priest in 1937. After his ordination, Father Misiuda continued his ministry with the Oblates at their monastery until September 1939.

After the German and Russian invasion of Poland, which began World War Two in September 1939, and the defeat and partition of Poland, many Poles of military age escaped to France to join the Polish Army in exile forming there. Father Misiuda was one of these. He completed the Polish Officer Cadet School in France and became chaplain of the Central Military Training Center in Loudéac. He was noted for his excellent sporting ability and especially his skill as a boxer. Brigade Staff Officer Władysław Klemens Stasiak would often serve as a sparring partner for Father Misiuda in the ring, and in his memoirs, he admitted that: "Many times only my superior height and longer arms rescued me from being knocked down to the canvas by Father Misiuda."

Shortly after completing the Polish Officer Cadet School, Padre Misiuda was transferred to be the chaplain of the 3rd Polish Light Artillery Regiment. With the German invasion of France and France subsequently becoming a divided country, Father Misiuda arrived in the unoccupied zone of France and ministered as a chaplain in the English hospital in Marseille until 1941. He then moved across the Mediterranean to the Poles, being held in the French internment camps in Algeria and Morocco in North Africa. Father Misiuda then travelled to the Spanish Internment Camp at Miranda del Ebro in Spain. Finally, Padre Misiuda made his way to the United Kingdom, where, in early 1942, he became chaplain of the Polish 2nd Infantry Battalion. Padre Misiuda then volunteered in the summer of 1942 to train as a parachutist and, on 15 September 1942, became the first Polish parachutist-trained chaplain. He was then assigned as the chaplain of the 1st Polish Independent Parachute Brigade, and eventually, he jumped with his unit into Holland in September 1944 to support the 6th British Airborne Division in the fighting at Arnhem.

After making a successful parachute landing, Padre Misiuda crossed the Rhine with the men of his battalion in small inflatable boats under enemy fire. He served in the frontlines of what has been described as a "caldron of fire" with his men, providing comfort and ministry while they fought to hold the Allied bridgehead open on the north bank of the Rhine River near Oosterbeek. However, by 25 September, it was recognized that the British and Polish airborne troops could not hold off the encircling German troops, and, in the darkness of the night of 25/26 September, a withdrawal of as many British and Polish paratroopers as possible was organized. Padre Misidua, realizing that there were not enough boats to take all the men across the Rhine, gave up his seat and decided to swim across the Rhine. However, as he was swimming across the river, he was hit and killed by German machine gun fire. Padre Misidua was posthumously awarded the highest Polish gallantry medal, the Cross of Valour, for his self-sacrificing service in the Allied bridgehead. The Cross of Valour is the Polish equivalent of the British Victoria Cross or the American Medal of Honor.

Padre Misidua's body was not recovered until May 1945, in a field, or polder, near Oosterbeek that was being drained of water after the Germans had flooded it during the winter of 1944-45. Padre Misidua's body was then buried in the Arnhem Oosterbeek Commonwealth War Graves Cemetery along with 73 of his fellow Polish parachutists and over 1400 British paratroops.

27 September 1944

BERNARD JOSEPH BENSON, SJ, Service no. 205968. Age 30. Chaplain 4th Class, Royal Army Chaplains' Department. Attached to 181st Airlanding Field Hospital, 1st Airlanding Brigade. Buried in the Arnhem Commonwealth War Graves Cemetery, plot 4, row B grave 10, Oosterbeek, Netherlands.

Bernard Benson was the son of Henry and Bridget Benson of Shipley, Yorkshire. As a boy, he attended St Bede's Grammar School in Bradford. Bernard entered into monastic life by becoming a member of the Roman Catholic monastic Society of Jesuits and was ordained a priest in the Leeds Diocese. Father Benson joined the Royal Army Chaplains' Department on 17 October 1941. He was one of the earliest chaplains to take parachute training and was assigned to the 1st Airborne Division and served with them in Tunisia, Sicily, and Italy. While serving in Tunisia, he arranged for German chaplains held as POWs to resume their ministry to the other German POWs, as required by the Geneva Convention.

In September 1944, Padre Benson was serving with the 1st Airborne Division attached to the 181st Airlanding Field Hospital. He landed on the Arnhem battlefield by glider on 17 September 1944 as part of Operation Market Garden. Shortly after landing, the 181st was moved to set up its hospital in the Dutch mental hospital in Wolfheze. However, this order was quickly changed, and the 181st was ordered into the town of Oosterbeek, where it took over the Schoonoord Hotel to use as its hospital. There was really no safe place for the wounded in the Arnhem bridgehead, and the hospital came under fire from a German self-propelled assault gun that fired four high explosive rounds into the upper level of the hotel. The commanding officer of the field hospital ordered that all wounded on the upper floors be brought down to the ground floor. Padre Benson, along with others, ran up the stairs to recover the wounded and began to clear the upper floor. It was announced that the upper floors were clear of any wounded, but Padre Benson and the soldier accompanying him did not hear the call to come downstairs. A further high explosive shell was fired into the upper floor of the hotel, and Padre Benson was hit on his right arm. The injury was so bad that his arm was nearly severed from his body. One of the 181st Field Hospital surgeons, Captain C. A. Simmons, operated on Padre Benson and had to amputate his right arm at the elbow. It is reported that Padre Benson had gone into shock and received a massive blood transfusion. His injury was so severe he was evacuated to the Dutch St Elizabeth Hospital for further treatment. However, another Para Padre, Father McGowan, who greeted Padre Benson when he arrived at St Elizabeth's, noted that Padre Benson seemed to have lost the will to live and was very upset that due to losing his right arm, he would no longer be able to carry on his ministry as a Catholic priest (the right arm was the only arm permitted in those days to provide blessings in the Roman Catholic Church).

Padre Benson's condition continued to decline, and he died in St Elizabeth's hospital on 27 September, just after all the able-bodied airborne troops were evacuated from the Arnhem bridgehead.

After Father Benson's death, the medical officer who had been treating him gave Anglican Chaplain Padre Selwyn Thorne the dead priest's crucifix. Padre Thorne was taken prisoner and placed in a POW Camp in Fallingbostel, where he came under the influence of a French Chaplain. In 1945 Padre Thorne converted to Catholicism and trained for the priesthood at St Edmund's College, Ware, and was ordained priest in 1951 for the Archdiocese of Westminster. After a curacy at Holy Trinity, Brook Green in Hammersmith, he joined Downside Abbey and took the name Father Columba. In the early 21st century, he donated Father Benson's cross to the Royal Army Chaplains Museum.

Next to St. Elisabeth's Hospital. The rearmost cross marks the grave of Father Benson.

Jesus Mercy ✠ Mary Help

Of your charity pray for the
repose of the soul of
Rev. Bernard Joseph Benson
Chaplain
1st Airborne Division
who died of wounds received at
Arnhem, 27th September, 1944,
Aged 30 Years.
Interred in Holland.

On whose soul, sweet Jesus have mercy.

Prayer:
O God who amongst Thy Apostolic Priests
raised up Thy servant Bernard Joseph to
the dignity of the priesthood, grant we
beseech Thee, that he may also be
admitted in Heaven to their everlasting
fellowship through Jesus Christ, Our
Lord. Amen.

May he rest in peace. Amen.

"This one thing I ask of you, that
wherever you may be you will always
remember me at the Altar of God."
St. Monica's dying request to St. Augustine

O most Lord Jesus, have mercy on
the souls in purgatory.

The Long, Cold, Wet Fall in the Netherlands and in the Hurtgen Forest

26 October 1944

IAN MACAULAY BA Hons, BTh, Service no. 121108. Age 28. Chaplain 4th Class, Royal Army Chaplains' Department. Attached to 1st Battalion Fife and Forfar Yeomanry. Buried in the Geel Commonwealth War Graves Cemetery, plot IV, row D Grave 22, Geel Belgium.

Ian Macaulay was born in Dublin in 1916 to Rev. James J. Macaulay and Margery Macaulay. Ian's father served as a Royal Army Chaplain during World War One. As well he went on to be the Moderator (the highest position in the Presbyterian Church) of the Presbyterian Church of Ireland in 1932. At the time of his election as Moderator, Rev JJ Macaulay was serving at Christ Church, Rathgar, in Belfast, Northern Ireland. Following their one-year term as Moderators, Presbyterian Clergy are given the honorific title of "Very Reverend" to indicate that they are former Moderators.

Ian Macaulay attended boarding school at Belfast's Campbell College as a boy. In 1933 Ian visited Canada on a tour sponsored by the Canadian Department of National Defence in Ottawa. He then went on to attend the

University of Cambridge, where he earned a Bachelor of Arts (Honours) degree, after which he began theological studies at the University of Edinburgh. However, some divinity students felt the call to serve their country very strongly and did not wait for their graduation. Ian Macaulay was one of these and joined the 1st Battalion of the Royal Scots Regiment (the oldest regiment of the line in the British Army) as a private soldier in early 1940. He was commissioned a platoon leader and served with this battalion as part of the British Expeditionary Force and was involved in the Battle of France. The battalion was, for all intents and purposes, wiped out on 27 May 1940 in battle with German forces while holding the southern flank of the British positions to facilitate the Dunkirk evacuation. However, Lieutenant Macaulay and a few others of the Royal Scots were able to evacuate from France and were returned to the United Kingdom. Lieutenant Macaulay was part of the leadership when the 1st Battalion of the Royal Scots was reconstituted in Bradford, England, in the summer of 1940 after the end of the battle of France. The 1st Battalion was then assigned to anti-invasion duties in various locations in southern England. Lieutenant Macaulay continued to serve with the Royal Scots until the Church of Scotland sought to ordain men who had completed or almost completed, their theological training, as there was a shortage of military chaplains. On 28 September 1941, Ian Macaulay was ordained Minister of Word and Sacrament in the Church of Scotland.

After his ordination, Rev Macaulay immediately volunteered for service with the Royal Army Chaplains' Department and completed the basic Chaplains' Course at Tidworth Barracks. Early in 1942, he was assigned as the chaplain to the 1st Fife and Forfar Yeomanry Regiment, 28th Armoured Brigade, part of the defence of the United Kingdom, as well being a unit for the experimentation with new armoured vehicles, most notably, the "Funnies" or specialized tanks that were to comprise the 79th Armoured division and play such an important role in the D-Day landings. The 1st Fife and Forfar Yeomanry Regiment became experts in the use of Churchill "Crocodile" flamethrower-equipped tanks.

The various tank troops and squadrons (equivalent to platoons and companies of an infantry unit) of the 1st Fife and Forfar Yeomanry Regiment, as it was for all the tanks of the 79th Armoured Division, were assigned on an as-needed basis to other Allied Divisions, Corps and Armies.

In August of 1944, the 1st Fife and Forfar Yeomanry was sent overseas to the continent and participated in the Allied advance into Northern France and Belgium. In Belgium in the early fall of 1944, they participated in the 1st Canadian Army's campaign to clear the Scheldt Estuary, which would permit the port of Antwerp to be used by Allied shipping (the port is actually 60 miles inland from the North Sea).

At least two troops each of both A and C Squadrons of the 1st Fife and Forfar Yeomanry Regiment were assigned to the 3rd Canadian Infantry Division battling to clear the Germans from the area north of Antwerp, in operation code-named "Operation Suitcase" designed to clear the area north of Antwerp, This area was between Bergen op Zoom (on the Scheldt Estuary) to the west and Breda to the east, and where the 1st FFY with their Churchill Crocodile flame-throwing tanks were invaluable in clearing dug-in German positions.

On the day of his death, Padre Macaulay went to visit the men of two troops of A squadron before their first action with the Canadian Algonquin Infantry Regiment, and a short service was held in the field alongside their tanks. They were located in Esschen (Essen), Belgium, just on the northern border with Holland and east of Bergen-op-zoom. Padre Macaulay then accompanied A Squadron into action and was soon under fire, although he was not riding in a tank but following beside and behind the tanks with the accompanying Canadian Infantry. It was noted that the ground where the A Squadron tanks were advancing was most unsuitable for tanks, as it was very waterlogged, but their flamethrowers were most effective in wooded areas where the German troops were hidden.

After that first battle, Padre Macaulay went to visit the troopers of C Squadron of the 1st FFY, who were also entering their first battle, and, on his way, encountered some wounded Canadian soldiers, whom he stopped to minister to. While he was tending their wounds, a German shell burst near him, and he died of shrapnel wounds within a half hour.

Padre Macaulay was regarded as a real gentleman and a very cheerful and eager person. The 1FFY felt his death left a gap in the regiment that was never fully filled afterward. Padre Macaulay is commemorated as a member who died in World War Two on a large plaque in St Giles (Presbyterian) Cathedral in Edinburgh, Scotland.

27 October 1944

JOHN RUDOLPH KILBERT, Purple Heart, Croix de Guerre, Service no. O-523437. Age 30. 1st Lieutenant, United States Army Chaplain Corps. Attached to the 9th Infantry Regiment, 2nd Infantry Division, Buried in the Arlington National Cemetery, section 12, grave 1616, Arlington, Virginia, USA.

John (Jack) Kilbert was born on 1 October 1914 in Philadelphia, Pennsylvania, to Rudolph Kilbert and Matilda Ella Kilbert (née Bookout), and he had a younger sister, Ruth. He attended Northeast High School in Philadelphia and was on the football and basketball teams there. He graduated from high school in 1933.

Pastor Kilbert was a graduate of Eastern Baptist Theological Seminary with a Bachelor of Theology degree in 1938, and he was ordained in the Baptist Church that same year. From 1936-1938 John served as a student pastor of the Manahawkin Baptist Church, in Manahawkin, New Jersey, along with the Surf City Baptist and the Beach Arlington Union Church, on Long Beach Island.

While ministering in this 3-point charge, he attended a Sunday School Halloween Party at the Baptist Church in the neighbouring community of Ship Bottom. He met his wife Margret (Margie) at the party, and within the family, the story is told that it was love at first sight for Jack. After the party, Jack and Margie went for a walk along the beach, and he told her that he was going to marry her. Margie replied that she did not want to be a minister's wife. She had just turned down an Episcopal Minister, and she was certainly not going to marry a Baptist Minister. However, Jack was not deterred. He went back to Philadelphia, where his parents lived, and ended his engagement to a tall blonde woman who sang in the choir at his church and who was considered perfect to be a minister's wife. Jack's mother was quite upset at her son's sudden change of heart at the breaking off of his engagement and sent her husband, Rudolph, to Ship Bottom to meet Margie, and when he came back, he told his wife, "If he doesn't marry her, I am going to." Jack continued to persist in his relationship with Margie, and they were married shortly after his graduation from seminary. After graduation and ordination, he became the pastor of the three congregations where he had trained. Jack and Margie lived in the neighbouring community of Surf City, N.J.

In the early fall of 1940, Jack and Margie moved to Philadelphia, where he became the pastor of the Geiger Memorial Brethren Church (the church that Jack's parents attended). As it is related to the Amish denomination, the Brethren denomination is strongly pacifist, and its young men of the draft age were generally conscientious objectors. However, some did go into the military and served in non-combatant roles, such as medics or chaplains. In the spring of 1943, Jack volunteered for the army, which caused quite a controversy at Geiger Memorial Church due to the congregation's pacifist beliefs. However, Jack was not put off, as being a chaplain was a non-combatant role. After training at the Harvard Chaplain School in the summer of 1943, he went overseas with the 9th Infantry Regiment of the 2nd Infantry Division. Chaplain Kilbert and his regiment trained in Northern Ireland and Wales for their part in the invasion of Europe.

Chaplain Kilbert landed with his regiment in Normandy on 7 June 1944 over Omaha Beach near Saint-Laurent-sur Mer and served with them in the Battle of Normandy and participated in the push to capture the port of Brest on the Brittany Peninsula in France. At the end of September, the

9th Infantry Regiment, along with Chaplain Kilbert and the rest of the 2nd Infantry Division, took up quarters near St Vith in Belgium to hold the front line along a very broad sector.

Chaplain Kilbert was awarded the Silver Star for his actions on the 29th of August, 1944. His 1st Battalion, 9th Infantry, was under attack by a German counter-attack. He left the aid station where he had been ministering and moved through German artillery fire to the front-line positions of his troops as they were being assaulted by German soldiers. For his steadying presence to the men of Company A, he was awarded the Silver Star, which was presented to his widow at the Custom House in Philadelphia on April 23, 1945.

Chaplain Kilbert's division was involved in the fighting in the Schnee-Eifel Mountain and the forest region near St Vith in the area where the borders of France, Belgium, and Germany meet in part of the German defences called the Siegfried Line. These defences included concrete bunkers built by the Germans to hold the Allies back.

The 9th Infantry waged incessant patrols and artillery duels with the German units doing the same in the area from their arrival at the end of September 1944. German night-time raids were a common occurrence, as there were significant gaps in the frontlines. The men of the 9th Infantry were also raiding into German territory on a regular basis. Because of the very long and rough terrain in the Schnee-Eifel region, the frontlines were not a continuous system of trenches. Instead, certain positions that overlooked road junctions, stream, and trail crossings were built or preferably captured from German-fortified strongpoints. These German Siegfried Line Fortifications were built of concrete and offered excellent protection from German mortar and artillery fire, as well as being easier to heat so the American GIs could keep dry, unlike the wooden fortifications that the GIs would have to dig out and build themselves. Generally, an American platoon of GIs would occupy the concrete bunkers and surround them with wire and mines, which allowed the men to defend themselves from attack from any direction by German patrols.

Chaplain Kilbert would have spent his time making the rounds during daylight hours to these various fortified bunkers manned by men of the 9th Infantry Regiment. Unfortunately, on 27 October 1944, after visiting the soldiers inside a former German bunker, Chaplain Kilbert was hit by a German mortar barrage and died instantly[9]. A medic who left the bunker to go to Chaplain Kilbert's aid was also killed.

Colonel CJ Hirschfelder wrote to Chaplain Kilbert's widow, "From the day Chaplain Kilbert joined the Regiment in Brest, France, he has done exceptionally find work. In the First Battalion to which he was assigned, he was known as their "Front Line Chaplain". His devotion to his work habitually carried him to where the fighting was hardest, knowing as he did the inspiration his presence always provided[10]."

Chaplain Kilbert was the second chaplain of the 9th Infantry Regiment who was killed in action. Chaplain Philip Edelen (see above), whom Chaplain Kilbert would have known, was killed in action on 10 June 1944.

21 November 1944

CLARENCE GIBSON STUMP, Purple Heart, Service no. O-540976. Age 30. Captain, United States Army Chaplain Corps. Attached to the 1st Battalion, 415th Infantry Regiment, 104th Infantry Division. Buried in the Mount Washington Cemetery, Independence, Missouri, USA.

Clarence Stump was born on 27 December 1914 in Independence, Missouri. He was the son of George Rufus Stump and Eula V Stump (nee Gibson) and had an older brother, Homer, as well as two younger brothers, Harold and Walter, and a younger sister, Evelyn. Clarence had been a member of Maywood Baptist Church in west Independence, Missouri, a town on the edge of Kansas City, where he was ordained to Gospel ministry. He graduated from William Jewell Baptist College in 1941. He had also been the assistant pastor of Rockwood Baptist Mission (later Church) in Independence City. However, he had decided to further his education and had enrolled in the Southern Baptist Seminary in Louisville, Kentucky, and it was from there that he volunteered for the Chaplain Corps in November 1943.

The 104th Infantry Division trained at Camp Adair, Oregon, for two years and became specialists in night fighting. The division embarked for France on 27 August

1944 and landed there on 7 September. Early in October, the Division was given the responsibility for holding 22 miles of wet, low country from the Belgian border to the Maas River. The fighting was hard, and the weather conditions in October and November 1944 were terrible: wet, cold, and muddy. Chaplain Stump and the men of his regiment were finally able to advance to the Maas River by 5 November. Shortly after that, they were located just inside the German border near Aachen. On 16 November 1944, the 104th launched "Operation Queen," and after hard fighting and taking many casualties due to extensive German mines and booby traps as well as mortar and artillery fire, they succeeded in capturing Stolberg, Germany, on 19 November. However, the fighting was even more fierce, and the 415th Regiment advanced slowly on Eschweiler, Germany, which was taken on 21 November. The 415th daily report indicates that Chaplain Stump was killed by a German "bouncing betty" or S mine. The S mine has a small charge of explosive which propels it about 3 feet in the air, when the main charge goes off, at the waist height of the man who stepped on it. Chaplain Stump triggered the S-mine while helping to evacuate wounded soldiers of the 1st Battalion of the 415th Infantry Regiment.

After the padre's death, it was written in the 104th Division history that "he frequently distinguished himself by his courage and devotion to the men he served. Chaplain Stump has left a heritage of heroism and Christian character which shall be an everlasting memorial." He also was eulogized by the Executive Board of the Missouri Baptist General Convention, which expressed sincere condolences to his family, the churches he had pastored, and the colleges he had attended. The Local Baptist Council of Kansas City described him as "a young man of great talent and unusual promise."

29 November 1944

EUGENE PATRICK O'GRADY, Bronze Star, Purple Heart, Service no. O-415524. Age 35. Captain, United States Army Chaplain Corps. Attached to the 115th Infantry Regiment, 29th Infantry Division. Buried in the New Cathedral Cemetery, plot HH-291-2, Baltimore, Maryland, USA.

Chaplain O'Grady was the son of Patrick J. and Della M. O'Grady (nee Donlon) and was born on 25 July 1909. He grew up in Baltimore with his five siblings. Eugene O'Grady studied at the American Seminary in Rome and was ordained there on 8 December 1935. His first assignment as a priest was in the Mount Washington neighbourhood in north Baltimore, Maryland. While serving there, the priest of the parish, Father Louis Stickney, described Father O'Grady as "the finest priest I have ever known".

On 31 January 1941, Chaplain O'Grady volunteered to join the US Army in January 1941 after learning that many of the men of his parish, who had joined the Maryland National Guard to supplement their incomes, were called to active duty even before America entered World War Two. Chaplain O'Grady served with the 29th Division for his whole time of service. To the men of the 115th Regiment, he was known as "Father Pat". Although only 35 years old, Father Pat had gone prematurely grey, so the men of his regiment were not sure how old he really was. No matter how old they thought he was, he was noted for tossing a baseball or kicking a soccer ball around with the men. He was noted for helping any of the soldiers he came in contact with, no matter their race or religious affiliation.

On D-Day 6 June 1944, Chaplain O'Grady landed on Omaha Beach in the 3rd wave while the beach was still under heavy German fire, but he survived and served with his regiment in the battles of the Normandy hedgerows. A battalion commander in the 115th Regiment commander said of Chaplain O'Grady's service in Normandy, "... without exaggeration that the single greatest contribution to the morale of his battalion had been the work of Chaplain O'Grady... a few words coming from him have on untold occasions, when the going was rough, changed the entire outlook of some individuals—buoyed them and spurred them on to greater efforts. Danger meant nothing to this chaplain...." However, five months of almost continuous frontline combat had exhausted the padre, and a Dutch priest who met him at that time encouraged him to take a rest. However, Father Pat said this was impossible as his "boys" needed him.

On 29 November 1944, Father Pat and his driver were in their jeep, loaded with hot coffee and doughnuts from the Red Cross and heading for the 3rd Battalion Aid Station located in an old manor house close to the Roer River, which was within view of the Germans on the other side of the River. Father Pat and his driver were spotted entering the courtyard of the manor house in their jeep, and as they began to unload it, the Germans launched a mortar attack on the grounds of the manor house. A mortar shell landed close to Chaplain O'Grady, and he was hit by a shell fragment in the head and killed instantly. Father Pat's death cast a pall over the whole regiment, as he had been with it since it was training in England for D-Day.

Padre O'Grady was buried by the Chief Chaplain of the 29th Infantry Division, Major Harold Donovan, who was also one of the padre's closest friends, as they had been commissioned together in January 1941. As the 115th Regiment was on the frontlines, the men of the regiment were unable to attend Father Pat's funeral. However, a few days later, the regimental commander permitted five men from each of the regiment's 19 companies to attend a solemn high requiem mass held in the Schandelen Church in Heerland, Holland.

Chaplain O'Grady is commemorated at the Camp Fretterd Military Reservation, Maryland, which is the location of the Chaplain Eugene P. O'Grady Chapel. Father Pat was the only Catholic chaplain from Baltimore to be killed during WWII and the only Maryland National Guard Chaplain to be killed as well.

The Battle of the Bulge and the Vosges Mountains Battle

18 December 1944

EDWIN WILLIAM HAMPTON, Purple Heart, Service no. O-553341. Age 36. 1st Lieutenant, United States Army Chaplain Corps. Attached to the 393rd Infantry Regiment, 99th Infantry Division Aged 36. Buried in the Kaufman Cemetery, Section 4, Kaufman County, Texas, USA.

Edwin Hampton was born on 9 March 1908 in Scurry, Texas, to William B Hampton and Sarah Hampton (nee Cave). Edwin had four brothers. Two were older, Roy and Charlie, and two younger, Henry and James. He had three sisters, two older, Christine and Evelyn, and one younger, Jeannette. James and Jeanette were twins. Edwin was married to Annie Mae Hampton (née Gassaway) in 1928, and they had a daughter, Sarah, who was born in 1939. Rev Hampton had served in a number of congregations, including Owenwood Church of Christ in Dallas. However, before entering the military, Chaplain Hampton was the minister at the Church of Christ in Winfield, Kansas.

Chaplain Hampton, along with the rest of his division, arrived in England in early October 1944, and refresher training courses were held for all of the units. On 2 November, the 393rd Regiment was moved aboard Landing

Ship Tanks (LST), and it was on one of these LSTs that Chaplain Hampton led a service using a Jeep's hood as his altar, and his sermon was about the obligations of soldiers to fight for a noble cause. After landing in France, the 393rd was trucked to near Aubel, Belgium, on 11 November 1944 and then on to the Losheim Gap near Krinkell to relieve the 9th Infantry Division opposite the German Siegfried Line. The 99th Division covered 22 miles of frontline, and there was a gap at the southern end of the line of several thousand yards between it and the next American division. On 16 December, the Germans launched their Ardennes Offensive directly at the 99th Division's line. The men of the 99th did all they could to hold back the German offensive but were overwhelmed by the attack. They were able to slow down the German advance for a few days, as small units were surrounded, but fought on. They were finally ordered to fall back to Elsborn while under heavy German shell fire. It was during this retreat that Chaplain Hampton and his assistant Specialist 5 Perry S Bogart were killed. As they were falling back towards more defensible positions, the two men stopped to change a tire on their jeep's trailer and came under an artillery barrage; a shell landed behind them, and both were decapitated by shrapnel from the burst.

There is some discrepancy as to when Chaplain Hampton and Specialist Bogart were killed. In his book *Snow and Steel*, Peter Caddick-Adams quotes the 394th's 3rd Battalion (note the different battalion number) Captain Charles Pierce as indicating they were killed fixing a tire on their trailer, before the retreat, in the initial opening salvos of the German artillery barrage that preceded the assault on the American positions. Captain Pierce indicated, "One moment, our battalion chaplain and his assistant were kneeling beside their disabled vehicle. The next moment they were headless, decapitated by an exploding shell as if by the stroke of a guillotine."

As happened with the British Chaplains in 1940 on the retreat to Dunkirk, whose dates of death vary according to accounts, it serves to remind the reader that during a retreat, reports of death and the circumstances often get delayed until a later date when they can be recorded properly.

18 December 1944

THOMAS HAMPTON REAGAN, Bronze Star, Purple Heart, Service no. O-020415.

Age 35. Lieutenant-Colonel, United States Army Chaplain Corps. Attached to Headquarters Company, 78th Infantry Division. Buried in the Henri-Chapelle American Cemetery, plot: B, row 15, grave 4, Plombières, Belgium.

Thomas Reagan was born on 17 May 1909 in McNeil, Arkansas, to Will Reagan and Josie E Reagan (nee Stringer). His father was a doctor in Waldo, Arkansas. Thomas attended Ouachita Baptist College in Arkadelphia, Arkansas, and graduated in 1930. He then attended Southwestern Baptist Theological Seminary in Fort Worth, Texas, and graduated in 1933. He was ordained a minister in the Southern Baptist denomination in late 1933.

In 1930, before entering seminary, Thomas Reagan joined the American Army Reserves as a 2nd Lieutenant. He was promoted to First Lieutenant (Reserves) Chaplain in 1934 after being ordained. He joined the regular Army in 1936 with the same rank as he had in the Reserves and then received a regular army promotion to captain in 1938. He was promoted in 1942 to Major and then received a further promotion on 29 May 1943 to Lieutenant-Colonel.

Chaplain Reagan was assigned to the Headquarters of the 78th Division as its senior chaplain and landed in England on 26 October 1944. The 78th had two weeks of further training in England before moving to France on 22 November 1944. The division was then moved to Tongeren, Belgium, and then on to Roetgen, Germany, where they arrived on 7 December and prepared for combat. On 13 December 13 when the 78th Division was assigned to take over positions previously held by the 1st Infantry Division. It was at Roetgen that the 78th Division went into battle for the first time.

As the first combat action of his division took place, Chaplain Reagan was at the front with the 2nd Battalion of the 309th Infantry Regiment who had attacked Kesternich, Germany. They were slowly making progress against a stubborn German defence of the town. On 14 December, the battalion commander Lt. Col. Wilson L. Burley, and assistant battalion commander, Maj. Mark H. Hudson were both killed, and Chaplain Reagan was severely wounded by German artillery fire. Chaplain Reagan was unable to be evacuated from Kesternich due to the heavy fighting and the lack of American artillery support. The American artillery could not fire in support of the trapped American troops but would have most likely broken up the German attack due to confusion as to whether other units of the 78th division were in Kesternich.

Due to his severe wounds and inability to be evacuated to a more advanced hospital, Chaplain Reagan died of his wounds two days after the German Ardennes offensive that began on 16 December 1944 smashed into Kesternich. The town was held by the Germans until the end of January 1945. Because of this, Lieutenant-Colonel Reagan's body was not recovered and buried until the Allies recaptured Kesternich on 1 February 1945.

Chaplain Reagan was the highest-ranking Allied chaplain killed in action in Northwest Europe in World War Two.

19 December 1944

CLYDE E KIMBALL, Silver Star, Purple Heart, Service no. O-415638. Age 36. Captain, United States Army Chaplain Corps. Attached to the 1128th Engineer Combat Group. Buried Henri-Chapelle American Cemetery, plot E, row 14, grave 39, Plombières, Belgium.

Clyde Kimball was born in 1908 and graduated from the Boston University School of Religious Education and Theology in 1933. Rev Kimball spoke four languages besides English, which helped with his studies, as they included Greek, Latin, and French, and during the war, he could get by in Icelandic, which he had learned as well. After ordination, he was a member of the New Hampshire Conference of the Methodist Episcopal Church, where he served in a number of congregations. At the time of his enlistment in the Army, he was the minister at the Methodist Episcopal Church in Concord, New Hampshire. He was married to Ellen A Kimball (nee Gates) and had two sons, Clyde Jr and Dana. He entered the Chaplain Corps in June 1941.

Chaplain Kimball was assigned to the 1128th Engineer Group, which was sent overseas in 1942 as part of the Allied occupation force in Iceland. While in Iceland – where he remained with his unit for 16 months, Chaplain Kimball performed the traditional duties of a chaplain, but with a degree of energy and devotion that surprised other chaplains. His monthly report for April 1943 reveals that through preaching or Communion services, hospital visits, and personal interviews, he had contact with 8,836 individuals. By the end of 1943, he reportedly had given over 500 services. While in Iceland, Chaplain Kimball even gave sermons on Radio Reykjavik. After Iceland, the 1128th was assigned to the United Kingdom for refresher training and preparing for action in Europe.

Rev Kimball is noted for his 1944 Good Friday service in a Congregational Church in a village in England as a "mingling of faiths... 150 African-American soldiers sang spirituals and wine was borrowed from a Catholic priest and communion wafers from some Episcopalians." On a typical day, Chaplain Kimball gave two to three services (sometimes travelling 40 miles through bad weather in an open Jeep), held Bible study groups, attended prescribed exercise drills, and provided spiritual direction and counselling for individual soldiers.

Chaplain Kimball was so dedicated to his ministry that it was not limited to his regiment. The local civilian population in the various villages and cities where he was stationed sometimes attended his services, and his fluency in French and familiarity with Icelandic attracted the natives. Local people expressed their affection and respect by requesting that he sign their Bibles. Some even gave him their Bibles (a few of which were rare) out of gratitude. While in Iceland, England, and Europe, Chaplain Kimball began a collection of rare bibles he found in bookstores. He continued collecting, rummaging through old bookshops, and making contact with printers and dealers. After one particularly successful book-buying excursion in Luxembourg, he declared: "Guess Bibles are my whiskey." He was most interested in rare Bibles with early European imprints. His purchases included a 1644 Icelandic Bible; in London, a Latin Bible printed in Venice in 1497, and also the famous "Treacle Bible" of 1568, so called because the word treacle is used instead of balm; and a Biblia Sacra, printed in Antwerp in 1574 by the firm of Christopher Plantin. After the war, his wife donated this collection of about 150 antique and rare bibles to the Boston University

School of Theology in memory of her husband.

Chaplain Kimball also had a great fondness for antiques and historic sites, and his observations were invariably accompanied by concern for their state of preservation. During a stay at a Luxembourg chateau, for example, he wrote stiffly of any soldier who did not pause to admire the objects adorning the interior and penned heavy criticism of those who handled them carelessly. Kimball was interested in genealogical research as well. While on leave in England, he visited his familial ancestral home (observing security regulations, he never wrote down the names of the villages or towns he visited) and carefully searched church records dating as far back as 1562.

Chaplain Kimball died during the Battle of the Bulge on 19 December 1944. During the heavy and desperate fighting, he brought personal supplies and offered spiritual comfort to detachments of isolated soldiers, travelling alone in an area that no longer had a fixed front line.

Chaplain Kimball heard that there was a group of wounded soldiers who could not get medical attention, and he set out to go to them. Along the way, his jeep was ambushed by advancing German troops, and he was mortally wounded. Kimball was awarded the Silver Star for his gallant service, as well as the Purple Heart.

After the war, a memorial window was installed in the Boston Methodist Church Chapel to commemorate Chaplain Kimball.

8 January 1945

JOHN J VERRET, SSE, Silver Star, Purple Heart, Service no O-477243. Age 32. Captain, United States Army Chaplain Corps. Attached to the 3rd Battalion, 507th Parachute Infantry Regiment, 17th Airborne Division. Buried in Saint Mary's Cemetery, Swanton, Vermont.

John Verret was born in Burlington, Vermont, to Alexander Joseph Verret and Anna Verret (nee Graves) on 7 July 1912. He had two brothers, Cyril and Omer, and three sisters, Elizabeth, Margaret, and Vivienne. His father owned a grocery store in Burlington.

Chaplain Verret was a Roman Catholic priest and a member of the Religious Society of St Edmund and was teaching school in the Edmonites private school, St Michael's in Colchester, Vermont, while becoming a member of the Order.

The Society of St Edmund is one of the smallest religious orders in the Roman Catholic Church. It was founded in France in 1843 in a rural region of France to revitalize the faith of people who had become increasingly alienated from the Catholic Church. Its founder, Father Jean-Baptiste Muard, began the Society at St. Mary's Abbey in Pontigny, one of the great Cistercian monasteries of France and the final resting place of Saint Edmund of Canterbury. The Edmundites take on assignments and challenges that local clergy are unable to do. The order moved to Vermont in the late 19th century as there was religious freedom in America that was not available in France at that time.

Rev Verret had been teaching at St Mary's Seminary in Washington, DC, following his ordination as a priest and was commissioned as a Chaplain on 10 August 1943. After his initial training at Chaplains School, he volunteered to become a paratroop chaplain and joined the 507th Parachute Infantry Regiment. Chaplain Verret helped design the regiment insignia of a shield that features a white parachute on a blue background and a blue streak of lightning on a white background to denote the infantry. The insignia below reads "Descende Ad Terram" (Down to Earth). Chaplain Verret trained with the 507th regiment and jumped into Normandy with it as part of the 82nd Airborne Division on D-Day.

After serving in Normandy and taking heavy casualties, the 507th was withdrawn to England for training and refitting, when it was hurriedly rushed back into combat on 17 December 1944 to counter the German Ardennes Offensive. As the Allies began to push the Germans back towards their initial positions, Chaplain Verret was there with them near the village of Laval, Luxembourg, west of Bastogne, Belgium, on a bitterly cold, snowy winter's day during the Battle of the Bulge. Chaplain Verret had just given last rites to his friend Major Davis, commanding officer of the 3rd Battalion, and had abandoned his foxhole to retrieve a badly wounded sergeant who had been injured in a German Nebelwerfer rocket barrage. Chaplain Verret carried the trooper to where an ambulance was waiting and was helping a corpsman load the wounded sergeant on his stretcher into the vehicle when another fusillade of rockets came in, with shrapnel instantly killing Chaplain Verret. The sergeant and the corpsman survived. It was reported that the men of the 507th were greatly affected by Chaplain

Verret's death, as he had been with the regiment almost since its formation.

Interestingly, Chaplain Verret appears to have two graves. One is in the St Mary's Cemetery in Swanton, Vermont, which is attached to the Roman Catholic Church of the Nativity of the Blessed Mother, where he had been one of the clergy before entering the military. This is recorded as his official grave. The other is in the Mount Calvary Cemetery Annex in Burlington, Vermont, where the rest of his family is buried and where he has a second gravestone.

20 January 1945

EDWIN ULYS MONROE, Bronze Star, Purple Heart, Service no. O-532213. Age 29. First Lieutenant, United States Army Chaplain Corps. Attached to the 1st Battalion 254th Infantry Regiment, 63rd Infantry Division. Buried in the Epinal American Cemetery and Memorial, plot A, row 8, grave 20, Dinozé, France.

Edwin Monroe was the son of George and Cora Monroe of Harrisonville, Missouri, and was born on 26 February 1915. He had two older brothers, George and John. He was a graduate of William Jewell College in Liberty, Missouri, and had graduated from two Baptist seminaries before being ordained in the Northern Baptist denomination. Though he had ministered in a Northern Baptist church in Peoria, Illinois, he was officially the minister of the Northern Baptist Church in Orange County, Indiana, immediately before volunteering for the military service, He had married his wife Doris Monroe (née Driggers) in August 1937, and they had a son, Gerald, and a daughter, Amelia.

Chaplain Monroe entered the Chaplain Corps in May of 1944 and, after training at the Army Chaplain School at Camp Van Dorn, Mississippi, was assigned to the 253rd Infantry Regiment, 63rd Infantry Division from July to October 1944. He was then transferred to the 254th Infantry Regiment in the same Division. Chaplain Monroe and the rest of his regiment embarked for England on 20

November 1944 and arrived five days later. After a period of refresher training, the 254th Regiment and Chaplain Monroe were shipped to Marseille, France, over a period from early December 1944 until early January 1945 due to a lack of available Allied transport.

After the 63rd Division re-assembling, the 254th moved to Willerwald, France, in the Moselle region. His Regiment was temporarily assigned to the 3rd Infantry Division for the attack on the town of Jebsheim as part of the Battle of the Colmar Pocket in Lorraine in eastern France. Chaplain Monroe was struck by fragments from a German artillery shell that landed on the road beside the jeep he was travelling in. The driver was not injured. Chaplain Munroe's funeral was officiated by the 63rd Divisional Senior Chaplain on 23 January. Chaplain Munroe was the first chaplain killed in action in the 7th US Army.

21 January 1945

ANTHONY EUGENE CZUBAK, Bronze Star, Purple Heart, Service no. O-511364. Age 33. Captain, United States Army Chaplain Corps. Attached to Headquarters Company, 7th Armoured Division. Buried in the Saint Francis Cemetery, Pawtucket, Providence County, Rhode Island, USA.

Chaplain Czubak was born on 4 March 1911 to Anthony Czubak and Sophia Czubak (nee Smolinski) in Providence, Rhode Island. He had six older brothers, Zygmunt, Matthew, Edmund, Stanley, Zdislaw, and Richard, and two older sisters, Cecelia and Adele. He attended the Providence College Roman Catholic Seminary, where he graduated in 1932, before being ordained a priest in the Diocese of Providence. In 1940 he was an assistant priest at St Patrick's Church in Valley Falls, Rhode Island. He was commissioned as a chaplain on 1 February 1943.

Chaplain Czubak was assigned to the 176th Infantry Regiment in March 1943, which was part of the 7th Armored Division. However, in an attempt to make the chaplains of the 7th Armored Division more efficient in serving the men of the division, in July 1944, just before embarking for France, they were assigned to the 7th Armored Division Trains (supply system). Chaplain

Czubak and the Divisional Supply troops landed over Omaha and Utah Beaches in Normandy during August 1944 and were assigned to the newly formed U.S. Third Army. It immediately went into battle in Northern France, where it was involved in the attack on Chartres, Dreux, Melun, and then crossing the Seine River. Chaplain Czubak and his division liberated Chateau-Thierry and Verdun at the end of August. Chaplain Czubak and the 7th Armored Division reached the Moselle River but were unable to cross and became engaged in the heavy fighting around Metz. The 7th was transferred to the 9th Army and moved into the Netherlands to support the airborne Operation Market Garden to seize the bridges over the Rhine River.

Chaplain Czubak and the Division continued to battle in the Netherlands for the month of October. In early November, the division was withdrawn from battle to rest and retrain, as it had taken so many losses that the new men needed to be better integrated into their units. In December, the 7th Armored was back in the frontlines facing the Germans across the Roer River when the Germans launched their Ardennes Offensive. The 7th was immediately sent south to the crossroads town of St. Vith in Belgium, where they held the town for seven days before withdrawing in the face of overwhelming German forces. Their defence of St Vith slowed the Germans' advance enough to ensure its failure. After again being withdrawn from the frontline for rest and refitting, the 7th Armored Division went back into battle to seize the town of St Vith that they had lost in December. On the morning of 20 January at 0730, the 7th began its attack in poor weather conditions, including extreme cold, snow squalls, and with visibility ranging from fair to poor. As well, the roads were covered with ice, which made the movement of the Division's tracked vehicles extremely difficult.

On 20 January 1945, Chaplain Czubak and the part of his division to which he was currently attached, the 17th Tank Battalion (part of Combat Command A of the 7th Armored Division), along with the 23rd Armored Infantry, moved out at about 9:30 am, and, along with the 2nd Battalion of the 517th Parachute Infantry Regiment, began their attack on the little town of Born south of Saint-Vith. Born was heavily defended by German soldiers of the 18th Volksgrenadier and 3rd Parachute Divisions supported by three tanks and some tank destroyers of the 12th SS Panzer Division. After a day of heavy fighting and significant American losses, the American forces finally took Born in the early evening of the short winter's day of 20 January. However, the next day, the Germans, who had been pushed out of Born, counter-attacked but were halted before re-entering Born by American artillery fire. It was during this counter-attack that Chaplain Czubak died. The Morning Report of the 7th Division Trains indicates Chaplain Czubak died on 22 January, but this is only because they were informed of his death by the 17th Tank Battalion staff on 22 January. The records are clear; however, he was killed in action on 21 January, killed by shrapnel from an artillery shell penetrating his chest and killing him instantly while he was on the battlefield, tending wounded soldiers. He was

anointed by a fellow chaplain and brought to an aid station, but he was deceased. Chaplain Czubak's remains were initially interred in what became the Henri-Chapelle Military Cemetery, but in 1948, upon the request of his parents, his remains were returned to Rhode Island, where his parents lived, and in April of that year, he was buried in the St Francis Cemetery in Pawtucket, Rhode Island.

The Harsh Winter of 1945 in Northwest Europe

28 February 1945

JOSEPH RÉMI ARCHIBALD JOSEPHAT DALCOURT, Bronze Star. Age 37. Chaplain 3rd Class, Canadian Chaplain Service. Attached to Le Régiment de la Chaudière, 8th Canadian Infantry Brigade. Buried in the Groesbeek, Holland Commonwealth War Graves Cemetery, plot IX row E grave 14, Groesbeek, Netherlands.

Joseph Dalcourt, known by his third name Josephat (to distinguish him from his father), was born on 3 October 1908 to Joseph Dalcourt and Philomène Dalcourt née Bérard in Saint-Barthelemy, Berthier, Quebec. He had four older brothers, Antonio, Pierre-Elphège, Charles-Édouard, and one younger sister, Dolorè. He grew up in Louisville, Quebec, and attended the local high school for two years, where he excelled in hockey and baseball. However, his grades were good enough that he switched to L'Assomption College, an all-male private school in L'Assomption, Quebec. After finishing his high school education, Josephat remained at L'Assomption College, where there was an arrangement that he could earn a Bachelor's degree from Laval University of Montreal (later known as Université de Montréal). Most unusually, Josephat earned a Bachelor of Science degree in 1929, when most of his contemporaries at L'Assomption College would have earned a Bachelor of Arts in the classics. After graduation, Josephat took a job teaching at a high school in Le Plateau, an area of Montreal; however, he felt the call to ordained ministry and began studying in 1930 for ordination as a Roman Catholic priest at the Diocese of Trois-Rivières Seminary. He was ordained a priest on 7 July 1935. After his ordination, Father Dalcourt served as vicar in the Sainte-Thècle Parish from July 1935 until May 1936.

Father Dalcourt was noted by his religious superiors as being a good priest, especially with younger families, and he was appointed the priest of the parish of l'Église du Très-Saint-Sacrement (Most Blessed Sacrament) in Trois-Rivières. This was a new church, built only in 1926, and served a growing congregation that would benefit from a young priest such as Father Dalcourt. However, within three years of his taking up his ministry, Father Dalcourt saw the young men of his church enter the French-speaking regiments of the Canadian army after World War Two began, and he felt he needed to be with them as they faced hardship and uncertainty. He sought permission from his bishop to join the Canadian Chaplain Service. This permission was granted, and he joined the Canadian Chaplain Service on 18 January 1940.

Shortly after his initial training at the Canadian Chaplains School, he was assigned to duty in the Montreal area serving the various army units there. In the early spring of 1941, Padre Dalcourt suffered from appendicitis and spent two weeks in hospital after having his appendix removed. He made a full recovery, and by the middle of June 1941, he was certified as fit to be sent overseas.

Despite his more mature years and the fact that Father Dalcourt had suffered yearly bouts of bronchitis during the winter months while in Quebec, as well as being diagnosed with mild hypertrophy or enlargement of his heart, he was certified fit for overseas and combat duty. Padre Dalcourt left Canada on June 20, 1941, and arrived in the United Kingdom on July 1, 1941. While serving in the United Kingdom, Father Dalcourt served mostly with the 3rd and 6th Canadian Division Infantry Reinforcement Units (CDIRU). While serving with these units, Padre Dalcourt also took part in the Officer Refresher Course in mid-1943, which brought longer-serving officers up to date with modern military combat field craft.

Padre Dalcourt had been made an acting Chaplain 3rd Class on October 1, 1943, and he was confirmed as a Chaplain 3rd Class on February 17, 1944. With this rise in rank, in April 1944, Padre Dalcourt was appointed the senior Roman Catholic chaplain of the Headquarters of the 2nd Canadian Base Reinforcement Group (2 CBRGrp) and moved to France with this unit in the late summer of 1944. This unit was safely behind the frontlines and was responsible for sending replacements to frontline units that incurred casualties. While serving as the senior chaplain (Roman Catholic) with the 2CBRGrp, Padre Dalcourt continuously applied to his CCS superiors to permit him to serve with a frontline regiment. For many weeks his requests were denied, but an opening for a Roman Catholic padre became available with Le Régiment de la Chaudière, whose padre had been worn out dealing with his chaplain duties from D-Day through to the end of October 1944 and had to be rotated back to a less physically and mentally taxing ministry. On 1 November 1944, Padre Dalcourt was assigned to the French-Canadian Le Régiment de la Chaudière.

Padre Dalcourt immediately became very involved with the men of his regiment. He was always visiting their frontline positions, bringing them both the sacraments and small gifts such as extra food or cigarettes. He survived many night visits to outposts under fire, and as Christmas 1944 approached, the men of Le Régiment de la Chaudière were on frontline duty and could not have the traditional Christmas midnight Mass. However, Padre Dalcourt did not let this fact hinder his bringing Christmas Mass to the men of his Regiment, even those posted in the most forward positions. That Christmas Eve, Padre Dalcourt performed an action that made him a legend with La Chaudières. While visiting one of the most forward outposts, he heard the clucking of chickens in a chicken coop in the area between Canadian and German front lines, so Padre Dalcourt crept out, on his own, into no man's land and captured the chickens as an extra Christmas present for the men of his regiment.

Padre Dalcourt served with his regiment during the fierce, wet, muddy, and miserable fighting in the Hochwald Forest on the border between Luxembourg and Germany during the winter of 1945. On 28 February 1945, he and his driver, Private Antonio Gauthier, were on their way back to the Regimental Headquarters in the Reichswald Forest. Padre Dalcourt, along with Padre Hickey of the North Shore (New Brunswick) Regiment, had just finished holding funeral Masses in a small German town called Bedburg for Canadian soldiers killed in the Battle of the Rhineland (Reichswald). Father Dalcourt, along with Private Gauthier, had been told that there were unrecovered soldiers' remains in some destroyed and burned-out American tanks along their route back to the La Chaudière HQ. These tanks were remnants of battles fought by the men of the 7th American Armoured Division in the Peel Marshes of southeast Holland between 30 September to 17 December 1944. They were attached to the British XXX Corps, and not much has been published about their battles due to them being American troops fighting under British command.[11]

Padre Dalcourt and his driver, Private Gauthier, took their jeep off the road and were bumping across the rough ground towards some of the destroyed American tanks when their jeep hit a German anti-tank mine that instantly destroyed the jeep and killed both men.

As has occurred in the accounts of a number of other chaplains' deaths, there can be a number of accounts that record slightly different accounts of a chaplain's death. There is an account that says Padre Dalcourt was riding in a Bren Carrier when it went over an anti-tank mine and was destroyed. However, Bren Carriers were not issued to chaplains in the Canadian Chaplain Service, whereas jeeps were. As well, this account is from a third-hand source.

Padre Dalcourt was buried the next day by Catholic Chaplains Hickey and McCarney in the same churchyard where he had buried other men of his regiment the day before. A memorandum was sent by the Principal Canadian Chaplain, Overseas, Honorary Colonel M.C. O'Neill, to all Roman Catholic chaplains in NW Europe requesting they offer a Mass in memory of Padre Dalcourt.

It should be noted that because of his losing his life while searching the American tanks on behalf of the American Army, Padre Dalcourt was posthumously awarded the

American Bronze Star. During World War Two, in the Commonwealth forces, the only awards after death that a soldier of any rank could receive were the most minor, a Mention in Dispatches, or the very highest, the Victoria Cross. However, other armies, such as the American and French, did award medals posthumously to foreign nationals if their work (or death) had been related to the soldiers or civilians of these nations.

In a letter received by a friend, Padre Dalcourt described his dedication to his soldiers. "I only have one desire, one mission: to be with my soldiers, under the reign of God and under the rain of the enemy."

13 March 1945

CLARENCE ALFRED VINCENT, C.Ss. R. Bronze Star, Purple Heart, Service no: O-543340. Age 29. Captain, United States Army Chaplain Corps. Attached to Headquarters Company, Division Trains, 7th Armoured Division. Buried in the Henri-Chapelle American Cemetery, plot H, row 12, Grave 49, Plombières, Belgium.

Clarence Vincent was born in Seattle, Washington, on 3 January 1916 to Alfred and Elizabeth Vincent (née Stachowiak) and had a younger brother named Robert. As a boy, Clarence and his family moved to Oakland, California, and he attended high school at Holy Redeemer junior seminary, an all-male high school. A year or so after high school Clarence decided to become a member of the Community of the Sons of the Most Holy Redeemer (which operated the Holy Redeemer school) and made his vows to the order on 2 August 1935. At his profession of faith, he made a vow to say the Seven Dolors Rosary all his life in thanksgiving for his vocation and for the grace of perseverance since the Blessed Virgin Mary grants seven graces to those who honour her daily by saying seven Hail Marys and meditating on her tears and 'dolors' or sorrows). Clarence was ordained a priest on 29 June 1940 at the Immaculate Conception Seminary in Oconomowoc, Wisconsin. The Congregation of the Most Holy Redeemer (which in Latin is the Congregatio Sanctissimi

Redemptoris or C.Ss. R.), commonly known as the Redemptorists, is a religious order of the Catholic Church, dedicated to missionary work. The Redemptorists are especially dedicated to Our Mother of Perpetual Help, the Virgin Mary.

Father Vincent, after his ordination, returned to Oakland and, from 1942-1944, taught at the Holy Redeemer minor seminary, from which he had graduated a few years before. He was widely admired as a teacher while at Holy Redeemer. His work with the young men at his school in Oakland gave him a natural instinct for dealing with soldiers. While teaching in Oakland, Father Vincent also volunteered to lead masses and offer confession at the numerous army camps in the San Francisco Bay area. He was described as being able to speak the soldiers' language but not demean himself, and the soldiers appreciated his open manner.

After enlisting in the army in the spring of 1944 and completing chaplain school, Chaplain Vincent served six months on large army bases in the USA but kept asking to be transferred to a combat unit, where he felt the most calling. He had initially been assigned duties with training units due to his wearing glasses. However, the need for chaplains was so great that Father Vincent's continual requests to be assigned to a combat unit were granted. He was transferred to 7th Armoured Division and left for Europe, and landed in Normandy with the division in August 1944. As with Chaplain Czubak (who died on 22 January and also of the 7th Armored Division), he entered combat in mid-August and accompanied his division through northern then eastern France, Belgium, Holland, and then Germany.

As the 7th Armored Division slowly fought to breach the strong fortifications of the German Siegfried Line,

Chaplain Vincent was reported in February 1945 as offering Mass in bombed-out churches, tents, and even in the cold of the open air. He was noted for hearing 500 confessions in a week and visiting all the units he could in his division. He was noted for being a "little fighting man" and an extrovert with "restless energy for action and a powerful drive to get things done."

In March of 1945, units of the 7th Armored Division were assigned to hold the west bank of the Rhine River south of Bonn and north of the recently captured Remagen Bridge to prevent Germans from sending torpedoes, small boats, frogmen, etc., downstream to destroy the most important bridge. The 7th Armored had listening posts and strong points all along the west bank of the Rhine to prevent German patrols from crossing the river. However, it was a quiet time for the 7th Armoured, and this included the Division's supply train to which Chaplain Vincent and the other chaplains were attached, as it had vehicles of various sorts that the chaplains could ride along into the other units of the division for services and pastoral visits. It was headquartered at Mehlem along the west bank of the Rhine.

On 13 March, a lone German bomber, one of many ordered to destroy the bridge at Remagen, was driven off its attack run by very heavy American anti-aircraft fire and turned and flew north over the American side of the Rhine. The pilot would have been flying quite low to avoid anti-aircraft fire and could not have helped but notice all the trucks, trailers, and jeeps of the 7th Division's supply train ahead of him in the town of Mehlem. The pilot dropped his bomb load as he flew over the town and its garrison of American troops and Chaplain Vincent, along with Private Palmieri Meringolo, were killed instantly, while others were injured by this attack.

Shortly after his death, Chaplain Vincent was posthumously awarded the Bronze Star for "distinguishing himself by meritorious service in connection with military operations against an enemy of the United States in Germany, from 21 February 1945 to 13 March 1945."

Operation Varsity – Across the Rhine

24 March 1945

JAMES WILLIAM KENNY, Service no. 287957. Age 32. Chaplain 4th Class, Royal Army Chaplains' Department. Attached to 224th Parachute Field Ambulance, 6th Airborne Division. Buried in the Reichswald Forest Commonwealth War Graves Cemetery, plot 37, row D, grave 11, Kleve, Germany.

James William Kenny, who was born on 27 September 1912, was one of 3 sons, the others being Bernard and Thomas, of James and Matilda Kenny of St Helier's Road, Blackpool. Mrs Kenny brought up her children on her own, as her husband had been killed in action in Egypt during World War I. James attended St Joseph's College in Blackpool and went on to the seminary at Ushaw College in County Durham. He was ordained a Roman Catholic priest on 29 July 1939 at English Martyrs in Preston in the Roman Catholic Diocese of Lancaster, appointed assistant priest to Monsignor R. L. Smith at Our Lady and St Joseph's Church in Carlisle and was an honorary Chaplain to the troops stationed at Carlisle Castle.

While at Our Lady and St Joseph Church, Father Kenny organised a youth club for the teenagers and outings for the children. However, World War Two intruded on this idyllic priestly ministry, and Father Kenny volunteered for the Chaplains Department.

After the obligatory Chaplain training at Tidworth, Padre Kenny joined the 6th Airborne Division in August 1943 and trained alongside the Paras over the next few months. As D-Day approached, Padre Kenny was deployed with the 224th Parachute Field Ambulance and, on 7 June, parachuted into Normandy to support the rest of the 6th Airborne Division, who had landed on 6 June. He was heavily involved in the fighting on the eastern edge of the Normandy battlefield, northeast of Caen at Vareville. During this fighting, Padre Kenny was reported to have carried a wounded paratrooper to safety after they had been caught between the frontlines. Padre Kenny was wounded in the leg in Normandy and spent time in the hospital recovering. However, he recovered from his wounds to return to the 6th Airborne Division in March 1945. The 6th Airborne had returned to Britain after almost three months of intense fighting in Normandy to replace the dead and wounded members and begin training for the next call for paratroops. Padre Kenny returned to the 224th Parachute Field Ambulance on 14 March 1945. He then travelled with other members of the 224th to Hill Hall Transit Camp, where the rest of the Field Ambulance was stationed, arriving there on 20 March.

On Palm Sunday, 24 March 1945, Padre Kenny jumped at 10 am with the 224th PFA near the southeastern end of the Diersford Forest to provide medical support to support the 3rd Parachute Brigade as it jumped across the Rhine. Padre Kenny was the 6th man out of the first stick, or plane load of parachutists over the drop zone. The Royal Army Chaplains Museum records that he and three others from his stick landed in trees and were killed by German gunfire almost immediately before they could cut themselves out of their parachute harnesses and fall to the ground.

On Blackpool's War Memorial are recorded two men called James William Kenny. Padre Kenny's father is listed as dying in World War One, and Father James William Kenny's name appears in the World War Two listings.

Paschal (Pat) Dupuy Fowlkes, Purple Heart, Serial no: O-483005. Age 30. Captain, United States Army Chaplain Corps. Attached to the 507th Parachute Infantry Regiment, 17th Airborne Division. Buried in the Netherlands American Cemetery, plot C, row 17, grave 20, Margraten, Netherlands.

Paschal (Pat) Fowlkes was the son of Frank V Fowlkes, a medical doctor, and his wife, Lucy Fowlkes (nee Meriwether). Pat was born on 26 July 1915 in Burkeville, Virginia. He had two brothers, Francis and Hyde, and a sister, Elizabeth. He married Elizabeth Rives Fowlkes (nee Williams on 22 June 1940, and they lived in Richmond, Virginia. They had two children, a son, Frank, and a daughter, Rives.

Pat Fowlkes attended the University of Virginia at Charlottesville and graduated from there in 1936. While at university, Pat was the editor-in-chief of the university's yearbook, Corks and Curls. He was also a member of the German Club, Vice-President of the Young Men's Christian Association, and a member of Epsilon Tau Alpha Fraternity. After graduation from university, Pat Fowlkes entered Virginia Seminary in 1938. He was ordained a deacon in 1940 and appointed Deacon-in-Charge, of St John's Church, in Mclean, VA, and Holy Comforter Church, Vienna, VA. After being made a priest, he became the Rector of the above two congregations.

Rev Fowlkes was commissioned in the US Army Chaplain Corps in 1942, and after completing Chaplain School, he was appointed chaplain to the 314th Troop Carrier Group of the US Army Air Force, serving in North Africa, Sicily, and finally, in the Italian campaign. However, Chaplain Fowlkes requested a transfer to the Airborne troops and was sent to England, where he qualified as a paratrooper and was assigned to the 507th Parachute Infantry Regiment, 82nd Airborne Division. However, due to Chaplain Fowlkes transferring from the Mediterranean theatre of operations and being in training, he did not participate in the Normandy or Holland parachute drops of the 82nd Airborne.

Chaplain Fowlkes' first time in combat with the 507th PIR took place during Operation Varsity, the crossing of the Rhine in March of 1945. Chaplain Fowlkes volunteered for the "last man, last plane" position, which meant he might be dropped a long way from the drop zone, but he could then proceed to minister to wounded men as he made his way towards the forming up area of his unit.

On 24 March 1945, Captain Fowlkes made a successful jump and had removed his parachute upon landing on the dropzone. His chaplain's assistant, Private 1st Class Bruce Davis, who had jumped just before Chaplain Fowlkes, had been shot and was severely wounded as he descended by parachute. Chaplain Fowlkes saw his assistant in trouble and ran to Davis' side to render first aid, but, in turn, the chaplain was struck and killed by enemy machine gun fire.

25 March 1945

WALTER TULLIEDEPH (TULLY) OGILVY, MA, Mention in Dispatches, Service no. 118329. Age 33. Chaplain 4th Class, Royal Army Chaplains' Department. Attached to 8th Battalion, The Parachute Regiment. Buried in the Reichswald Forest Commonwealth War Graves Cemetery, plot 37, row B, grave 5, Kleve, Germany.

Walter Tulliedeph Ogilvy, or "Tully" as he was called, was the son of Walter Tulliedeph Ogilvy, Senior, and Nora Ogilvy (nee Archdale), and born on 16 January 1912 at Tanfield Vicarage, County Durham. His father died just eight days later in Streatham, Surrey, England, at the very young age of 29. However, Tully, as a boy, turned out to be an exceptional student and earned a scholarship to Harrow School and then to Brasenose College, Oxford, from which he earned a BA and an MA.

Before he became a deacon at Canterbury Cathedral, his first job was Senior Modern Language Master at Dover College. He was ordained a deacon in 1937 and was made a priest on 18 December 1938 by the Archbishop of Canterbury Cosmo Lang. Rev Ogilvy continued to teach at Dover College and was the assistant chaplain to the college when he was ordained as a deacon. The students affectionately nicknamed him 'Watto' due to his initials. He became the College's chaplain in 1938.

Rev Ogilvy joined the Royal Army Chaplains' Department in February 1940. He had his initial chaplain training at Tidworth and then was posted to Northern Ireland. However, in 1941 he was flown to the Middle East to join the 32nd Armoured Tank Brigade. He served in Palestine and Alexandria and then was assigned to the besieged town of Tobruk in Libya before being listed as missing at Cyrenaica in June 1942. While serving in North Africa, he received a Mention in Dispatches award. After being reported missing in action, his status was changed to captured and being held as a Prisoner of War in Camp 75 at Bari, Italy, where he became very unwell with diphtheria. However, as a non-combatant, the Geneva Convention required him to be repatriated as soon as possible to the United Kingdom if not needed to minister to prisoners of war, and as he was so sick, he was repatriated in less than a year.

In April 1943, without any prior notice, he turned up on his sister Mary's doorstep, having been repatriated to the United Kingdom. Padre Ogilvy was a very sick man, and it was reported he had to be "supported by two six-foot squaddies" from the local barracks when he knocked on his sister's front door. He was sent immediately to Horton Emergency Hospital, and while he recuperated there, he acted as the hospital chaplain.

Once he had recovered, he must have reached a high standard of fitness because he volunteered for the airborne forces and attended parachute training course number 117 between 21 May and 8 June 1944. After graduating from parachute training, he was posted to the 8th (Midland) Parachute Battalion, 6th Airborne Division in Normandy, to help replace the chaplains the Division had lost, those either wounded or killed in the initial battles around D-Day. However, he landed in Normandy not by parachute but over the landing beaches, as regular infantry soldiers did. He provided support, encouragement, and ministry for the rest of the summer of 1944 as the 6th Airborne Division held the extreme eastern edge of the Normandy frontline. Padre Ogilvy returned to Britain with the 6th Airborne for the replacement of the dead and wounded from the Normandy campaign and the restarting of intense training so the division would be ready when next called upon.

This call came sooner than was expected as the Germans launched the Ardennes Offensive in December 1944, and Padre Ogilvy and the 6th Airborne were rushed from training in England to the northern flank of the Allied lines to hold the Germans back from breaking through to Antwerp.

Padre Ogilvy jumped with the 6th airborne Division across the Rhine in Operation Varsity on Palm Sunday, 25 March 1945. He was killed by German gunfire while tending to the wounded airborne soldiers in the drop zone. He was wearing a Red Cross Armband, indicating his non-combatant status, but this often was not always visible from a distance or because of the way the person wearing it was in relation to those shooting at him.

26 March 1945

LOREN LEA STANTON, Bronze Star, Purple Heart, Service no O-511823. Age 31. Captain, United States Army Chaplain Corps. Attached to the 30th Infantry Regiment, 3rd Infantry Division, Buried in the Lorraine American Cemetery and Memorial, plot D row 37, grave 26, Saint-Avold, France.

Loren Stanton was born in Chanute, Kansas, on 26 March 1914 to Asa M Stanton and his wife, Eva A Stanton (nee Lea). He had two younger brothers, Paul and Mark. Loren lived in Parsons, Kansas, with his family, and they attended St John's Episcopal Church there. Loren married Florence Rosalie Taylor in the late 1930s. Upon finishing his undergraduate degree, Loren enrolled at the Episcopal Theological School in Cambridge, Massachusetts, affiliated with Harvard University, and graduated in 1940. His candidacy for ordination was shortened to one year, and his time as a deacon was shortened to 6 months by his bishop in Kansas. This indicated that the bishop had high confidence in his ability to help lead a parish immediately after ordination. Rev Stanton was ordained an Episcopal priest in 1940 and was appointed the Rector of St John's Episcopal Church in Parsons, the same church he had worshipped in as a child. Rev Stanton served at St John's from 1940-1943 and then was commissioned in the Chaplain Corps on 4 March 1943.

After his initial training at the Harvard University Chaplain School, Chaplain Stanton was assigned to the

30th Infantry Regiment. He joined his regiment in Italy after it was removed from combat there in preparation for the invasion of southern France in August 1944. After landing on the French Riviera at Saint-Tropez, the unit proceeded up the Rhone Valley, through the Vosges Mountains, and reached the Rhine River at Strasbourg at the end of November 1944. It remained on the defensive in the frontlines during the Battle of the Bulge in December 1944 and then went into action in clearing the Colmar Pocket in late January 1945. It gradually advanced over the winter of 1945 towards the Siegfried Line positions south of Zweibrücken. The 30th Regiment took part in the waterborne crossing of the Rhine on 26 March 1945. As he was crossing the Rhine in an assault landing craft, it was hit by enemy shell fire and capsized, and Chaplain Stanton was drowned. Loren Stanton was killed in action on his 31st birthday.

In 1946, Chaplain Stanton's widow married Mr Delbert Hosack, who had a daughter named Mary Jo from a previous marriage.

Capture – Freedom – Recapture – Death

5 April 1945

Rowland Arthur Koskamp, Bronze Star, Purple Heart, Service no O-517319. Age 29. Captain, United States Army Chaplain Corps. Attached to the 110th Infantry Regiment, 28th Infantry Division. Buried in Lorraine American Cemetery and Memorial, plot K, row 17, grave 9, Saint-Avold, France.

Rowland Koskamp was a native of Oostburg, Wisconsin, born on 24 February 1916 to Dennis and Francis Koskamp. He was the oldest of 5 children, the only son among sisters Ruth, Joyce, Doris, and Carolyn, and he attended the Cedar Grove Reformed Academy near Oostburg. In school, he was active in sports, playing basketball and baseball, which he was particularly good at. He excelled in oratory and won recognition in district finals. Chaplain Koskamp was a willing partner in anything that might produce some excitement and would provide some additional learning. After graduating from high school, he had enough education to teach elementary school for a couple of years. He then worked with his father in a shoe repair shop that also sold farm equipment, such as harnesses and halters, and had a small inventory of men's work shoes and boys' and women's shoes. He also served as a substitute rural mailman, filling in as circumstances warranted. He entered Hope College in 1933 and then went on to graduate from Western Theological

Seminary in 1940. While in seminary, he married Florence Vandenberg. His first assignment, in September of 1940, was to go to Raritan, New Jersey, to replace the retiring pastor of The Third Reformed Church. In 1942 Chaplain Koskamp and his wife Florence had a baby girl they named Karen Jane.

Chaplain Koskamp was noted for being an excellent leader for the young people of the congregation. He served as pastor in Raritan until April 1943, when he requested a leave of absence from the church to join the army as a chaplain. After training at the Chaplain School, he was assigned to the 28th Infantry Division and moved to England with the division in October 1943. Chaplain Koskamp and the 28th Division landed over the beaches in Normandy on 22 July 1944. The division pushed eastwards and was involved with the liberation of Paris and was granted the honour of parading through the city on 29 August 1944. Chaplain Koskamp was awarded the Bronze Star in October 1944 for his service to the men of his division as they fought across France. The division arrived in Luxembourg in October 1944.

A letter written by Chaplain Koskamp to his family in America reflects his gentle nature, his dedication, and his ability to find humour in the insanity of war. Chaplain Koskamp wrote: "Our division is finally off the secret list, so it can now be told that we've been in France, Belgium, Luxembourg, and Germany. We hit the Siegfried Line, and for two weeks, I lived in one of the pillboxes on the line. What structures are they? Kind of cramped, though, for a two-week stay. Since that time, I've established a rest camp for men of the battalion. I had a lot of fun with that and plenty of opportunities to serve the men in it. It was located in a schoolhouse along with the battalion aid station. We served hot meals and gave them sleeping accommodations, movies, and the opportunity to write letters. And above all, the opportunity to attend services which were deeply appreciated by the majority of them."

On the morning of 16 December 1944, the 28th Infantry, like all of the other American units, was caught off guard by the surprise German Ardennes Offensive. Chaplain Koskamp's assistant, PFC Carl Montgomery, tried to get Chaplain Koskamp to leave the aid station and retreat as the overwhelming German forces advanced towards the schoolhouse described in his letter. However, Chaplain Koskamp would not leave the wounded men and continued to give them water and cigarettes and do whatever he could for them. PFC Montgomery had been Koskamp's assistant throughout the war, and thus he could not bring himself to leave him. The aid station was surrounded, and Chaplain Koskamp and the medical staff, along with all the wounded, had to surrender. As he spoke German, Captain Koskamp went out of the heavily damaged aid station to arrange the surrender with a German officer. However, the Germans were in a hurry to get the POWs away from the front line and would not even let them put on their great warm coats.

Chaplain Koskamp and PFC Montgomery, along with 3,000 other Americans, were marched to a railroad station behind the German lines. Sixty men were put in each box car for an eight-day train ride that would take them to their POW camp. At one point during their train ride to the prison, they were parked in a marshalling yard when some U.S. planes attacked. The German guards ran off till the attack was over, leaving the American prisoners locked in the box cars, and some of the prisoners were killed by this friendly fire. When they arrived at the POW camp, the officers were separated from the enlisted men, and Padre Koskamp was separated from Private Montgomery. At the officers' POW camp, which was called Hammelburg 13B (Oflag XIII-B), Chaplain Koskamp took on the role of keeping up the morale among the POWs and was known for his ability to work with the men in all conditions.

Keeping busy in the POW camp is essential, yet often difficult as men have little strength for physical activity. One of the things that Chaplain Koskamp and the other chaplains – 2 Roman Catholics and 4 Protestants – did was to set up a Toastmasters Club where soldiers would learn to speak publicly to a group. Each speaker would share a story, and those in attendance would evaluate the speaker on grammar and presentation style. These small activities would be vital to keeping morale high in the camp, where conditions were not good. For example, the small amount of food they received was terrible, and the average man would lose 30-40 pounds while a prisoner. Another important function that Chaplain Koskamp undertook in the POW camp was to provide his fellow prisoners with updated new reports about the progress of the war. As a chaplain, Captain Koskamp was allowed to travel to different sections of the POW camp. In one section, some Serbian officers had managed to hide a radio. When Chaplain Koskamp visited their section, they would update him on the news that they had gotten from the BBC in

London. He would then pass this information along to the men in the other sections of the camp.

On 27 March 1945, after three months in the camp, Chaplain Koskamp and the other prisoners were surprised when a group of American soldiers broke through the fence of the POW camp without a shot being fired: the German guards had fled since a few days before the Allies had crossed the Rhine River.

A special task force (Task Force Baum) of 200 American soldiers in armoured vehicles and trucks was sent by General George Patton through German lines the 60 miles to the Hammelburg Camp to liberate his son-in-law, Major John K Waters, who had been taken captive in Tunisia in 1943. Due to poor maps and German resistance, only just over half of the task force reached the camp and breached its perimeter to the cheers of the 1,500 prisoners – a number much higher than the three hundred POWs that Task Force Baum leaders were expecting to liberate, and it meant that Task Force Baum did not have room in their remaining vehicles to transport them all back to American lines.

The majority of the American POWs were given the choice of walking back to Allied lines or remaining in the POW Camp in the hope that the American Army would liberate them in a few days. The men, including Chaplain Koskamp, held a conference to decide what to do. It was 50 miles to the Rhine River, where the U.S. troops were. After a few miles marching towards the Rhine in very cold and snowy conditions, many of the POWs on foot decided to return to Hammelburg camp, as they expected U.S. forces would liberate them in a few days since they were too weak and without warm enough clothing for the march to the Rhine in winter. However, some small groups of American officers decided to continue to attempt the 50-mile journey to the Rhine River.

Chaplain Koskamp had decided to return to the POW camp. When he and the others returned to the POW camp, their hope of being liberated shortly was shattered as the Germans guards had returned to the camp and quickly recaptured the returning prisoners and sent them on a 100-mile march away from the frontlines to a POW camp near Nuremberg, Germany.

On 5 April, Chaplain Koskamp and the other prisoners were still on their forced march, yet coming near to their destination. While still outside of Nuremberg, they witnessed an American heavy bomber raid on the city. They had thought they were safe as they were still protected in a wooded area outside. However, the Germans had changed their plans for this column of POWs, and as the American heavy bombers turned for home, Chaplain Koskamp and the others were marched to a railway marshalling yard on the edge of town. Unfortunately, the marshalling yard was the target of a follow-up American raid by medium bombers, and the POW column was caught in it; 30 men were killed and many more injured. Among those killed was Chaplain Koskamp.

Chaplain Koskamp was not the only chaplain in the group of POWs who had been marched from Hammelburg: there were also Roman Catholic and other Protestant chaplains. While tending the wounded, Roman Catholic Chaplain Mark Moore was told that one of the protestant chaplains, Koskamp, had been killed. Chaplains Moore, Curtis, and Stonesifer tried desperately to aid Chaplain Koskamp; however, he was indeed dead. Chaplain Moore anointed Chaplain Koskamp's forehead with oil, and all the other chaplains offered prayers for the dead over his shattered body.

On 20 December 1944, it was reported in the Raritan, New Jersey newspaper, that Chaplain Koskamp was missing in action. In March 1945, hope was given when it was reported that he was a POW. In late April 1945, Chaplain Koskamp's wife Florence was notified by the War Department through a telegram that her husband had been freed from the POW camp at Hammelburg. Unfortunately, this information was incorrect. Some of the POWs who had been liberated by Task Force Baum had been able to walk to freedom and cross into American-held territory and reported that Chaplain Koskamp had been freed and was among those walking to the American lines. They did not realize that Chaplain Koskamp had returned to the Hammelburg POW camp with many others. Thus, with the information from his wife, the local newspaper mistakenly reported that Chaplain Koskamp had been freed and more news would be forthcoming shortly. However, there was no further word on Chaplain Koskamp until the end of May 1945, after the war in Europe had ended, when Florence received another telegram from the War Department saying that her husband had been killed. Mrs Koskamp notified the pastor at the Third Reformed Church, who was filling in for her husband, of Rowland's death on Saturday evening, who announced it

the next morning during the service. Those in attendance were shocked as the last news they had was that he had been freed from being a POW.

In the short space of over four months, and with just a month left in the war in Europe, Chaplain Koskamp had served in battle, been taken prisoner, freed, taken prisoner again, and finally killed by bombs of his own country.

Victory and Death

It has to be more than a coincidence; some might even say the Divine Providence, that story of the murder of Canadian Padre Walter Brown on the evening of June 6, 1944, which began my interest in the chaplains killed in World War 2 ends with the death of a chaplain who has a connection to my discovery of Padre Brown's story. This first investigation of Rev Brown's death was based on the groundwork of Dr Christopher McCreery, as recounted in that section of this study. While corresponding with Dr McCreery, it again was more than coincidental that I learned that his second cousin was Canadian Chaplain Albert McCreery, the last Commonwealth Chaplain killed in Northwestern Europe in World War 2.

4 May 1945

ALBERT EDMUND MCCREERY. Age 27. Chaplain 4th Class, Canadian Chaplain Service. Attached to the Canadian 22nd Armoured Regiment (Canadian Grenadier Guards), 4th Canadian Armoured Division. Buried in the Holten Commonwealth War Graves Cemetery, plot XII row B Grave 5, Overijssel, Netherlands.

Albert was born on 4 January 1918, the son of Samuel J and Lauretta McCreery of Ingersoll, Ontario. After Albert was born, his parents moved from the town to a nearby farm. Albert had two older sisters, Margaret and Ava, and a younger brother, Kenneth. Albert's father was a member of the Church of Ireland (Anglican), and his mother was a devout Baptist. Albert and his siblings were brought up according to their mother's denomination. As Albert grew up, he sang in the church choir of First Baptist Church in Ingersoll and showed his leadership abilities at an early age when he became president of the Baptist Young People's Union at the church. Albert, like most youths of his time, also enjoyed summer and winter activities such as baseball and swimming in the summer and skating and hockey in the winter. Of course, in a time when farming was a very labour-intensive activity, Albert would also have been involved in helping to plant and harvest the crops on the family farm.

Albert completed his primary education and enrolled in the Ingersoll High School. However, the demands of his family life on the farm meant that Albert left high school after a year and went to work for the Hydro-Electric Company in Kitchener, Ontario. Albert was good at school, so he took night school courses and earned his high school diploma. In 1935, Albert had saved enough money to resume his full-time education by attending the Toronto Bible College, where he had the distinction of receiving a perfect 100% on his Latin and Hebrew examinations, although his grades in other subjects were only average. Part of the curriculum of the Toronto Bible College required the students to minister at congregations of the Baptist Home Mission Board, and, in between his terms of study, Albert pastored congregations ranging from Niagara Falls and Burford in southern Ontario, and Haileybury in northeastern Ontario. Albert did well in these missions, and this helped him to decide to go on to the Baptist seminary at McMaster University in Hamilton, Ontario. However, in 1938, Albert deferred entrance to seminary and became the pastor of a congregation in Northwestern Ontario at Eagle River. Albert entered McMaster University Baptist Seminary in the fall of 1939, just as World War Two began. Albert, even with his somewhat unusual educational background, did well enough at McMaster to progress into his second year. He was very studious, and his only extra-curricular activities were the McMaster Christian Union and the Chess Club. During World War Two, all male university students were required to be in the Canadian Officer Training Corps unless they registered as conscientious objectors. Albert did not register as a conscientious objector as some theological students did and took all the training during the school year and during the summer camps. In September 1942, Albert decided to enter the Canadian Army.

Albert enlisted as an ordinary soldier, assigned for armoured vehicle training, but obviously, he showed promise as a leader – perhaps due to his life experiences as a Baptist pastor in remote parts of Ontario – and he was sent to Officer Cadet School at Camp Borden, Ontario. He graduated in February 1943 as a 2nd lieutenant and, in May, was promoted to 1st lieutenant before being sent overseas to the United Kingdom in June 1943. After his arrival, he was named a tank commander and was trained in the operation and command of a Sherman tank. While Albert was undergoing tank training in England, he continued to provide ministry to the men of his unit. He was so highly regarded in this respect that the commanding officer of his training unit wrote a letter of support to the Baptist Chaplaincy Committee towards his ordination. While Albert had not completed the official syllabus to be ordained at McMaster University, wartime often led to exceptions being made. Albert was ordained on 17 May 1944 by special dispensation in the Baptist Temple at Aldershot, England. Albert was ordained by Canadian Rev H/Major Stuart Ivison, a McMaster graduate and Baptist minister, then serving as an assistant to the Principal Canadian Chaplain (Overseas). By chance Rev H H Bingham, Executive Secretary of the Baptist Convention of Ontario and Quebec (the denomination's governing body), who happened to be on an official visit to England, was also present.

Chaplain McCreery left his training as a tank commander and took up his ministry as a chaplain in a number of reinforcement units in the United Kingdom until he was sent to serve with the 1st Canadian Army in Northwest Europe in September 1944. Padre McCreery served in a number of staff appointments with various higher headquarters of the Canadian Army until April 1945, when he was transferred to the Canadian Grenadier Guards (22nd Armoured) Regiment after their chaplain was wounded in action. It was most fitting that Padre McCreery, who had originally trained as a tank crew commander, was chosen to minister in an armoured regiment.

A few short weeks after joining the Grenadier Guards, Padre McCreery was to lose his life. On 4 May 1945, just four days before the end of the war in Europe on 8 May, Padre McCreery received word that some wounded men were in need of help. The records are not clear as to whether those in need of assistance were wounded Canadian or German soldiers. What Chaplain McCreery knew was that they needed help. Others of his regiment were sceptical of this information, as there was no hard evidence or indication of where exactly these wounded soldiers were, but Padre McCreery said they needed him, and he was going to go, accompanied by Lieutenant Norman A Goldie of the Canadian Grenadier Guards.

As with so much of the minutiae of war, different stories get passed on. In Chaplain McCreery's case, one story says that he went out into no man's land to help a German tank crew who had been badly burned escaping from the vehicle, which had been set on fire by Canadian anti-tank gunfire. This version of his death indicates that Padre McCreery was shot by other German troops who did not know he was a non-combatant while approaching the tank. However, another version is recounted in *The History of the Canadian Grenadier Guards* by Colonel A Fortescue Duguid, which notes that Padre McCreery and Lieutenant Goldie set off "to bring in wounded Germans said to have been abandoned somewhere on a side road." Whatever the situation, Chaplain McCreery and Lieutenant Goldie set off to try and locate these wounded men, and that was the last time they were seen alive.[12] A few days later, Padre McCreery's body, with a number of fatal bullet wounds, was found, in marshy terrain northeast of Groningen, Holland, between the Dutch/German border and the North Sea. Lieutenant Goldie's body has never been found. Chaplain McCreery was initially buried in the Lutheran churchyard in the German hamlet of Wiefelstede west of Bremen under a small wooden cross before being moved to the CWGC Cemetery at

Holten. It is more than likely Padre McCreery was one of the last, if not the last, Canadian to die in combat in Northwest Europe in World War Two.

After World War Two ended, McMaster University received an anonymous financial gift in memory of Albert McCreery. It set up a bursary enabling theological students "to get the training which [Albert] was not permitted to receive" due to the war.

5 May 1945

RALPH A ANTONUCCI, Purple Heart, Service no. O-518099. Age 31. Captain, United States Army Chaplain Corps. Attached to the 196th Field Artillery Battalion Group. Buried in Mount Calvary Cemetery, plot G Lot 871 Cheektowaga, New York, USA.

Ralph Antonucci was the son of Pasquale and Dalinda Antonucci of Buffalo, New York, and was born there in 1914. He had two younger brothers, Anthony and Claude, and three younger sisters, Mary, Frances, and Anna. Ralph attended public schools in Buffalo and graduated high school in 1931. He then studied for his BA degree at Niagara University and then for the priesthood at St. Bonaventure University Seminary. Ralph was ordained a Roman Catholic priest on 3 June 1939, and afterwards, he served as assistant pastor of Holy Cross Church, and at Our Lady of Loretto Church in Buffalo, before entering military service in May 1943.

After his training at the US Army Chaplain's school, Chaplain Antonucci served in a number of locations in the United States and England before being assigned to the 196th Field Artillery Battalion Group in France. This artillery group was a unit that moved between various American Divisions in NW Europe as their extra firepower was needed for attack or defensive missions. They served with the 2nd, 4th, 8th, 9th, 83rd, and 99th Infantry Divisions and the 5th Armoured Division.

Captain Antonucci served with the 196th across northern France, Belgium, and Germany. On 2 May 1945, west of Magdeburg, in central Germany, fighting had stopped as the Americans and Russians had met at the Elbe River. Chaplain Antonucci was invited to go on a sightseeing flight with the airborne observation pilot of the 196th Artillery Group, Major Keith C. Morrison, in an L4H Piper Cub spotting plane. However, the small plane was attacked and shot down by 2 Russian (LAG-3) fighters over Seehausen. It is likely the Russian planes were unfamiliar with the American plane and did not pay attention to the white stars on the top of both wings. Both Major Morrison and Chaplain Antonucci were badly wounded in the attack by the Russian fighters and the subsequent crash of their light plane. Chaplain Antonucci died in hospital on 5 May, and Major Morrison on 8 May, the day that Victory in Europe was announced. Chaplain Antonucci was one of the last American soldiers to be killed in World War Two in Europe.

Conclusion

As is to be expected, during times of heavy fighting, and especially the confusion of the retreat, such as the British and French experienced in May 1940, the losses of all troops greatly increased. During the retreat to Dunkirk and the channel ports, the British Army lost six chaplains. As I have noted, there is confusion about the timing and manner of some of their deaths due to the inability of rapidly retreating troops and their headquarters to keep proper records.

Travelling the world's oceans by ship, the main method of transportation across the globe during World War Two, was also incredibly dangerous between 1939 and early 1944 until the Allies were able to gain control of the seas and find effective methods of dealing with the German U-boat menace. Thousands of men were lost to the U-boat attacks, including chaplains travelling to the various theatres of war. It is hard to believe, but until early 1943, the British had ships travelling on the South Atlantic from South Africa to ports in North Africa sailing without being part of a defended convoy. These unescorted ships were easy targets for German U-boats, and many were sunk, including the SS Laconia, which brought about the death of Padre William Copland in September 1942.

As the American build-up of troops in the United Kingdom grew, more and more troops were being transferred across the North Atlantic, some to become replacement garrison troops in Iceland and others for combat divisions in Great Britain. But the convoys that carried these troops were still not well escorted, as American industry rushed to build more warships and the United States to train their crews. As well, the crews of the merchant ships had to learn how important it was to stay with the convoy within the cover of the armed warships escorting the convoy. This is evidenced by the loss of 9 American chaplains, as well as hundreds of other American soldiers and sailors, in the sinking of the SS Dorchester and the SS Henry J Mallory in one week in early February 1943. Considering how relatively few chaplains there were in relation to the millions of Americans in the American Army, this week was a disaster for the US Army Chaplain Corps.

The British sustained 21 chaplains killed between 6 June 1944 and 31 August 1944. A huge loss rate forced the headquarters of the British Army Chaplains Department and the Canadian Chaplain Service to issue stern orders that chaplains were not to go right to the front lines, as they were irreplaceable due to the shortage of qualified replacements. This is illustrated by the much lower loss rate of British and Canadian chaplains in the final nine months of the war, with only 9 Padres in total killed in action, three of whom, along with one Polish Chaplain, were killed in the fighting at Arnhem during Operation Market Garden.

During the Battle of the Bulge (16 December 1944 to 31 January 1945), the Americans lost a significant number of chaplains in the surprise offensive by the Germans in an attempt to split the Allied Armies and recapture the port of Antwerp. This included the highest-ranking American chaplain to be killed in Northwest Europe in WW2, Lieutenant Colonel Thomas Reagan, and five other American chaplains as well. Also, a significant number were taken prisoner by the Germans, and this led to the death of Chaplain Koscamp in April 1945, even though he was captured during the Battle of the Bulge.

Airborne operations with troops parachuting or landing in gliders behind the frontlines are inherently very dangerous, and this danger is just as much for the chaplains that landed with the airborne troops. Parachutists do not give any indication to enemy soldiers attempting to repel this invasion of who is a non-combatant and who is not. So all parachutists are targets for enemy fire, and this led to some of the last deaths of American chaplains in Northwest Europe in the Allied offensive to cross the Rhine River in March of 1945.

While chaplains, as priests, pastors, and ministers, are called by God and set apart for their vocation of serving others, it does not mean they are not also human and can make human mistakes. Padre Williams, of 45 Commando, preaching the worst possible sermon two days before his unit was to land in France on D-Day, is a prime example of this. His ill-chosen words led to his being excluded from the invasion with the troops he had trained so hard with and to his overwhelming sense of shame that led him to take his own life on 5 June 1944. This humanness of the chaplains also led Canadian chaplain Albert McCreery, newly arrived at the frontlines in mid-April 1945, to disregard the advice of the experienced men of the regiment he served with, to rush off, with another officer, to a vague report of wounded soldiers in need. This lack of listening to the battle-experienced troops led to the deaths of Padre McCreery and the officer who accompanied him.

After the Battle of Normandy, it became clear to the commanders of the Chaplain Services of both the Commonwealth and American Armies that finding replacement clergy for those wounded or killed in action, or taken prisoner of war, was becoming very difficult. For the Americans, the demands of the war in the Pacific were also putting a strain on the number of chaplains available to replace those lost in combat. There were also needs of congregations of all denominations on the home front for clergy to serve in their local churches. As well, the work of the clergy on the home front was vital in supporting and encouraging their parishioners in war work. Clergy were also needed to provide comfort when families received official notices of family members missing, wounded or killed in action, or taken prisoner of war.

Of course, chaplains were an independent-minded group of individuals, and they felt their calling by God to minister to the men of their units who were right on the frontlines, and many did not heed the orders to not approach the frontlines. As you will have read, this meant that the chaplains suffered a significant number of killed and many more wounded by enemy fire or accidents while travelling to and from the various units. However, after the Battle for Normandy, the loss rate of chaplains did decrease as the chaplains' superiors impressed upon them how vital their ministry was and that they were not easily replaced.

History indicates that the Cold War between Russia and the rest of Western Europe, the United States, and Canada began after World War Two ended. However, Chaplain Antonucci's death in the shooting down of the American light observation plane that he was in by Russian aircraft while he was on a short sightseeing tour over Germany gives an idea that this lack of understanding and communications between Russia and the West began even in the last days of World War Two in Europe.

After World War Two, unlike after World War One, chaplains became an integral part of the Table of Organization of both American and Commonwealth armies. Never again would Chaplain units in the Allied Armies have to be reformed almost from scratch as conflicts continued around the world. Chaplains served in Korea, with one, Father Emil Kapaun, who was taken prisoner of war by the North Koreans and died in captivity. Following this, he was awarded the United States of America's highest military honour, the Medal of Honour, for his heroic work while a POW. He has also been nominated for sainthood in the Roman Catholic Church. During the Vietnam War, Chaplains also served, but with great difficulty, due to the lack of a frontline and having units scattered across the whole country. Again, chaplains were wounded and killed in action. Three American Army chaplains were awarded the Medal of Honor for their heroism in the face of the enemy.

The wars of the 21st century also continue to have chaplains serving the men and now women on the frontlines. These men and women of God no longer have even the minimal protection of the Red Cross on their helmets and on their sleeves, as the new form of warfare, using IEDs and snipers, does not follow any of the "rules of warfare" that at least provided a modicum of protection to the chaplains who served in World War Two. In fact, in Iraq, chaplains, according to a document captured from ISIS in 2006, were regarded as a prime target of snipers, as it was felt their being killed or wounded would demoralize the men and women of the unit they served with.

Chaplains are often criticized in the 21st century for serving in the armies of the world. After all, they ultimately serve the "prince of peace," Jesus Christ. However, in their defence, Chaplains feel that Armed Forces members are worthy of being served by men and women of God, just as much as any person in their own home country. As long as there are people of faith in the military, be it Christian, Jewish, Muslim, Buddhist, Hindu, Sikh, or even Pagan, there will be chaplains who will minister to their spiritual and moral needs and provide a caring presence in what can often seem an impersonal war machine of the military.

End Notes

1. A visit of the Canadian Veterans Affairs Minister https://www.youtube.com/watch?v=VkECdVZyS4o&list=WL&index=5inister to the Commonwealth War Graves Commission Headquarters on 1 November 2016.
2. http://freepages.rootsweb.com/~cacunithistories/military/HR_Mallory_Navy_Stories.htm
3. Ibid.
4. https://www.pegasusarchive.org/normandy/frames.htm/Lord_Lovat_Biography
5. Western News, November 10, 2005 "Junk Store Find Remembrance Treasure" published by the University of Western Ontario, London, Ontario, reprinted with permission
6. https://www.ww2-airborne.us/units/401/401.html
7. Ibid.
8. Ibid.
9. Official Letter from Colonel CJ Hirshfelder, 9th Infantry Regiment to Margaret Kibert, 14 November, 1944.
10. Ibid.
11. https://www.7tharmddiv.org/us-troops-in-hollandaise#2ad30id
12. Caddick-Adams, Peter;1945: Victory in the West, Penguin Books, Pg 508

Bibliography

Books

Balkoski, J. (2013). *Our Tortured Souls: The 29th Infantry Division In The Rhineland, November-December 1944.* Stackpole Books.

Carpenter, A. E., & Eiland, A. A. (2007). *Chappie: World War Ii Diary Of A Combat Chaplain.* Mesa, AZ: Mead Pub.

Crosby, D. F. (1994). *Battlefield Chaplains.* Lawrence, Kan: University Press of Kansas.

Cross, C., & Arnold, W. R. (1945). *Soldiers Of God*: [by] Christopher Cross, in collaboration with Major General William A. Arnold. New York: E.P. Dutton & Company, Inc.

Dempsey, M., & Burns, Oates & Washbourne. (1947). *The Priest Among The Soldiers.* London: Burns Oates.

Faulkner, R. L. (2015). *Wehrmacht Priests. Catholicism And The Nazi War Of Annihilation.* Cambridge: Harvard University Press.

Fowlkes, P. D., & Carroll, R. F. (2018). *Chaplain: The World War Ii Letters Of The Army Air Corps Chaplain Paschal Dupuy Fowlkes.* Politics and Prose Bookstore, Washington DC.

Gillate, D. (2019). *With the 8th Rifle Brigade from Normandy to the Baltic: June 1944 – May 1945.* S.L.: Tredition GMBH.

Gushwa, R. L., & United States. (1978). *The Best And Worst Of Times.... 1920-1945.* Washington, D.C: Govt. Print. Off. [for] Department of the Army, Office of the Chief of Chaplains.

Hayden, M. (2005). *German Military Chaplains In World War II.* Atglen, PA: Schiffer Pub.

Hickey, R. M. (1980). *The Scarlet Dawn.* Fredericton, N.B: Unipress.

Hoegh, L. A., Doyle, H. J., & National Timberwolf Association. (2004). *Timberwolf Tracks: The History Of The 104th Infantry Division, 1942-1945*. Washington: Infantry Journal Press.

Johnstone, T., & Hagerty, J. (1996). T*he Cross On The Sword: Catholic Chaplains In The Forces*. London: G. Chapman.

Kilan, M. (2016) *The Story of the Paratrooper Chaplains of the 1st Independent Parachute Brigade*. Biblioteka Narodowa, Poland

McLuskey, J. F., & SCM Press. (1997). *Parachute Padre: Behind German Lines With The SAS: France 1944*. Stevenage: Strong Oak Press.

Mueller, T. (2009). *The Wisconsin 3,800: Our Men And Women Buried Or Mia In The Lands They Liberated In World War II*. Indianapolis, Ind: Dog Ear Pub.

Oliver, K. (1986). *Chaplain At War*. Chichester: Angel Press.

Parker, L. (2019). *Nearer My God To Thee: Airborne Chaplains In The Second World War*. Helion & Company, Warwick, UK.

Reynolds, A., & Trew, S. (2019). To *War Without Arms: The Journal Of Rev Alexander Reynolds, May-November 1944*. Sabrestorm Publishing, Devizes, Wiltshire, UK.

Robinson, A. C. (2008). *Chaplains at war: The Role Of Clergymen During World War II*. London: Tauris Academic Studies.

Roekel, C., & Arriëns, J. (1998). *The Torn Horizon: The Airborne Chaplains At Arnhem*. Oosterbeek: Published by Jan and Wedela ter Horst and Chris van Roekel..

Roland, Charles. (2010). *History Teaches Us To Hope: Reflections On The Civil War And Southern History*. University Press of Kentucky.

Sampson, F. L. (1989). *Look Out Below!: A Story Of The Airborne By A Paratrooper Padre*. Sweetwater, Tenn: 101st Airborne Division Association.

Smyth, J. S. (1968). *In This Sign Conquer: The Story Of The Army Chaplains*. Place of publication not identified: publisher not identified.

Snape, M. (2005). *God And The British Soldier: Religion And The British Army In The First And Second World Wars*. London: Routledge.

Steven, W. T. (1958). *In This Sign*. Toronto: Ryerson Press.

United States. (1944). *The Chaplain Serves: A Narrative And Factual Report Covering The Activity Of The Chaplain Corps*, as coordinated by the Chief of Chaplains, for the calendar year 1943.

Weston, L. E. (2001). *The Fightin' Preacher*. Alexander, NC: Mountain Church.

Wilson, T. D. (2018) *No Guns, Just God's Glory*. OREP Editions, Bayeux, France.

Wright, R. S. (1941). *Front Line Religion*. London: Hodder and Stoughton.

Wright, R. S. (1943). *The Greater Victory: Further Broadcast Talks*. London: Longmans, Green and Co.

Wright, R. S. (1944). *The Padre Presents: Discussions about Life in the Forces*. McLagan and Cummings Ltd.

Unpublished Manuscripts / Manuscrits non publiés

Cavanaugh, Paul W., S.J. American Priest In A Nazi Prison: The Personal Narrative Of An American Catholic Chaplain As A Prisoner Of War In Germany, Property Of 106 Division Association

Chaplain Hobson Matthews Diary in the possession of the Royal Army
Chaplaincy Department Museum.

415th Infantry Regiment After Action Report from 1November 1944 inclusive.

Websites / Sites web

www.7-star-admiral.com/0185_SSgt_Rice_war_diary_part2.html

ww2talk.com/forums/topic/32550-ss-leibstandarte-and-chaplain-the-rev-reginald-podmore-rachd/

chaplainshill.org/encyclopedia/macdonald-ernest-w/

www.facebook.com/WW2Researcher/posts/1913273218792313

forum.axishistory.com/viewtopic.php? t=126116

www.fourchaplains.org/george-l-fox/

freepages.rootsweb.com/~cacunithistories/military/HR_Mallory_Navy_Stories.htm

www.indianamilitary.org/228th/Diaries/CharlesBlakeney/CharlesBlakeney.htm

www.film.iwmcollections.org.uk/record/33715

www.mcmaster.ca/ua/alumni/ww2honourroll/mccreery.html

www.pegasusarchive.org/normandy/frames.htm/Lord_Lovat_Biography

www.polishwargraves.nl/langri/2159.htm?fbclid=IwAR2OeqtO8AKXjnHXddYPLr-6hFvMePvww8nYVGOCT23oj0el5zZKmmQqljo

www.scotsatwar.org.uk/rohprints/e.htm

www.swzygmunt.knc.pl/MARTYROLOGIUM/POLISHRELIGIOUS/vENGLISH/LISTs/POLISHRELIGIOUS_list_01.htm us.army.39.45.soforums.com/t2908-capitaine-aumonier-catholique-John-J-Verret-507-pir.htm

www.raritan-online.com/koskamp-article.htm

https://www.7tharmddiv.org/us-troops-in-holland.htm#2ad30id

Newspapers / Journaux

Ashbury Park Press, New Jersey, USA 22 October, 1942 edition.

B.U. Bridge, 25 October, 2002, Vol VI, No 9. Piscitello, Dawn. Gift of war hero grad's rare Bibles forms core of STH library's collection.

InfoTrac Custom Newspapers. Gale. Library of Michigan. 12 Jan. 2009 "SOLDIER OF GOD: The last Canadian hero The final Canadian casualty on European battlefields was very probably Albert E. McCreery of Ingersoll, Ont., a padre to the Canadian Grenadier Guards. Unarmed, he died in German territory as he looked for injured soldiers from his homeland.(FOCUS)." Globe & Mail (Toronto, Canada) (May 6, 1995): D4. InfoTrac Custom Newspapers. Gale. Library of Michigan. 12 Jan. 2009

Lewiston *Daily Sun*, Maine, 7 June, 1943 edition.

Personal Correspondence / **Correspondance personnelle**

Ian Bruce Macaulay, Ottawa, Canada about the descendants of Hugh William Walker, specifically Rev Ian Macaulay.

www.ingramcontent.com/pod-product-compliance
Lightning Source LLC
Chambersburg PA
CBHW052053110526
44591CB00013B/2189